THE *InterActive* READER™ PLUS

TEACHER'S GUIDE

Active Reading Strategies for All Students

Grade 8

McDougal Littell
A HOUGHTON MIFFLIN COMPANY
Evanston, Illinois   Boston   Dallas

ISBN 0-618-31026-6

Copyright © 2003 by McDougal Littell Inc.
Box 1667, Evanston, Illinois 60204
All rights reserved. Printed in the United States of America.

6 7 8 9 – PB0 – 08 07 06 05

Table of Contents

What Is *The InterActive Reader™ Plus*?

A book that allows students with different abilities to develop stronger reading skills by encouraging the use of a variety of comprehension strategies.

Every student is on the same page, but strategic help varies across three levels:

The InterActive Reader™ Plus

Includes

- Literature selections from the Grade 8 *Language of Literature* broken into short, manageable sections
- Reading support throughout
- A consumable format that allows students to mark the text with their notes and questions
- In-book activity sheets

The InterActive Reader™ Plus with Additional Support

Includes

- All of the features of *The InterActive Reader™ Plus*
- Special reading support for your struggling readers, including
    - a brief summary with every section
    - more contextual background information
    - extra reading checks
- Page layouts that are the same across all books

The InterActive Reader™ Plus for English Learners

Includes

- All the features of *The InterActive Reader™ Plus*
- Special support for English Learners, including
    - a brief summary with every section
    - more contextual background information
    - special language and culture notes
    - extra reading checks
- Page layouts that are the same across all books

The InterActive Reading Process

The InterActive Reader™ Plus encourages students to write in their books!

All levels of *The InterActive Reader™ Plus* provide students and teachers with a unique resource that fosters reading comprehension. *The InterActive Reader™ Plus* encourages students to engage or *interact* with the text. Activities before, during, and after reading a selection prompt students to make personal connections; ask themselves questions; clarify their ideas; and visualize objects, persons, and places—all thinking processes performed by proficient readers.

The following features help students interact with the text:

Before Reading

Connect to Your Life and **Key to the Selection** give students concrete ways to begin thinking about the selection they will read.

FOCUS Appearing before each "chunk" of text, the Focus serves as a mini-preview and sets the purpose for reading.

Additional Support for Struggling Readers and English Learners

As the story begins ... Every chunk of text begins with a brief summary of the section.

During Reading

MARK IT UP ⬙ **KEEP TRACK** Using a system of stars, question marks, and exclamation marks, students monitor their understanding as they read.

Pause & Reflect Students read until the Pause & Reflect symbol appears, signaling them to stop and answer the questions in the margins. These questions allow students to follow up on the purpose-setting statement in the Focus and to learn and practice a variety of reading skills and strategies, including

- summarizing
- inferring
- questioning
- predicting
- visualizing
- connecting
- clarifying
- evaluating

- drawing conclusions
- stating opinions
- locating main ideas
- making judgments
- analyzing
- identifying cause-and-effect relationships
- understanding an author's purpose
- distinguishing fact from opinion

MARK IT UP ⬙ This activity invites students to underline, circle, or highlight key words or passages that help clarify meaning.

 Frequently, students are told to reread a key passage aloud to themselves or to a partner to focus on a particular idea, author's intent, or author's use of language.

 Often, students are told to reread a key passage and then given a question that checks their comprehension.

Additional Support for Struggling Readers and English Learners

 Reading Check These questions at key points in the text help students clarify what is happening in a selection.

MORE ABOUT . . . These notes provide key background information, such as historical context, political situations, and scientific background, needed for understanding the selection.

WHAT DOES IT MEAN? Possibly confusing words, phrases, references, and other constructions are clearly explained in these notes.

 Reader's Success Strategy Specifically for struggling readers, these notes give useful and fun tips and strategies for comprehending the selection.

English Learner Support **Language** Support for English Learners involves a wide range of vocabulary, language, and culture issues that are covered in these special notes.

After Reading

 Challenge At the end of most selections, a Challenge activity requires students to reenter the selection to analyze a key idea and to answer a higher-level question.

SkillBuilder Pages During and after reading a selection, students are encouraged to complete the SkillBuilder pages that follow each lesson. The three SkillBuilder pages help students practice and apply important skills.

• **Active Reading SkillBuilder** Comprehension skills are reinforced through graphics and other visual representations, requiring students to use their understanding of the selection to extend their reading skills.

• **Literary Analysis SkillBuilder** Literary elements are reinforced through graphics and other visual representations, requiring students to use their understanding of the selection to extend their literary skills.

• **Words to Know SkillBuilder** (for most selections) Words underlined and defined in the selection are reviewed, requiring students to use the words contextually and in original sentences.

Ongoing Assessment In addition to increasing students' involvement in the reading process, *The InterActive Reader™ Plus* offers you, the teacher, a window on students' progress and problems. Students' notes, responses, and other markings should be looked at regularly as part of the ongoing informal assessment process.

Who Will Benefit?

The InterActive Reader™ Plus helps students with differing abilities to access authentic text.

The InterActive Reader™ Plus
(for on-level and above-level students)

- On-level students will find appropriate support or scaffolding to hone their reading process strategies and skills. The interactive activities enable students to construct meaning and to recognize *how* that meaning was constructed.

- Above-level students will be able to sharpen their analytical reading skills using this level. Being able to write in the book allows these students to annotate authors' use of tone, mood, symbols, and other literary concepts addressed by the College Board.

The InterActive Reader™ Plus with Additional Support
(for below-level readers)

Struggling readers will achieve best in this level. Summaries, additional background information, extra vocabulary support, and extra interactive activities will provide the necessary help for these students. Allowing students to work in pairs or small groups and partner-reading followed by talking through their answers to questions in the side columns will not only build reading competence but also reading confidence!

Three levels of books . . . yet the SAME text on the SAME page . . . and *all* students receive the differentiated support they need for their reading abilities.

The InterActive Reader™ Plus for English Learners
(for students learning English)

Students learning English will achieve best in this level. Extra assistance to meet their specific needs will allow these students to break through the word-level barrier to focus on the meaning and ideas of the selection.

How is *The InterActive Reader™ Plus* best used in the classroom?

Because all three levels contain the *same* literary selections with the *same* page numbers, you can easily use them in a single classroom. As you introduce a selection or discuss a "chunk" of text, there will never be any confusion by students, for they will have their own customized side-column activities based on their reading abilities. *The InterActive Reader™ Plus* changes the level of support, not the literature.

Lesson Planning

You may wish to use the following sequence for a lesson using all levels of *The InterActive Reader™ Plus:*

Before Reading

- Assign the **Connect to Your Life** and **Key to the Story** activities for the whole class. Students may complete them independently or with partners before sharing their answers with the group.

During Reading

- Read aloud the **Focus** and **Mark It Up** to clarify the "reading with pen in hand" activity that is suggested.
- Read aloud or think aloud or model the thinking strategy required to complete the **Mark It Up** task for the first section.
- Encourage all students to read through the side-column notes and to answer questions and mark anything that puzzles or confuses them. Struggling readers and English learners will find summaries and notes especially for them.
- At the Pause & Reflect, discuss as a group the questions listed in the side column or have students work with partners to answer the questions.
- Beginning with the next section, again read the **Focus** and **Mark It Up.** At this point you may have some students working independently while you assist others with think-alouds or other strategies.
- Use the SkillBuilder pages along with the reading if appropriate. For example, an Active Reading SkillBuilder on predicting is best filled out while students read. They can then check the accuracy of their predictions as they finish the selection.

After Reading

- You may wish to work together as a whole class on the **Challenge** activity, or you may find pairs or small groups most effective.
- Use the SkillBuilder pages as an effective review and reinforcement of the vocabulary, reading, and literary skills covered.

Suggested Reading Options

A variety of methods can be used with *The InterActive Reader*™ *Plus*.

The InterActive Reader™ *Plus* allows you to choose from a number of different reading options as you assign students work. Each Lesson Plan in this Guide suggests one of the following options, the suggestion being based on the nature of the selection itself. However, any reading options may be used at any time. Options marked with an asterisk (*) are especially effective with Students Acquiring English.

Independent Reading

Students can read independently, using the questions in the margins of their books for guidance and focus. Though most often this option is used with students who need little support, all students should have some opportunities to read independently. In this situation, *The InterActive Reader*™ *Plus* may be used as a take-home text.

Note: If *The InterActive Reader*™ *Plus* is being used in conjunction with *The Language of Literature,* you may wish to begin the prereading activities, such as Connect to Your Life and Build Background, in class; the main anthology can then be left at school while students carry home their smaller and less cumbersome readers.

Partner/Cooperative Reading*

Students can read in pairs, pausing at the indicated places to discuss the questions, write answers, and compare notations and highlighted passages. Alternatively, students can read in small groups, pausing in the same manner to discuss the selection and respond to prompts. In either setting, encourage students to discuss the strategies they use as they read.

Teacher Modeling*

Read aloud the first part of a selection, discuss key events or concepts that are important for comprehension, and then have students continue reading on their own. For particularly challenging selections, reading aloud can continue further into the selection, or there could be an alternating of silent reading and teacher read-aloud.

Oral Reading*

This option works well for plays, speeches, or selections that contain an abundance of dialogue. It can also work well with narrative passages, providing an aural dimension to the comprehension process.

Audio Library*

Recordings of almost all selections in *The InterActive Reader*™ *Plus* are provided as part of the *Language of Literature* core program. You may find it useful to have students read along with these recordings.

Note: In order to familiarize students with the lesson structure and format of *The InterActive Reader*™ *Plus,* you might consider reading aloud the beginning of each selection and modeling the Focus and Pause & Reflect activities provided.

Reciprocal Teaching

Reciprocal teaching refers to an instructional activity that teaches students concrete, specific, "comprehension-fostering" strategies they will need whenever they approach the reading of a new text. The activity consists of a dialogue between students and teacher, with each taking a turn in the role of the teacher or leader. Classroom use of this activity has been found to improve the reading comprehension of both good and struggling readers.

Step 1: Have everyone silently read a short passage (one or several paragraphs) of a new text. Model the following four thinking strategies using only the part of the reading that has been read.

- **Questioning** – Ask the class to think of a question that everyone can answer because everyone has read the same text. Model by generating a question for the class. Call on a student to answer your question. Ask that student to then generate a question for the class and to call on another student to answer her question. Repeat this procedure until you think all students are thoroughly familiar with the facts and details of the passage. (If students do not ask a question beginning with *why,* model one for them to move their thinking from literal to inferential comprehension.)

- **Clarifying** – Model for the class a confusion you need to clarify; for example, a word or a phrase that caused you to pause as you initially read the passage. Think aloud as you discuss your mental engagement with this section, explaining to the class how you figured it out. Ask students if they found any confusing parts when they read the passage. Have a dialogue about the problem-solving methods used by students to make sense of confusing parts.

- **Summarizing** – After students have comprehended the passage as a result of the reciprocal questioning and clarifying strategies, ask them to think of a one-sentence summary for the passage. Ask a volunteer to share his summary statement. Encourage others to revise, if needed, the shared summary by elaborating and embellishing its content. Identify the best summary through a dialogue with class members.

- **Predicting** – Now that students know what the first passage in the reading means, ask them to predict what the author will discuss next.

Step 2: Ask everyone to silently read another portion of text. Have a student volunteer repeat Step 1, serving as the teacher/leader, over this new portion.

Step 3: In groups of four, have students silently read the next portion of text, taking turns role-playing the leader and following the 4-step procedure.

Teacher's Role: Guide students' practice by monitoring the student dialogue in each group during steps 2 and 3. Remind students of the procedure and give additional modeling of the steps.

Reciprocal Teaching training provides students with explicit ways to interact with new text. *The InterActive Reader™ Plus* extends this powerful technique by focusing on additional strategies: connecting, visualizing, and evaluating. You will notice that students connect and visualize while clarifying and evaluate in order to predict.

For each Lesson Plan in *The InterActive Reader™ Plus,* one of the above comprehension strategies is modeled. An ongoing review of all of the strategies provides a helpful reminder to students and encourages their pursuit of independent reading.

Strategies for Reading

These strategies can help you gain a better understanding of what you read. Whenever you find yourself having difficulty making sense of what you're reading, choose and use the strategy that seems most likely to help.

PREDICT   Try to figure out what will happen next and how the selection might end. Then read on to see how accurate your guesses are.

VISUALIZE   Visualize characters, events, and setting to help you understand what's happening. When you read nonfiction, pay attention to the images that form in your mind as you read.

CONNECT   Connect personally with what you're reading. Think of similarities between the descriptions in the selection and what you have personally experienced, heard about, or read about.

QUESTION   Question what happens while you read. Searching for reasons behind events and characters' feelings can help you feel closer to what you are reading.

CLARIFY   Stop occasionally to review your understanding of what you read. You can do this by **summarizing** what you have read, identifying the **main idea,** and **making inferences**—drawing conclusions from the information you are given. Reread passages you don't understand.

EVALUATE   Form opinions about what you read, both while you're reading and after you've finished. Develop your own ideas about characters and events.

Reaching Middle School Readers

One of the many challenges of middle school teaching is accommodating the wide range of reading abilities and interests among students. For those students who are hooked on reading, the challenge is to provide a steady diet of rich materials. But for many students, reading is a chore that requires enormous effort and yields little success.

Students who are not able to read at grade level often do not succeed in school. While much of the focus of the early grades is on learning to read, the focus shifts in the middle grades to reading to learn. Students who do not have a strong foundation in basic decoding and comprehension skills become struggling readers. Their poor reading ability denies them access to the content of the textbooks; as a result, they fall behind in almost every subject area. Below-level reading ability most often is the result of inadequate decoding skills, poor comprehension, or a combination of both.

Decoding skills provide readers with strategies for determining the pronunciation of the written word. Basic decoding skills involve matching letters and letter combinations with spoken sounds and blending those sounds into words. As students encounter longer—multisyllabic—words, they need to divide these words into manageable chunks or syllables.

Decoding is an enabling skill for comprehension. Comprehension is a process of constructing meaning from text. Readers integrate the information in the text with their prior knowledge to make sense of what they read. Specific comprehension skills and strategies, such as main idea, sequence, and visualizing can help students recognize the relationships among ideas, figure out text structures, and create pictures of what they read.

This book provides some basic tools and strategies that will help you help your students to become readers. The lessons and articles can be used as needed, or they can be organized into mini-units of instruction.

Developing Fluency in All Readers

Reading fluency is the ability to automatically recognize words so that attention can be focused on the meaning of the written material. Fluency involves both decoding and comprehension skills; fluent readers decode text with little or no effort as they construct meaning from that text. Teachers can usually spot readers who struggle with decoding the text. Other readers, however, may be able to say the words and sound as though they are reading, but they have little or no understanding of what they read. These readers often go unnoticed, especially in the content areas.

Fluency is a developmental skill that improves with practice. The more students read, the better readers they become. The reading level at which a student is fluent is called his or her *independent reading level*. However, a student's independent reading level may vary with the type of material he or she is reading. For example, reading a short story is often easier than reading a textbook.

A key part in developing reading fluency is determining a student's independent reading level and then providing a range of materials at that level. Developing Fluent Readers on pages 14–16 offers diagnostic tools for determining reading levels and tips for improving fluency.

Helping All Readers Break the Code

There are many reasons that some students struggle with reading. Often poor readers spend most of their mental energy trying to figure out, or decode, the words. With their brains focused on the letters and corresponding sounds, there is little attention left to think about what the words mean. Until readers achieve a basic level of automaticity in word recognition, they are not reading for meaning.

Although most middle school students do have a knowledge of basic phonics, some students fail to develop strategies for using the letter-sound correspondences. They often have difficulty decoding new words, and multisyllabic words are especially problematic. As students encounter longer words they need to be able to break these words into parts.

The lessons on applying multisyllabic rules in Teaching Decoding Strategies on pages 111–121 provide students with strategies for tackling longer words. These lessons also provide a basic review of phonics within a model of direct instruction. You can expand this review for students who need more intensive work in this area. You can also skip the basic phonics instruction and focus on multisyllabic word attack strategies.

Using the Most Effective Teaching Strategies

Choosing *how* to teach something is as important as deciding *what* to teach. While a variety of methods are sound, some methods are more effective in teaching specific skills and strategies than others.

Decoding skills need to be taught explicitly and systematically through direct instruction. These skills can be taught to mastery. The lessons in Teaching Decoding Strategies offer an efficient set of steps and teaching script for short but effective lessons in these skills.

Comprehension skills, however, are developmental skills that are not easily mastered. Students will continue to grow in their understanding of increasingly difficult reading materials throughout life.

Comprehension skills can be modeled so that students are shown the thinking processes behind these skills. The Comprehension Mini-Lessons provide passages and teaching script to model basic comprehension skills.

Establishing a Reading Process

Good readers are strategic in how they approach reading. They consciously or unconsciously do certain things before, during, and after reading. Poor readers, however, often possess few or none of the strategies required for proficient reading. To help struggling readers, establish a routine for reading that involves strategies before, during, and after reading.

- **Before Reading** New ideas presented in reading materials need to be integrated with the reader's **prior knowledge** for understanding to occur. Have students preview the material to see what it is about. Discuss what they already know about the topic and have them **predict** new information they might learn about it. Talk about a **purpose** for reading and have students think about reading strategies they might use with the material.

- **During Reading** Good readers keep track of their understanding as they read. They recognize important or interesting information, know when they don't understand something, and figure out what to do to adjust their understanding. Poor readers are often unaware of these **self-monitoring strategies.** To help these readers become more involved in their reading, suggest that they read with a pencil in hand to jot down notes and questions as they read. If students own the reading materials, they can mark the text as they read. *The InterActive Readers*™ that accompany *The Language of Literature* are ideal for this type of work.

- **After Reading** Provide opportunities for readers to reflect on what they have read. These can involve group or class discussion and writing in journals and logs.

Creating Independent Readers

As you work to give students the skills they need to read for themselves, you can also incorporate some basic routines into your classroom that will help your students extend their understanding.

- **Read aloud.** People of all ages love a good story. Read aloud to your students and hook them on some authors and genres they might not have tackled themselves. For most material, students' listening comprehension is more advanced than their comprehension of written material. Listening helps them develop the thinking skills needed to understand complex text.

- **Write daily.** Writing is a powerful tool to understanding. Encourage students to use writing to work through problems, explore new ideas, or respond to the literature they read. Encourage students to keep journals and learning logs.

- **Read daily.** Allow time for sustained silent reading. Set aside classroom time for students to read self-selected materials. Students who read become better readers, and students are more likely to choose to read if they can pursue ideas they find interesting.

- **Build a classroom library.** If possible, provide a wide range of reading materials so that students are exposed to diverse topics and genres. Respect students' reading choices. Struggling readers need first to view themselves as readers.

- **Promote discussion.** Set ground rules for discussion so that all opinions are heard. Model good discussion behaviors by asking follow-up questions, expanding on ideas presented, and offering alternate ways of viewing topics.

When teachers allocate time to these experiences, students see literacy as possible.

Developing Fluent Readers

Good readers are fluent readers. They recognize words automatically, group individual words into meaningful phrases, and apply phonic, morphemic, and contextual clues when confronted with a new word. Fluency is a combination of accuracy (number of words identified correctly) and rate (number of words per minute) of reading. Fluency can be taught directly, and it improves as a consequence of students' reading a lot of materials that are within their instructional range.

Understanding Reading Levels

Every student reads at a specific level regardless of the grade in which he or she is placed. Reading level in this context is concerned with the relationship between a specific selection or book and a student's ability to read that selection. The following are common terms used to describe these levels:

- **independent level**—The student reads material in which no more than 1 in 20 words is difficult. The material can be read without teacher involvement and is likely to be material students would choose to read on their own.
- **instructional level**—The student reads material in which no more than 2 in 20 words are difficult. The material is most likely found in school and read with teacher involvement.
- **frustration level**—The student reads material in which significantly more than 2 in 20 (or 89%) of the words are difficult. Students will probably get little out of reading the material.

If students read only material that's too easy, growth in skill, vocabulary, and understanding is too slow. If students read only difficult material, they may give up in frustration much too early.

Providing Reading Materials in the Student's Instructional Range

Most states have testing programs that provide information about each student's reading ability. Once you determine a student's general reading level, you can work with the library media teacher to identify reading materials that will be within the student's instructional level. To develop fluency, students should read materials that contain a high proportion of words that they know already or can easily decode. Work with each student to develop a list of books to read, and have students record their progress on a Reading Log.

Repeated Oral Readings

Repeated oral readings of passages is a strategy that improves fluency. Oral reading also improves prosody, which is the art of sounding natural when you read, or reading with appropriate intonation, expression, and rhythm.

Beginning readers sound awkward when they read aloud. They pause and halt at the wrong places; they emphasize the wrong syllables; they may read in a monotone. Repeated oral readings can increase fluency and prosody as students 1) identify words faster and faster each time they read; 2) correctly identify a larger percentage of words; 3) segment text into appropriate phrases; 4) change pitch and emphasis to fit the meaning of the text.

To improve fluency and prosody, select passages that are brief, thought provoking, and at the student's current independent level of reading. You may choose narrative or expository text, or have the student choose something he or she enjoys. Performing a play, practicing to give a speech, reading to younger students, and rereading a passage to find evidence in support of an argument are all activities that provide opportunities to reread. For the following exercise, you may choose to pair students together and have them read to each other, or use this as a one-on-one teacher-student or tutor-student activity.

1. Select an excerpt within the student's reading level that ranges from 50–200 words in length.

2. Have the student read the passage aloud to a partner. The partner records the number of seconds it takes to read the whole passage, and notes the number of errors. Reverse roles so that each student has a chance to read to the other.

3. Read the passage aloud to the students so that students can hear it read correctly.

4. As homework, or as an in-class assignment, have students practice reading the passage out loud on their own.

5. After practice, have each student read aloud again to his or her partner, who records the time and the number of errors.

6. After repeated practice and readings the student will read the passage fluently, that is, with a moderate rate and near 100% accuracy.

Example Excerpt

I have a little dream
For the flying of a plane.
I have a little scheme,
I'll follow yet again.

There is a little heaven,
Just around the hill.
I haven't seen it for a long time,
But I know it's waiting still.

from Dragonwings
by Laurence Yep

Repeated Silent Readings

Having students silently read and reread passages that are at their instructional level also improves fluency. As they practice, students will recognize words more quickly each time, will group words into meaningful phrases more quickly, and will increase their reading rate. One nice thing about repeated silent reading is that a student can do it individually. Many students enjoy timing themselves when they read and seeing improvement over time. Have them keep a record on a piece of graph paper.

Modeling

Students benefit from repeated opportunities to hear English spoken fluently. By listening to live models or tapes, listeners can understand the rhythm of the language and the pitch and pronunciation of particular words and phrases. They can hear when to pause, when to speed up, and what words to emphasize. In addition, you can model

or ask an experienced reader to read passages aloud. At most advanced levels, this technique is particularly useful to introduce students to various forms of dialect. As you play the tapes aloud, have students read along silently or chorally, or pause the tapes after each paragraph and have the students try reading the same passage aloud.

Phrase-Cued Text

Less proficient readers may not know when to pause in text. They may pause in the middle of a phrase, or run through a comma or period. They may not recognize verb phrases, prepositional phases, or even phrases marked by parentheses or brackets as words that "go together." This makes their reading disjointed and choppy, or gives it a monotone quality. Some poems have essentially one phrase per line and can be used to demonstrate to students how to phrase text. Or, you may take a passage and have students rewrite it with one phrase per line, so that they pause at the end of each line. Alternatively, you can show them how a passage should be read by inserting slash marks or blank spaces at appropriate places to pause. Choose passages of about 50–100 words in length from fiction or nonfiction selections. For example, you can take a passage like the following:

Example Modeling

When the man entered the room, he failed to notice the trembling brown fox crouching in the corner next to the refrigerator. When the man opened the door of the refrigerator to grab a cold soda, the fox leapt between his feet and the door and scrambled for a hiding place on the shelf behind the lettuce.

And present it to students in this way:

When the man entered the room,/he failed to notice/ the trembling brown fox/ crouching in the corner/ next to the refrigerator. When the man opened the door of the refrigerator/ to grab a cold soda,/ the fox leapt between his feet and the door/ and scrambled for a hiding place/ on the shelf /behind the lettuce.

Have students read and then reread the passage, stopping to pause at each slash mark.

Informal Reading Inventory

An informal inventory can give an initial idea of a student's reading level. Teachers often use an Informal Reading Inventory (IRI) to place students in the appropriate textbook.

To conduct an IRI, you need at least one 100-word passage from the material in question and 10 comprehension questions about the material. If you want more than one passage, select them randomly from every 30th page or so. Have the student read the same passage twice—the first time orally to assess oral reading skills. The student should read the passage a second time silently, after which he or she answers questions for assessment of reading comprehension.

Suggestions for administering an IRI:

1. Tell the student he or she will read the passage out loud and then again silently, and then you will ask some questions.

2. Give the student a copy of the passage and keep one for yourself. Have the student read the passage. As the student reads out loud, note on your copy the number of errors he or she makes:

   Mispronunciations: Words that are mispronounced, with the exception of proper nouns.
   Omissions: Words left out that are crucial to understanding a sentence or a concept.
   Additions: Words inserted in a sentence that change the meaning of the text,
   Substitutions: Words substituted for actual words in the text that change the meaning of a sentence.

Use these criteria for assessing reading levels after oral reading:

- Fewer than 3 errors—The student is unlikely to have difficulty decoding text.

- Between 4 and 9 errors—The student is likely to have some difficulty and may need special attention.

- More than 10 errors—The student is likely to have great difficulty and may need placement in less challenging material.

3. Have the student read the passage again, silently.

4. When the student finishes, ask the comprehension questions you have prepared ahead of time. Tell the student that he or she can look back at the passage before answering a question.

5. Note the number of correct responses. Use these criteria for assessing reading level after silent reading:

- Eight or more—The student should be able to interpret the selections effectively.

- Five to seven—The student is likely to have difficulty.

- Fewer than five—The student needs individual help or alternate placement.

6. Evaluate results from oral and silent reading to decide how good a match the material is for a student's independent or instructional level.

Another approach allows you to assess the student's choice for independent reading. Have the student independently select a book he or she would like to read. The student should open to a random page in the middle of the book (that has not been read before) and begin reading silently from the top of the page. Ask the student to extend one finger for each time he or she comes across an unfamiliar word. If, by the end of that page, the student has five or more fingers extended, the book is probably too difficult for that student. You may want to suggest that the student find a book more suitable to his or her reading level.

Research/Related Readings

The following research supports the philosophy and pedagogical design of *The InterActive Reader™ Plus*:

Beck, I., et al. "Getting at the Meaning: How to Help Students Unpack Difficult Text." *American Educator: The Unique Power of Reading and How to Unleash It* 22.1–2 (1996): 66–71, 85.

California Reading Initiative and Special Education in California: Critical Ideas Focusing on Meaningful Reform. Sacramento: California Special Education Reading Task Force, California Department of Education and California State Board of Education, 1999.

Carnine, D., J. Silbert, and E. J. Kame'enui. *Direction Instruction Reading*. Columbus: Merrill, 1990.

Honig, B., L. Diamond, and L. Gutlohn. *Teaching Reading Sourcebook*. Novato, CA: Arena, 2000.

Irvin, Judith L. *Reading and the Middle School Student*. 2nd ed. Boston: Allyn & Bacon, 1998.

Langer, J. A., and A. N. Applebee. "Reading and Writing Instruction: Toward a Theory of Teaching and Learning." *Review of Research in Education*. Ed. E. Rothkopf. Washington, D.C.: American Educational Research Association, 1986.

Lapp, D., J. Flood, and N. Farnan. *Content Area Reading and Learning: Instructional Strategies*. 2nd ed. Boston: Allyn & Bacon, 1996.

Lyon, G. Reid. "Learning to Read: A Call from Research to Action." *National Center for Learning Disabilities*. 9 Nov. 1999 <http://www.ncld.org/theirworld/lyon98.html>

Palinscar, A. S., and A. L. Brown. "Interactive Teaching to Promote Independent Learning from Text." *The Reading Teacher* 39.8 (1986): 771–777.

Palinscar, A. S., and A. L. Brown. "Reciprocal Teaching of Comprehension-Fostering and Comprehension-Monitoring Activities." *Cognition and Instruction* 1.2: 117–175.

Pearson, P. D., et al. "Developing Expertise in Reading Comprehension." *What Research Says to the Teacher*. Ed. S. J. Samuels and A. E. Farstrip. Newark: International Reading Association, 1992.

Rosenshine, B., and C. Meister. "Reciprocal Teaching: A Review of the Research." *Review of Educational Research* 64.4 (1994): 479–530.

Simmons, D. C., and E. J. Kame'enui, eds. *What Reading Research Tells Us About Children with Diverse Needs: Bases and Basics*. Mahwah: Lawrence Erlbaum, 1998.

Tierney, R. J., J. E. Readence, and E. K. Dishner. *Reading Strategies and Practices: A Compendium*. 4th ed. Boston: Allyn & Bacon, 1995.

Tompkins, Gail. *50 Literacy Strategies: Step by Step*. Upper Saddle River: Merrill, 1998.

Lesson Plans

Before Reading

Have students do the Connect to Your Life and Key to the Story activities on page 2 of *The InterActive Reader.*™ Use the following suggestions to prepare students to read the story.

Connect to Your Life Before students fill out the chart, have them discuss experiences they have had taking care of another person. Ask: *What are some advantages of taking care of someone? What are some disadvantages?* Once students have completed the chart, ask for volunteers to share what they have written.

Key to the Story Ask for volunteers to share what they have written in their concept webs. You may want to fill out a concept web yourself and share it with students. Students may mention changes such as starting a new grade in school, being trusted with more responsibilities at home, or learning new skills through after-school activities. They may also mention changes they have noticed within themselves, such as becoming more patient or independent.

BUILD BACKGROUND Connect to Science Tell students that the story they are about to read includes a character named Raymond, who has a medical condition called *hydrocephalus.* The symptoms of this disorder include a swelling of the head caused by too much fluid collecting in the skull. Sometimes, the excess fluid damages the brain, as in Raymond's case. Explain that hydrocephalus may be caused by an infection, a tumor, a major head injury, or a malformation of the brain before birth. Childhood hydrocephalus is fairly rare and affects only about 1 out of every 1,000 children.

WORDS TO KNOW

clutch

periscope

prodigy

relay

sidekick

Additional Words to Know

admiring
  p. 5, line 46

stagecoach
  p. 6, line 64

liable
  p. 7, line 101

tradition
  p. 15, line 381

VOCABULARY PREVIEW: Words to Know in Context

You can help students learn the Words to Know by reading aloud the following sentences or writing them on the board. Then show students how to use context clues to help them figure out the meaning.

clutch: I *clutched* the broken string of beads tightly in my hands, trying to make sure no more fell on the floor.

periscope: A submarine uses a *periscope*—a long, thin tube that contains a lens—to see above the surface of the water.

prodigy: Antonio was a *prodigy* at age eight, playing violin solos with the local symphony orchestra.

relay: The last runner in the four-person *relay* waited anxiously as her three teammates completed their parts of the race.

sidekick: Everywhere he went, his *sidekick* followed him like a shadow.

---

admiring: Everyone was *admiring* Arnetta's bike after she repaired and repainted it.

stagecoach: In the 1800s, horse-drawn carriages called *stagecoaches* carried mail and passengers in the western United States.

liable: If you go out in the hot sun and don't drink enough water, you are *liable* to faint.

tradition: We eat pumpkin pie every Thanksgiving; it's a *tradition* in our family.

VOCABULARY FOCUS: Using Words with Multiple Meanings

Teacher Modeling Remind students that they can use the context of a multiple-meaning word to figure out which meaning is the right one. Then use the following modeling suggestions for the multiple-meaning word *dash* (page 4, line 27).

You could say I know that a dash is a punctuation mark, and I've heard of people adding a dash of salt to a recipe, but those meanings don't make sense in the passage "There is no track meet that I don't win the first place medal. I use to win the twenty-yard dash when I was a little kid in kindergarten. Nowadays, it's the fifty-yard dash." The character is talking about racing in track meets, and I know dash can mean "a short, fast race," so that's what I think it means in this passage.

Student Modeling Now have students follow your lead. Ask a volunteer to model using context clues to determine the meaning of *scales* (page 6, line 88).

A student might say When I think of scales, I usually think of the kind of scales on a fish, or a scale you use to weigh something. Those meanings don't make sense here, though, because "she is practicing the scales on her piano over and over and over." I know that scale can also mean "a series of musical notes," so since the sentence mentions a piano, that definition must be the right one.

> **Mini-Lesson**
> See pages 108–109 of this Guide for additional work on **Using Words with Multiple Meanings.**

During Reading

COMPREHENSION FOCUS

Key Points	Strategies for Success
Target Skill ➡ Cause and Effect "Raymond's Run" contains a complicated series of causes and effects that change Squeaky's feelings about her brother, her rival, and herself. Sorting through these causes and effects can give students a better grasp of the plot.	**Mini-Lesson** Before students read "Raymond's Run," you may want to teach the **Cause-and-Effect** lesson on pages 130–134 of this Guide. • As students read, have them stop after the *Pause & Reflect* on page 9 and discuss some of the causes and effects in the story so far. • After reading, students can complete the **Active Reading SkillBuilder** on page 17 of *The InterActive Reader.*™
Compare and Contrast Toni Cade Bambara uses vivid comparisons and contrasts between many characters in the story—Squeaky and Cynthia Proctor, runners and May Pole dancers, and finally Squeaky and Gretchen. Analyzing and discussing these similarities and differences will give students a clearer understanding of the characters.	One of the reasons Squeaky is such a lively character is that she has strong opinions on who she is and who she is not. Draw a Venn diagram on the board. Have students use it to compare and contrast Squeaky with another character in the story, such as Cynthia Proctor.

Suggested Reading Options

• An oral reading of "Raymond's Run" is available in *The Language of Literature* Audio Library. ◠
• Partner/Cooperative Reading (see page 8 of this Guide).
• Additional options are described on page 8 of this Guide.

RECIPROCAL TEACHING SUGGESTION ➡ Visualizing

Teacher Modeling *Pause & Reflect, page 12* Model for students how they can pay attention to the images that form in their minds as they read.

You could say In lines 173–193, Squeaky is describing the May Pole dance, and I can use my imagination to picture it. She says the dancers wear white dresses made out of organdy, which I know is a lightweight fabric. They also wear white shoes, which Squeaky says can't be taken out of the box until May Day, so that must mean they get dirty really easily. The girls dance around a May Pole, but Squeaky describes it as "prancing" and says the girls get their expensive clothes dirty and sweaty. No wonder she wants to get to the park after the dance is finished!

Student Modeling *Pause & Reflect, page 14* Have students reread lines 292–330, in which Squeaky describes her feelings during the race. Ask them to point out words and phrases that help them envision the scene. Offer these prompts: *How does Squeaky feel before, during, and after the race? What does she hear? What memories, images, and smells come to her mind?*

Encourage students to use the other five reading strategies when appropriate as they proceed through the rest of the selection. (See page 10 of this Guide.)

ENGLISH LEARNERS

1. Explain that the author often uses slang expressions, many of which can be figured out through context. For example, in lines 250–251, Squeaky says, "I pin number seven to myself and stomp away, I'm so burnt." If students look for context clues in the paragraph, they will realize that *burnt* means angry in this case.

2. Students might benefit from reading along with the recording of the story provided in *The Language of Literature* Audio Library. ◯

After Reading

Recommended Follow-Up

- Thinking Through the Literature, page 41, *The Language of Literature*
- Choices & Challenges, pages 42–43, *The Language of Literature*
- SkillBuilders, pages 17–19, *The InterActive Reader*™

Informal Assessment Options

Retell Have small groups of students retell the story from Gretchen's point of view. How might the descriptions of Squeaky and Raymond differ if Gretchen were the main character in the story?

Spot Check Look at the notes students made in the margins of the story. Invite them to explain their answers and discuss any questions they still have about the story.

Formal Assessment Options in *The Language of Literature*

Selection Quiz, page 20, Unit One Resource Book

Selection Test, pages 7–8, Formal Assessment Book

For more teaching options, see pages 32–43 in *The Language of Literature* Teacher's Edition.

Additional Challenge

1. **Plan a Sequel**
   Divide students into small groups, and have each group outline a sequel to "Raymond's Run." Ask: *What happens to the relationship between Squeaky and Raymond? What about the relationship between Gretchen and Squeaky? Does Squeaky become a spelling-bee champion, a pianist, a coach, or something else altogether? And what happens at the next year's May Day race?*

2. **MARK IT UP ⬦ Examine a Character**
   Direct students to look at lines 1–67 and lines 349–381. Have them mark words and phrases that describe Raymond—his physical appearance and his actions. Then ask: *How do the descriptions change as the story progresses? How did your impression of Raymond change from the beginning of the story to the end? What does Raymond do that makes Squeaky call him "a great runner in the family tradition"?*

Before Reading

Direct students' attention to the Connect to Your Life and Key to the Story activities on page 20 of *The InterActive Reader.*™ Use the following suggestions to prepare students to read the story.

Connect to Your Life
Ask students to discuss the difference between being lonely and being alone. Ask: *When have you felt lonely? Do you ever like to be alone? When?* Then write the words *lonely* and *alone* on the board and work with students to brainstorm a list of words related to each one. Finally, have students complete the activity on page 20. Ask them to share their responses in small groups.

Key to the Story
Ask students to share what they know about orphanages. Then read aloud the Key to the Story, and have students jot down their ideas about what they think orphanages are like. Encourage them to think about images they have received from books, movies, or television. Invite volunteers to share their ideas.

BUILD BACKGROUND Connect to Geography
Explain to students that the story takes place in an isolated rural location in the North Carolina mountains. North Carolina's mountain region is made up of many mountain ranges, including the Blue Ridge Mountains. All of these are part of the larger Appalachian Mountain chain. Have students locate these mountains on a map of the United States. Ask them to predict what the landscape and climate might be like in the story, based on this information.

WORDS TO KNOW

- abstracted
- blunt
- clarity
- communion
- ecstasy
- impel
- inadequate
- instinctive
- kindling
- predicated

VOCABULARY PREVIEW: Words to Know in Context

You can help students learn the Words to Know by reading aloud the following sentences or writing them on the board. Then show students how to use context clues to help them figure out the meaning.

abstracted: *Abstracted* with thoughts about the game, I didn't look where I was going and bumped into the wall.

blunt: His comments about my new shirt were *blunt,* as if he did not care whether he hurt my feelings.

clarity: In the country, the *clarity* of the air lets you see many stars at night.

communion: Soldiers often become close friends, trusting each other and sharing a deep *communion.*

ecstasy: A look of *ecstasy* lit up the child's face when she saw the pile of birthday presents.

impel: I felt *impelled* to donate money to help the family whose house had burned down.

inadequate: We ran out of food because our supplies were *inadequate.*

instinctive: A mother's love for her child is a natural, or *instinctive,* reaction.

kindling: If you gather *kindling,* such as dry wood or twigs, you'll have an easier time lighting a campfire.

predicated: She ran for mayor with no *predicated,* or established, record in city government.

VOCABULARY FOCUS Word Parts: Prefixes

Teacher Modeling Remind students that they can sometimes figure out the meaning of an unfamiliar word by thinking about the word parts it contains. Then use the following modeling suggestions for the word *subtropics* (page 22, line 27).

You could say I'm not sure what subtropics *means, but I've seen the prefix* sub- *before in words such as* submarine. *I know the prefix means "below" or "under." The tropics are a hot, humid region near the equator. So* subtropics *must mean "a region below the tropics."*

Student Modeling Now have students follow your lead. Ask a volunteer to model using the strategy to figure out the meaning of the word *undersized* (page 23, line 40).

A student might say I'm not familiar with the word undersized. *However, I recognize the prefix* under- *from words such as* underground *and* underpaid. *I know the prefix can mean "below" or "less than normal." Therefore, a boy who looks* undersized *is probably smaller than normal.*

Mini-Lesson
See pages 100–101 of this Guide for additional work on **Word Parts: Prefixes.**

During Reading

COMPREHENSION FOCUS

Key Points	Strategies for Success
Target Skill ➡ Making Inferences It is important that students be able to make inferences in order to understand the story's key events and the characters' motivations.	**Mini-Lesson** Before students read "A Mother in Mannville," teach the **Making Inferences** lesson on pages 138–140 of this Guide. • Read aloud lines 320–346 on page 32. Ask students what they can infer about Jerry's feelings for the narrator from the fact that he lies to her about his mother. Ask: *How do you think Jerry feels about the narrator? Why do you think he lies to her? What clues from the story helped you make your inferences?* • As students read, have them use the **Inference Chart** on page 139 of this Guide to record other inferences.
Characterization Students' ability to discern the characters' personalities and motives by interpreting clues in the text is crucial to their understanding of events.	Remind students that authors show what characters are like by describing them directly, by having other characters describe them, or by showing the characters' words and actions. At the *Pause & Reflect* on page 23, work with students to note clues about the two main characters and the traits they reveal. Have them jot down these clues in the margins and add to their notes as they read.

Suggested Reading Options

• An oral reading of "A Mother in Mannville" is available in *The Language of Literature* Audio Library. ◯
• Independent Reading (see page 8 of this Guide).
• Additional options are described on page 8 of this Guide.

RECIPROCAL TEACHING SUGGESTION ➡ Connecting

Teacher Modeling *Pause & Reflect, page 26* To help students understand the narrator's respect for Jerry, model for students the connecting strategy.

You could say *In lines 104–111 on page 25, the narrator describes Jerry's integrity and recalls her father, who also possessed that quality. When I read the passage, I think about my own mother, who raised two children on her own and was always honest, brave, and trustworthy. My memories help me relate to the narrator's feelings and experiences.*

Student Modeling *Pause & Reflect, page 30* Have several students model the connecting strategy to identify with the narrator's feelings for Jerry. Offer this prompt: *Have you ever felt protective toward a friend or family member? How would you react if you thought someone had hurt your loved one's feelings?*

Encourage students to use the other five reading strategies when appropriate as they proceed through the rest of the story. (See page 10 of this Guide.)

ENGLISH LEARNERS

1. Make sure students understand that the narrator is a writer who lives alone and travels to do her work and that Jerry is a boy who lives in an orphanage because he has no parents to care for him.

2. Students might benefit from reading along with the recording of "A Mother in Mannville" provided in *The Language of Literature* Audio Library. ⌒

After Reading

Recommended Follow-Up

- Thinking Through the Literature, page 66, *The Language of Literature*
- Choices & Challenges, pages 67–68, *The Language of Literature*
- SkillBuilders, pages 33–35, *The InterActive Reader*™

Informal Assessment Options

Retell Have pairs of students retell the story from Jerry's point of view. Offer these prompts:

- *What did you do for the woman?*
- *How did you feel when she complimented your work?*
- *How did you feel when she had you take care of her dog?*
- *Why did you tell her you had a mother?*
- *How did you feel when she left?*

Spot Check Look at the notes students made in the margins. Ask students who used the **?** notation whether they were able to clear up their confusion, and if so, how.

Formal Assessment Options in *The Language of Literature*

Selection Quiz, page 34, Unit One Resource Book

Selection Test, pages 11–12, Formal Assessment Book

For more teaching options, see pages 59–68 in *The Language of Literature* Teacher's Edition.

Additional Challenge

1. Examine Setting

Discuss with students how the story's setting affects its plot and characters. Ask: *Why is the setting important in the relationship between the narrator and Jerry? How does the setting affect the narrator's weekend trip?* Then ask students how the story might be different if it took place in a big city. Ask: *How might the characters meet? How would a city setting affect their relationship? Do you think they would be as close?*

2. ▐▐ MARK IT UP ⟫ Identify Figurative Language

Tell students that a simile is a comparison that uses the words *like* or *as*. A metaphor is an implied comparison that does not contain *like* or *as*. Point out the simile on page 22, lines 20–21 ("soft as the May winds that stirred the hemlocks"), and the metaphor on page 26, lines 138–139 ("the clear well of his eyes"), to help students recognize these types of figurative language. Then have students underline other similes and metaphors they find in the story. Discuss some of the examples they identify. Have students tell why each example is effective.

Before Reading

Have students do the Connect to Your Life and Key to the Story activities on page 36 of *The InterActive Reader.*™ Use the following suggestions to prepare students to read the story.

Connect to Your Life
Guide students in a discussion about a time when they planned something that turned out differently from what they expected. You might ask them to think about a surprise they planned for someone in their family and how it turned out. Or you might ask them to think about a trip they planned and what actually happened. After students fill out the chart, let them share their incidents and the results.

Key to the Story
The story is about two men who have the idea of kidnapping a mischievous child for money. Ask volunteers to read examples of the words they used in the word web. Have a brief discussion about the word *ransom.* You might say: *Think of various stories you've read about or seen on TV or in the movies that involved a ransom. Why did the ransom take place and how did it end?*

BUILD BACKGROUND Connect to History
Explain to students that this story was published in 1910, when methods of catching criminals were less sophisticated. The kidnappers in "The Ransom of Red Chief" did not have to worry about being identified through fingerprints or about being located by helicopters or infrared devices. Most likely, the criminals in the story also counted on the isolation of Alabama in 1910. In contrast, Alabama at present is part of a national communications network that includes telephones, cell phones, TV, radio, fax machines, and computers.

WORDS TO KNOW

- collaborate
- commend
- comply
- diatribe
- impudent
- palatable
- pervade
- proposition
- ransom
- surreptitiously

VOCABULARY PREVIEW: Words to Know in Context

You can help students learn the Words to Know by reading aloud the following sentences or writing them on the board. Then show students how to use context clues to help them figure out the meaning.

collaborate: The teacher asked us to choose a partner who would *collaborate* on the science project.

commend: The officer praised the boys' honesty when he told their parents, "I would like to *commend* you for having such truthful children."

comply: If you do not *comply* with the rules, you will be cut from the team.

diatribe: Today's newspaper has an angry *diatribe,* or criticism, about the plan to raise taxes.

impudent: He was rude to the teacher and got in trouble with the principal for his *impudent* actions.

palatable: The most *palatable* foods on the menu include favorites like pizza, hamburgers, sandwiches, and milk shakes.

pervade: The smell of bacon *pervaded* the entire house even though the kitchen windows were wide open.

proposition: Tom made Michael a *proposition* he couldn't refuse—$50 for walking his dog in the evening.

ransom: The hijackers listed their demands, including a large sum of money, in a *ransom* note.

surreptitiously: I handed Jane the note *surreptitiously* so that no one else would see it.

VOCABULARY FOCUS: Using Context Clues

Teacher Modeling Remind students that they can use context clues to figure out the meaning of unfamiliar words. Then use the following modeling suggestions for the word *reconnoiter* (page 43, line 161).

You could say *I don't know the word* reconnoiter, *but I can look for clues by reading the surrounding sentences. The narrator says that he will go up to the top of the mountain and* reconnoiter. *He is going to do something, but what is it? The next sentence says, "I went up on the peak of the little mountain and ran my eye over the contiguous vicinity." He is on top of the little mountain looking at the area near the mountain. From these clues and others in the paragraph, I can conclude that* reconnoiter *means "to inspect or observe an area."*

Student Modeling Now have students follow your lead. Ask a volunteer to model using context clues to determine the meaning of the word **yeomanry** (page 43, line 164).

A student might say *In the sentence, "Over toward Summit I expected to see the sturdy yeomanry of the village armed with scythes and pitchforks beating the countryside for the dastardly kidnappers," I'm not familiar with the word* yeomanry. *I know that Summit is the town where Red Chief was kidnapped. I also know that the word* sturdy *means "strong and powerful." The phrase "armed with scythes and pitchforks" tells me that someone is armed with farming tools, so* yeomanry *probably means townspeople or farmers.*

> **Mini-Lesson** See pages 96–99 of this Guide for additional work on **Using Context Clues.**

During Reading

COMPREHENSION FOCUS

Key Points	Strategies for Success
Target Skill ➡ Making Inferences In order to understand the irony and humor in this story, students must be able to make inferences about how the character of Red Chief influences all that happens.	**Mini-Lesson** Before students read "The Ransom of Red Chief," you many want to teach the **Making Inferences** lesson on pages 138–140 of this Guide. • Read aloud lines 43–53 on page 39 and the speech on page 41. Then ask students what they can infer about the little boy from these lines and the speech. • Tell students that the writer uses hints, or clues, throughout the story to help the reader make inferences about characters and the way they feel. • After students have read the story, have them complete the **Inference Chart** on page 139.
Antiquated Language Students may have difficulty understanding O. Henry's formal style and antiquated vocabulary and diction.	Tell students that they may need to reread some passages and/or work with classmates to paraphrase sections of the text into modern, everyday language.

Suggested Reading Options

• An oral reading of "The Ransom of Red Chief" is available in *The Language of Literature* Audio Library. ◯
• Partner/Cooperative Reading (see page 8 of this Guide).
• Additional options are described on page 8 of this Guide.

RECIPROCAL TEACHING SUGGESTION ➡ Clarifying

Teacher Modeling *Pause & Reflect, page 44.* Have students reread lines 162–177. If some students are confused about the narrator's reaction in this passage, model the clarifying strategy.

You could say *I'm not sure what is happening in these lines. Why is Sam so excited towards the end of the passage and why does he say, "Heaven help the wolves"? I can reread the passage, paying close attention to the details the narrator gives. Sam expected to see a town made frantic by the child's disappearance but instead finds a "peaceful landscape." Towards the end of the passage, he comes to the conclusion that "it has not yet been discovered that the wolves have borne away the tender lambkin from the fold. Heaven help the wolves!" I believe he sees himself as the wolf who has stolen a precious child. When he says, "heaven help the wolves," he is thinking about what the townspeople might do to the kidnappers, but also about what Johnny is already doing to them.*

Student Modeling *Pause and Reflect, page 54.* Have students reread lines 430–435 and then model the clarifying strategy. Offer these prompts: *Why do you think Mr. Dorset tells the kidnappers that his neighbors believe Johnny is lost and that he could not be "responsible for what they would do to anybody they saw bringing him back"? Use details from the story and what you have learned about Johnny to answer this question.*

Encourage students to use the other five reading strategies when appropriate as they proceed through the rest of the selection. (See page 10 of this Guide.)

ENGLISH LEARNERS

1. Students may have difficulty with some of the vocabulary in this story. Let them know that the writer has adopted a fairly wordy style, and that they will often be able to follow the plot even if they don't know the meaning of every single word. You may need to stop and help students define difficult words as they read the selection.

2. Students might benefit from reading along with the recording of the story provided in *The Language of Literature* Audio Library. ◯

After Reading

Recommended Follow-Up

• Thinking Through the Literature, page 80, *The Language of Literature*
• Choices & Challenges, pages 81–82, *The Language of Literature*
• SkillBuilders, pages 55–57, *The InterActive Reader*™

Informal Assessment Options

Retell Have students work in pairs to retell the selection from the point of view of Johnny (Red Chief) and Bill Driscoll.

Spot Check Review the comments and responses students have written on the side margins, paying special attention to *Pause & Reflect* questions. Invite students to explain their answers and discuss any questions they still have about the story.

Formal Assessment Options in *The Language of Literature*

Selection Quiz, page 41, Unit One Resource Book

Selection Test, pages 13–14, Formal Assessment Book

For more teaching options, see pages 69–82 in *The Language of Literature* Teacher's Edition.

Additional Challenge

1. **Analyze Humor**
   Ask students to identify and read aloud passages in the story that they found humorous. Then lead students in a discussion of how the author created humor through such devices as exaggeration and reversing expectations.

2. **▌▌MARK IT UP ⬦ Identify Character Traits**
   Write the following list of adjectives on the board. Have students decide which of these words describe Bill Driscoll and then have them circle details in the story that reveal each of those traits.

friendly	brave	ignorant
quick-tempered	foolish	smart

Before Reading

Direct students' attention to the Connect to Your Life and Key to the Story activities on page 58 of *The InterActive Reader.*™ Use the following suggestions to prepare students to read the story.

Connect to Your Life
Read aloud the directions on page 58 and have students add an example to their chart. Invite volunteers to share their responses. Then ask: *Would you put yourself in danger to do a good deed for someone you cared about? Why or why not?*

Key to the Story
Have students use a map of North America to gauge the distance between their city or town and the Yukon territory of northwestern Canada. Ask students what they think the climate is probably like in this region. Then have them read the paragraph on page 58 and shade the map. Discuss what hardships gold-seekers of the late 1800s might have faced in the Yukon, far from large cities and supplies.

BUILD BACKGROUND
Sled Dogs Ask students what they know or have heard about dogsledding. Explain that today it is a popular sport as well as a means of transportation in such areas as northern Canada, Alaska, and Siberia. If possible, show students a picture from an encyclopedia or magazine of a sled dog team. Point out that the most important dog on the team is the lead dog, who must be fast, smart, and reliable. Discuss why these qualities might be important in a lead dog.

WORDS TO KNOW

antic
capsize
commissioner
flounder
liable
peer
prospector
stampede
summit
yaw

Additional Words to Know

adjoining
    page 62, line 61
resolved
    page 62, line 78

VOCABULARY PREVIEW: Words to Know in Context

You can help students learn the Words to Know by reading aloud the following sentences or writing them on the board. Then show students how to use context clues to help them figure out the meaning of the boldfaced words.

antic:	Dani is famous for her crazy *antics.* She is always playing tricks and practical jokes.
capsize:	When we put too many things in the boat, it *capsized.* We spent 20 minutes getting it turned right side up again.
commissioner:	The police *commissioner* was in charge of the entire police department.
flounder:	When a big wave knocked me over, I *floundered* in the deep water, trying to regain my balance.
liable:	Tell Alex not to walk on that icy sidewalk. If he does, he is *liable* to slip and fall.
peer:	Brianna *peered* through her telescope at the stars.
prospector:	The old *prospector* searched for gold for years.
stampede:	When the bell rang, a *stampede* of 15 eighth graders rushed to the cafeteria.
summit:	I reached the *summit* of the mountain, enjoyed the view for a few minutes, and then started climbing back down again.
yaw:	The truck suddenly *yawed* to the right to keep from hitting a pothole; a moment later the truck was back on course again.

adjoining:	That fence separates our property from the *adjoining* plot of land.
resolved:	After a long discussion, the band *resolved* to play in the summer concert whether it was raining or not.

VOCABULARY FOCUS Word Parts: Suffixes

Teacher Modeling Remind students that they can sometimes use their knowledge of suffixes to help them determine the meaning of an unfamiliar word. Demonstrate this strategy by using the word *cautiously* (page 63, line 121).

You could say I'm not sure what the word cautiously *means, but I recognize the suffix* -ly *from words such as* nicely. *I know that it usually means "in a certain way." Since* cautious *means "careful,"* cautiously *must be an adverb that means "in a way that is careful." Walt is looking "cautiously" at the camp of dangerous men, so this meaning makes sense.*

Student Modeling Now have students follow your lead. Call on a volunteer to model how to use the suffix *-ly* to figure out the meaning of the word *evidently* (page 63, line 118)

A student might say I recognize the suffix -ly *in this word. I know it can mean "in a certain way." The word* evident *means "easy to see or understand" or "clear."* Evidently *must mean "in a way that is clear" or "obviously." This makes sense in the sentence.*

> **Mini-Lesson**
> See pages 100 and 102 of this Guide for additional work on **Word Parts: Suffixes.**

During Reading

COMPREHENSION FOCUS

Key Points	Strategies for Success
Target Skill ➡ Narrative Elements The unfamiliar story setting, the unusual problems faced by the main character, and the fast-paced sequence of events may hinder students' ability to follow the plot.	**Mini-Lesson** Before students read "The King of Mazy May," you may wish to teach or review the **Narrative Elements** lesson on pages 147–150 of this Guide. • Have students read aloud pages 61–62. Then discuss with students the setting, characters, and conflict. Make sure students understand how the setting creates a problem for the main character. • After reading, students can also complete the **Story Map** on page 148 of this Guide.
Spatial Distances Students' ability to imagine the distances mentioned in the story is crucial to their understanding of the main conflict as well as the danger Walt faces as he flees his pursuers.	At the *Pause & Reflect* on page 60, help students relate the distances to their own experiences. For instance, have them visualize three hundred yards as the length of three football fields end to end, and fifty miles as the distance between your community and another familiar town. Have students note additional spatial references as they read, and make similar comparisons to help them visualize the setting or events.

Suggested Reading Options

- An oral reading of "The King of Mazy May" is available in *The Language of Literature* Audio Library. ◯
- Partner/Cooperative Reading (see page 8 of this Guide).
- Additional options are described on page 8 of this Guide.

RECIPROCAL TEACHING SUGGESTION ➡ Predicting

Teacher Modeling *Pause & Reflect, page 67* Model using story clues to predict what the next part of Walt's journey will be like.

You could say *Walt has shown skill, bravery, and determination so far in his attempt to reach Dawson and evade the stampeders. However, although he has made it to the Yukon, night is falling and the stampeders are still after him. The first eight miles from Walt's claim to the Yukon were extremely difficult. The crooked paths prevented the dogs from running at top speed. I predict that he will face more dangerous obstacles in his quest to reach Dawson.*

Student Modeling *Pause & Reflect, page 70* Have volunteers model how to use story clues to predict whether Walt will reach Dawson safely or whether the stampeders will overtake him. Offer this prompt: *What advantage has Walt gained? How long has he been steering the sled? Do you think he will be able to keep his lead?*

Encourage students to use the other five reading strategies when appropriate as they proceed through the rest of the story. (See page 10 of this Guide.)

ENGLISH LEARNERS

1. Before students read, clarify the following: why prospectors came to the Yukon, how they recorded their claims, and how and why those claims were often "jumped." Also briefly summarize Walt's main problem and how he attempts to solve it.

2. Students might benefit from reading along with the recording of the story provided in *The Language of Literature* Audio Library. ◯

After Reading

Recommended Follow-Up

- Thinking Through the Literature, page 157, *The Language of Literature*
- Choices & Challenges, page 158, *The Language of Literature*
- SkillBuilders, pages 73–75, *The InterActive Reader*™

Informal Assessment Options

Retell Have pairs of students retell the story by role-playing an imaginary conversation that might take place between Walt and his father about Walt's adventure.

Spot Check Look at the notes students made in the margins of the story. Invite them to explain their answers and discuss any questions they still have about the story.

Formal Assessment Options in *The Language of Literature*

Selection Quiz, page 80, Unit One Resource Book

Selection Test, pages 23–24, Formal Assessment Book

For more teaching options, see pages 148–158 in *The Language of Literature* Teacher's Edition.

Additional Challenge

1. Examine Point of View
Have students rewrite one of these sections from Walt's or a stampeder's point of view: page 66, lines 181–202; pages 69–70, lines 300–320.

2. ⃞‖MARK IT UP〉 Analyze Character
Ask: *What qualities enabled Walt Masters to succeed in his struggle against the stampeders?* Have students mark passages in the story to support their views.

3. ⃞‖MARK IT UP〉 Explore the Setting
Have students highlight details that help them picture the setting. Discuss what they think they might like and dislike about living in the Yukon Territory in the 1890s.

Before Reading

Direct students' attention to the Connect to Your Life and Key to the Poems activities on page 76 of *The InterActive Reader.*™ Use the following suggestions to prepare students to read the poems.

Connect to Your Life
Invite volunteers to share examples of advice they have been given. Then ask: *What are some subjects you could give advice about to someone younger?* Students may mention tips for succeeding in school, doing well in sports, or getting along with siblings. Have students read the directions and the example on page 76. Then have them complete their charts.

Key to the Poems
Ask a volunteer to read aloud the excerpt from "Mother to Son." Discuss how the poet uses direct address, dialect, and other elements to make the words sound like spoken English. Ask students why they think the poet might have wanted his words to sound this way.

BUILD BACKGROUND
Connect to the African-American Experience Explain to students that the poetry of both Langston Hughes and Gwendolyn Brooks tells about the experience of growing up African American in the early part of the 20th century. Hughes, who became an important literary figure during the 1920s, often portrayed the everyday life of African Americans in his poems. Brooks's collection *A Street in Bronzeville* describes the lives of the people who live in a poor Chicago neighborhood. The work of both poets shows an awareness of prejudice and of the need for justice.

Strategies for Reading Poetry

- Notice the form of the poem: the number of lines and their shape on the page.
- Read the poem aloud a few times. Listen for rhymes and rhythms.
- Visualize the images and comparisons.
- Mark words and phrases that appeal to you.
- Ask yourself what message the poet is trying to send.
- Think about what the poem is saying to you.

FOCUS ON POETRY

Before having students read "Mother to Son" and "Speech to the Young/Speech to the Progress-Toward," you may want to have them read the feature "Poetry" on pages 187–191 of *The Language of Literature.* That lesson shows how the key elements of poetry work together to produce emotion and meaning. It also suggests some strategies students can use when reading poetry. The activities below will prepare students for reading "Mother to Son" and "Speech to the Young/Speech to the Progress-Toward."

- **Free Verse** Read aloud the excerpt on page 76. Explain that the informal, conversational format the poet uses is called free verse. Discuss why a poet might use free verse. Students may answer that a *free-verse* poem might sound more like actual speech or that the reader of a *free-verse* poem might pay more attention to the message of the poem rather than its rhythm and structure. Have students listen for other signs of free verse in both poems as they read.

- **Speaker** Point out to students that the *speaker* of a poem is the "voice" the reader hears telling the story or the ideas of the poem. Sometimes the speaker is the poet; other times the speaker is a "character" the poet creates within the poem. Read aloud the excerpt on page 76. Ask students who the speaker seems to be, and how they can tell. Encourage students to listen for clues about the speakers in both poems as they read.

VOCABULARY FOCUS Word Parts: Compound Words

Teacher Modeling Remind students that they can often use the meanings of the smaller words within a compound word to help them figure out its meaning. Model using the invented word **harmony-hushers** (page 79, line 5).

You could say *I'm not sure what* harmony-hushers *means, but I see that it has the smaller words* harmony *and* hushers *in it. I know* harmony *can mean "a pleasing combination of sounds or colors" or "a state of agreement; a lack of discord." I also know that* hush *means "to make quiet." In this poem the term seems to refer to a person who tries to silence signs of harmony or happiness.*

Student Modeling Call on a volunteer to model figuring out the invented word **sun-slappers** (page 79, line 3).

A student might say *I can see that this unfamiliar word is made up of two smaller words I know,* sun *and* slappers. *To* slap *is to "strike or smack." Since you can't literally strike the sun, a* sun-slapper *is probably someone who tries to strike down or spoil the joy of others.*

 **Mini-Lesson** See pages 100 and 103 of this Guide for additional work on **Word Parts: Compound Words.**

During Reading

COMPREHENSION FOCUS

Key Points	Strategies for Success
Target Skill ➡ Making Inferences Both poets rely on readers to make inferences about the speaker and the themes in the poems.	**Mini-Lesson** Before students read the poems, you may want to teach or review the **Making Inferences** lesson on pages 138–140 of this Guide. • Use the *Pause & Reflect* questions on pages 78–79 to help students make inferences. Ask: *What values and traits does each speaker seem to possess? How can you tell?* Students may mention perseverance, patience, and a positive outlook. • During or after reading, have students complete the **Active Reading SkillBuilder** on page 80.
Figurative Language Figurative language and imaginative word play help convey the message of each poem. Students may need help interpreting the figurative language.	Read aloud lines 10–13 on page 78 and then ask: *Why does the speaker compare life to a staircase? What details show you that her life has been difficult?* Then read aloud lines 2–5 on page 79 and ask students to give synonyms for the figurative language in these lines (for example, "criticizers" for "down-keepers").

Suggested Reading Options

• Oral readings of "Mother to Son" and "Speech to the Young/Speech to the Progress-Toward" are available in *The Language of Literature* Audio Library. ◯
• Oral Reading (see page 8 of this Guide).
• Additional options are described on page 8 of this Guide.

RECIPROCAL TEACHING SUGGESTION ➡ Connecting

Teacher Modeling *Pause & Reflect, page 78* Model using the questioning strategy to help students interpret the imagery in "Mother to Son.".

You could say *In line 14, I wonder why the speaker says, "don't you turn back." I ask myself:* What does she mean by "turn back"? *As I reread, I see that her life has been so difficult that sometimes "there ain't been no light," or hope. She probably fears that her son might feel hopeless at times, too. "Turn back" probably means "to give up."*

Student Modeling *Pause & Reflect, page 79* Have students model using the strategy to understand "Speech to the Young/Speech to the Progress-Toward." Offer these prompts: *Which words or expressions in this poem are confusing to you? Do you understand the advice the speaker is giving?*

Encourage students to use the other five reading strategies when appropriate as they proceed through the poems. (See page 10 of this Guide.)

ENGLISH LEARNERS

1. Discuss with students why the staircase in "Mother to Son" is a good comparison for life. Then have them work with English-proficient partners to restate in their own words the poet's message in "Speech to the Young/Speech to the Progress-Toward."

2. Students might benefit from reading along with the recordings of "Mother to Son" and "Speech to the Young/Speech to the Progress-Toward" provided in *The Language of Literature* Audio Library. ◯

After Reading

Recommended Follow-Up

- Thinking Through the Literature, page 195, *The Language of Literature*
- Choices & Challenges, page 196, *The Language of Literature*
- SkillBuilders, pages 80–81, *The InterActive Reader*™

Informal Assessment Options

Retell Have students retell "Mother to Son" by using a different metaphor, such as a road or a ladder, to restate the speaker's message about life. Then have them work in pairs to retell "Speech to the Young/Speech to the Progress-Toward" as a conversation between the speaker and a "down-keeper."

Spot Check Look at the notes students made in the margins. Make sure their answers show an understanding of what they have read. Pay particular attention to question 2 on page 78 and question 2 on page 79, as both of these check comprehension.

Formal Assessment Options in *The Language of Literature*

Selection Test, pages 29–30, Formal Assessment Book

For more teaching options, see pages 192–196 in *The Language of Literature* Teacher's Edition.

Additional Challenge

1. ▌▌▌**MARK IT UP**⟩ **Understand Imagery**
Both poems contain powerful images that reflect the theme of overcoming obstacles with perseverance and a positive outlook. Have students underline images of darkness and light in each poem. Discuss how these images help convey the underlying message.

2. ▌▌▌**MARK IT UP**⟩ **Compare Tones**
Tell students that the tone of a work expresses the writer's attitude toward the subject. Words such as *amused, sad,* and *encouraging* can be used to describe different tones. Ask students to describe the tone the speaker uses in each poem. Have students underline details that support their answers.

Before Reading

Direct students' attention to the Connect to Your Life and Key to the Story activities on page 82 of *The InterActive Reader.*™ Use the following suggestions to prepare students to read the story.

Connect to Your Life
Tell students that "Flowers for Algernon" is a story about a mentally retarded man who bears the brunt of his coworkers' ridicule. Discuss possible reasons why people sometimes make fun of those who are different. Then ask: *What are good ways to respond to people who make fun of others?* Have students complete the activity and share their responses.

Key to the Story
Ask students: *Do you think intelligence is a significant part of someone's personality? Why or why not?* Then read aloud the Key to the Story on page 82, and have students place their checkmarks on the scales on the page.

BUILD BACKGROUND
Connect to Psychology Explain to students that intelligence is generally defined as the ability to acquire and apply knowledge. However, scientists have long argued about exactly what this means. Some believe humans have different kinds of intelligence, such as linguistic, mathematical, or musical intelligence. Another controversial issue is whether it is possible to measure intelligence, as with an IQ test. People with certain developmental disabilities—or those who have suffered particular illnesses or injuries—have abnormally low IQs, and are considered to be mentally retarded. Charlie, the narrator of this story, is one of those people.

WORDS TO KNOW

- absurd
- hypothesis
- impair
- introspective
- naïveté
- opportunist
- proportional
- regression
- sensation
- shrew
- specialization
- statistically
- syndrome
- tangible
- vacuous

VOCABULARY PREVIEW: Words to Know in Context

You can help students learn the Words to Know by reading aloud the following sentences or writing them on the board. Then show students how to use context clues to help them figure out the meaning.

absurd: It is *absurd,* or ridiculous, to use a hammer to swat flies.

hypothesis: The science teacher asked us to write down a *hypothesis,* or theory, to guide our research.

impair: If your eyesight is *impaired,* you might need to wear glasses.

introspective: Whenever I walk along the lake, I become *introspective,* thinking about the way I feel that day.

naïveté: The young lawyer's *naïveté* showed he knew nothing about politics; he was as trusting as a little child.

opportunist: The con artist is an *opportunist* who takes advantage of trusting people.

proportional: Her success in school is *proportional* to the time she spends studying.

regression: Instead of showing an improvement, my scores on tests seem to show a *regression.*

sensation: The new band caused a *sensation,* exciting audiences in city after city.

shrew: The woman in the story was a mean old *shrew* with a nagging voice.

specialization: The surgeon's *specialization* is heart surgery.

statistically: It is *statistically* true that women live longer than men.

syndrome: Al has a rare *syndrome* that causes him to become weak and dizzy.

tangible: The detective wanted concrete, *tangible* evidence to make a strong case.

vacuous: The *vacuous* look on his face showed that he didn't understand a word.

VOCABULARY FOCUS Word Parts: Roots

Teacher Modeling Remind students that they can sometimes figure out the meaning of an unfamiliar word if they recognize its root from other, familiar words. Model using the word **suspicion** (page 102, line 608).

You could say *The word* suspicion *begins like the word* suspect, *which I know can mean "to think or believe something is true." The two words appear to have the same root,* susp-, *so they may have similar meanings. In this sentence,* suspicion *could mean "belief." The dictionary confirms my guess and explains that both words come from the Latin word* suspicere, *meaning "to watch."*

Student Modeling Ask a volunteer to model using roots to figure out the meaning of **sensibility** (page 112, line 903).

A student might say *I wonder what the word* sensibliity *means. I notice that it is similar to the word* sense, *which means "ability to feel." Sensibility must have something to do with sensing or feeling. When I look it up in the dictionary, I see that it means "keen awareness of feeling" and that it has its root in the Latin word* sentire, *which means "to feel."*

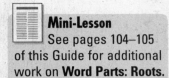
Mini-Lesson See pages 104–105 of this Guide for additional work on **Word Parts: Roots.**

During Reading

COMPREHENSION FOCUS

Key Points	Strategies for Success
Target Skill ➡ Compare and Contrast The story revolves around narrator Charlie Gordon's profound mental and emotional transformation. To follow the plot, students must be able to discern similarities and differences between the "old" Charlie and the "new" Charlie.	**Mini-Lesson** Before students read "Flowers for Algernon," you may wish to teach the **Compare and Contrast** lesson on pages 135–137 of this Guide. • At the *Pause & Reflect* on page 93, help students note subtle improvements in Charlie's writing ability. As they continue reading, have students identify the aspects of Charlie's life that change as well as those that stay the same. • Have students complete the **Venn Diagram** on page 136 of this Guide.
Making Inferences In the first part of the story, the narrator's limited mental ability prevents him from perceiving the other characters' motivations or the significance of their actions. As a result, Charlie's descriptions of other characters and events are not reliable. Readers must make inferences about the real feelings and actions of these other characters in order to understand story events.	Read aloud lines 251–257 on page 91. Ask students what they can infer about Joe Carp and Frank Reilly and their feelings toward Charlie. Continue to work with students at each *Pause & Reflect* to help them make inferences about events or characters described in that section. • Have students keep track of their inferences by using the **Active Reading SkillBuilder** on page 125 of *The InterActive Reader.*™

Suggested Reading Options

• An oral reading of "Flowers for Algernon" is available in *The Language of Literature* Audio Library. ◯
• Partner/Cooperative Reading (see page 8 of this Guide).
• Additional options are described on page 8 of this Guide.

RECIPROCAL TEACHING SUGGESTION ➡ Evaluating

Teacher Modeling *Pause & Reflect, page 93* Model using the evaluating strategy to help students form opinions about how Charlie's co-workers treat him.

You could say *Charlie enjoys the company of the other men at work. Their jokes make him laugh, and he believes they like him. However, he doesn't realize that their jokes are at his expense. They think he's dumb, and they enjoy making fun of him. I think they treat him cruelly.*

Student Modeling *Pause & Reflect, page 107* Have students model the evaluating strategy to form opinions about the effects of Charlie's new intelligence. Offer this prompt: *How do others react to Charlie's growing intelligence? Do you think having the operation was a good idea? Why or why not?*

Encourage students to use the other five reading strategies when appropriate as they proceed through the rest of the story. (See page 10 of this Guide.)

After Reading

Recommended Follow-Up

- Thinking Through the Literature, page 246, *The Language of Literature*
- Choices & Challenges, pages 247–248, *The Language of Literature*
- SkillBuilders, pages 125–127, *The InterActive Reader*™

Informal Assessment Options

Retell Have students work in groups of three to retell the events in this story as an imaginary conversation between the two doctors and Miss Kinnian. Each student should select a different character to role-play.

Spot Check Look at the notes students made in the margins to check for understanding. Ask students who used the **?** notation if they were able to clear up their confusion, and if so, how.

Formal Assessment Options in *The Language of Literature*

Selection Quiz, page 23, Unit Two Resource Book

Selection Test, pages 37–38, Formal Assessment Book

For more teaching options, see pp. 220–248 in *The Language of Literature* Teacher's Edition.

Additional Challenge

1. **Explore the Title**
   Ask: *Why do you think the author called this story "Flowers for Algernon"?* Have students write an explanation, using examples from the story to support their points.

2. **⦚ MARK IT UP ⟩ Author's Style**
   Ask: *How does the author's use of language reflect the intellectual changes in Charlie? What are some specific ways in which Charlie's voice changes throughout the story?* Have students underline examples of Charlie's voice, describing these details in the margin (e.g., better spelling, improved vocabulary, references to new scientific knowledge). Also ask them to mark places in the text where the shift in voice is especially noticeable.

Before Reading

Direct students' attention to the Connect to Your Life and Key to the Story activities on page 128 of *The InterActive Reader.*™ Use the following suggestions to prepare students to read the story.

Connect to Your Life
Explain to students that the conflict in this story begins with a disagreement over capital punishment. Define this term and point out that its use in the United States is also highly controversial. Brainstorm with students a list of other controversial issues they know about. Then ask: *What are your opinions about these topics?* Have students fill out the chart and share their responses in small groups.

Key to the Story
Ask a volunteer to read aloud the sentence from the story and the directions on page 128. Then work with students to come up with several words related to the two circled words, and use them to help students define *voluntary* ("brought about by free choice") and *enforced* ("brought about by force"). Then discuss what they think the sentence means, whether they agree, and why.

BUILD BACKGROUND **Connect to Biography** Tell students that Russian author Anton Chekhov (1860–1904) believed that writers should portray life and its problems realistically. He also worked to help solve some of the real economic and social problems facing Russia during the late 1800s. For example, he was a doctor as well as a writer, and he ran a free clinic for poor peasants for many years.

WORDS TO KNOW

- capricious
- haphazardly
- humane
- immoral
- incessantly
- obsolete
- posterity
- rapture
- renunciation
- stipulated

VOCABULARY PREVIEW: Words to Know in Context

You can help students learn the Words to Know by reading aloud the following sentences or writing them on the board. Then show students how to use context clues to help them figure out the meaning.

capricious: The monkey's behavior was *capricious*—sometimes she'd start to eat her food and then suddenly throw it against the wall.

haphazardly: The teacher selected books *haphazardly,* without purpose or planning.

humane: The captain insisted on the *humane* treatment of prisoners of war, showing them mercy and kindness.

immoral: The criminal was sentenced to five years in jail for his *immoral,* or evil, behavior.

incessantly: George beat the drums *incessantly;* it seemed he would never stop.

obsolete: Do you think CDs will become *obsolete* someday, like record players and typewriters?

posterity: Recycling paper, cans, and plastic helps to protect the environment for *posterity,* or future generations.

rapture: Filled with *rapture,* the audience jumped to its feet, clapping and shouting with delight at the wonderful concert.

renunciation: The king decided to give up his throne; this act of *renunciation* shocked his people.

stipulated: The contract stated that the project would begin on July 1; although we wanted to start sooner, we had to wait until the *stipulated* date.

VOCABULARY FOCUS Word Parts: Prefixes

Teacher Modeling Remind students that they can often use their knowledge of prefixes to help figure out the meaning of an unfamiliar word. Model using the word ***disapproved*** (page 130, line 11).

You might say *I'm not sure what this word means, but I recognize the prefix* dis- *from words such as* disagree. *I know it often means "not." I also know that* approve *means "to consider right or good" or "to think highly of."* Disapproved *probably means "not approved," which makes sense here. Many of the banker's guests did not think that capital punishment was right or good.*

Student Modeling Call on a volunteer to model using prefixes to figure out the meaning of the word ***compressed*** (page 139, line 268).

A student could say *I'm not sure what* compressed *means, but the prefix* com- *is familiar to me from words such as* companion. *I know it can mean "with" or "together." Pressed can mean "pushed" or "squeezed";* compressed *probably means "squeezed together." This meaning makes sense in the sentence.*

Mini-Lesson
See pages 100–101 of this Guide for additional work on **Words Parts: Prefixes.**

During Reading

COMPREHENSION FOCUS

Key Points	Strategies for Success
Target Skill ➡ **Sequence** Anton Chekhov uses an extended flashback in this story. It is important that students follow the sequence of events in order to understand the story and to appreciate how the lawyer changes during his fifteen years of confinement.	**Mini-Lesson** Before students read "The Bet," you may want to teach the **Sequence** lesson on pages 127–129 of this Guide. • Read aloud the first paragraph in the story on page 130. Ask students to identify the setting and the characters and to note the introduction of the flashback. • During or after reading, students can complete the **Active Reading SkillBuilder** and **Literary Analysis SkillBuilder** on pages 141–142 of *The InterActive Reader.*™
Characters' Beliefs To make sense of the story's outcome, students must understand what opinions the characters hold about life imprisonment and capital punishment, what the banker and the lawyer each hope to prove with the bet, and what conclusions the lawyer reaches by the end of his term of imprisonment.	At the *Pause & Reflect* on page 131, work with students to paraphrase the opinions expressed by the banker and the lawyer at the party. At the *Pause & Reflect* on page 133, discuss with students what each of these characters hopes to prove by winning the bet. After completing the story, use the *Pause & Reflect* questions on page 140 to help students summarize the lawyer's beliefs as expressed in his letter.

Suggested Reading Options

• An oral reading of "The Bet" is available in *The Language of Literature* Audio Library. 🎧
• Shared Reading (see page 8 of this Guide).
• Additional options are described on page 8 of this Guide.

RECIPROCAL TEACHING SUGGESTION ➡ Predicting

Teacher Modeling *Pause & Reflect, page 136* Model using story clues and prior knowledge to predict what the banker will see through the window of the cell.

You could say *I know the lawyer has been confined to his room for fifteen years. I think that staying inside for so long would probably give someone a pale or sickly appearance. I also predict that his room will be filled with books and papers from all the reading and writing he has been doing.*

Student Modeling *Pause & Reflect, page 138* Have students model predicting what the banker might do next. Offer this prompt: *What does the banker plan to do to the lawyer? What do you think he might find in the note? How might this affect his plans?*

Encourage students to use the other five reading strategies when appropriate as they proceed through the rest of the story. (See page 10 of this Guide.)

ENGLISH LEARNERS

1. Before students read, summarize the main conflict: two men disagree over which is worse, death or life imprisonment. To prove that it is "better to live somehow than not at all," one man bets that he can endure fifteen years of voluntary imprisonment.

2. Students might benefit from reading along with the recording of the story provided in *The Language of Literature* Audio Library. ◯

After Reading

Recommended Follow-Up

- Thinking Through the Literature, page 293, *The Language of Literature*
- Choices & Challenges, pages 294–295, *The Language of Literature*
- SkillBuilders, pages 141–143, *The InterActive Reader™*

Informal Assessment Options

Retell Have students retell the story from the lawyer's perspective. You may wish to have students share the task of retelling with a partner.

Spot Check Look at the notes students made in the margins of the story. Invite them to explain their answers and discuss any questions they still have about the story.

Formal Assessment Options in *The Language of Literature*

Selection Quiz, page 47, Unit Two Resource Book

Selection Test, pages 43–44, Formal Assessment Book

For more teaching options, see pages 285–295 in *The Language of Literature* Teacher's Edition.

Additional Challenge

1. **Write a Dialogue**
   Have students write a dialogue that might take place between the banker and the lawyer if they were to meet one year after the lawyer's disappearance.

2. **MARK IT UP** ⟩ **Identify the Theme**
   Remind students that a story's theme is the message conveyed by the author about life or human nature. Then ask: *What are some possible themes for this story? What do you think the author is saying about freedom and greed?* Have students mark passages in the story to support their views.

Before Reading

Direct students' attention to the Connect to Your Life and Key to the Story activities on page 144 of *The InterActive Reader.*™ Use the following suggestions to prepare students to read the story.

Connect to Your Life
Guide students in a discussion about homelessness. Ask: *Where have you seen homeless people? Why do you think some people become homeless?* Have students read and complete the Connect to Your Life activity, and then share their responses with the class.

Key to the Story
Write the word *treasure* on the board and ask: *What do you think of when you hear this word? Is a treasure always something that is worth much money?* List students' responses in a web on the board. Then read the directions on page 144 and have students complete the activity.

BUILD BACKGROUND Homeless People Explain to students that to be *homeless* means to have no permanent address. Many homeless people find shelter in abandoned buildings or cars; others go to homeless shelters or live on the streets. Many have families, and some have jobs. (In some communities, people with low-wage jobs can't keep up with rising housing costs.) Homelessness can be a difficult cycle to break, since getting better-paying jobs often requires training or transportation that homeless people don't have and can't afford. Estimates of the number of homeless people in the United States range from 600,000 to 3,000,000.

WORDS TO KNOW

ajar

beckon

commence

gnarled

impromptu

ominous

probe

tentatively

tremor

vault

Additional Words to Know

panic
    page 154, line 272

eerie
    page 154, line 273

VOCABULARY PREVIEW: Words to Know in Context

You can help students learn the Words to Know by reading aloud the following sentences or writing them on the board. Then show students how to use context clues to help them figure out the meaning of the boldfaced words.

ajar: The door was not closed, but standing *ajar* by about six inches.

beckon: Samantha *beckoned* to Ramón, waving her hand at him.

commence: A movie often *commences* with the title and opening credits.

gnarled: His fingers are rough and *gnarled* like the roots of a tree.

impromptu: It's an *impromptu* party; nobody did any planning for it.

ominous: The weather report didn't mention rain, but those huge, black clouds are an *ominous* sign for our picnic.

probe: Shelly *probed* the bottom of the old canoe with her hand, searching for leaks.

tentatively: I *tentatively* poked at the cafeteria food, not sure if I would like it.

tremor: David was so nervous that his hands shook with a *tremor* that he couldn't stop.

vault: Sara dashed across the yard and *vaulted* over the fence to escape the dog that was chasing her.

---

panic: Carlos did not *panic* during the accident; instead, he remained calm and still.

eerie: The old, empty house was creepy and scary; it gave me an *eerie* feeling to walk by it at night.

VOCABULARY FOCUS: Understanding Idioms

Teacher Modeling Remind students that they can often figure out the meaning of an unfamiliar idiom by looking for context clues in the surrounding words or sentences. Model using the idiom *hit those books* (page 146, line 29).

You could say I'm sure Mr. Ridley doesn't want Greg to literally hit the books with hands, so this must be an idiomatic expression. Mr. Ridley is upset by Greg's poor grade in math and refuses to let his son play basketball until the grade improves. Hit those books *must mean "study hard."*

Student Modeling Now have students follow your lead. Ask a volunteer to use context clues to figure out the meaning of the idiom *let up* (page 149, line 98).

A student might say I'm not sure what this expression means. Greg has been scared by a noise in the abandoned house and considers leaving, but he decides to wait until the rain lets up. He probably means he'll wait until the rain stops or lightens up; let up *must mean "stop" or "diminish."*

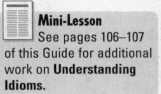
Mini-Lesson See pages 106–107 of this Guide for additional work on **Understanding Idioms.**

During Reading

COMPREHENSION FOCUS

Key Points	Strategies for Success
Target Skill ➡ Compare and Contrast The author creates a parallel between Lemon Brown and Greg's father. Understanding this comparison is crucial to story comprehension.	**Mini-Lesson** Before students read "The Treasure of Lemon Brown," teach or review the **Compare and Contrast** lesson on pages 135–137 of this Guide. • At the *Pause & Reflect* on page 158, read aloud lines 383–384. Ask students to think about the lesson Lemon Brown is teaching Greg. Then ask: *How would you compare this lesson with the lesson Greg's father is trying to teach him? What does Lemon Brown say is important for a father to leave his son? What is important to Greg's father?*
Dialect The author uses dialect to make Lemon Brown's speech more realistic. Students' ability to comprehend what this character says is important to their understanding of the story.	Suggest that students try reading Lemon Brown's words aloud. Explain that when read aloud, the lines might be easier to understand. Also remind students that they should strive to get an overall meaning of what the character says. They can underline difficult passages as they read and figure them out after they have read the entire story.

Suggested Reading Options

• An oral reading of "The Treasure of Lemon Brown" is available in *The Language of Literature* Audio Library. ◯
• Independent Reading (see page 8 of this Guide).
• Additional options are described on page 8 of this Guide.

RECIPROCAL TEACHING SUGGESTION ➡ Connecting

Teacher Modeling *Pause & Reflect, page 147* Model using the connecting strategy to help students understand Greg's mood at the beginning of the story.

You could say *I see that Greg is upset because his father has forbidden him to play basketball until his grades improve. Even though Greg doesn't question his father's authority, he's frustrated because he wants to play. I understand how he feels; I feel frustrated and upset sometimes when I can't do what I want to do.*

Student Modeling *Pause & Reflect, page 147* Have a student volunteer model the connecting strategy to identify with Greg's feelings. Offer this prompt: *Why does Greg go walking in the rain instead of going into his house? Do you ever feel like being alone when you are upset?*

Students can also complete the **Active Reading SkillBuilder** on page 159 of *The InterActive Reader™* during or after reading.

Encourage students to use the other five reading strategies when appropriate as they proceed through the rest of the story. (See page 10 of this Guide.)

ENGLISH LEARNERS

1. Make sure students understand these terms:

   knitted, page 146, line 27

   stock-still, page 149, line 104

   rest a spell, page 151, line 175

   getting their nerve up, page 155, lines 300–301

   till the coast is clear, page 155, lines 302–303

   saw fit, page 157, line 351

2. Students might benefit from reading along with the recording of "The Treasure of Lemon Brown" provided in *The Language of Literature* Audio Library. ◯

After Reading

Recommended Follow-Up

- Thinking Through the Literature, page 345, *The Language of Literature*
- Choices & Challenges, pages 346–347, *The Language of Literature*
- SkillBuilders, pages 159–161, *The InterActive Reader™*

Informal Assessment Options

Retell Have students work in small groups to dramatize the story, role-playing Greg, Mr. Ridley, Lemon Brown, and the thieves. Explain that a dramatization relies on dialogue more than narration.

Spot Check Review the notes students made in the margins to check for understanding. Invite students to ask any questions they still have about the story.

Formal Assessment Options in *The Language of Literature*

Selection Quiz, page 10, Unit Three Resource Book

Selection Test, pages 49–50, Formal Assessment Book

For more teaching options, see pp. 334–347 in *The Language of Literature* Teacher's Edition.

Additional Challenge

1. **⟦||| MARK IT UP ⟧ Analyze Character Traits**
   Ask: *What qualities of a good parent does Lemon Brown seem to have?* Tell students to consider how Lemon Brown feels about his dead son and how he treats Greg. Have students mark passages in the story to support their views.

2. **⟦||| MARK IT UP ⟧ Identify Figurative Language**
   Have students find and mark examples of figurative language, such as similes metaphors, and personification (for example, "angry, swirling clouds" page 146, line 2; "like the distant thunder" page 146, line 31; "the flashlight danced crazily" page 153, line 250; "like dry twigs being broken" page 149, lines 104–105). Then discuss with students what makes each example so effective.

Before Reading

Direct students' attention to the Connect to Your Life and Key to the Poem activities on page 162 of *The InterActive Reader.*™ Use the following suggestions to prepare students to read the poem.

Connect to Your Life
Have students close their eyes, and then ask: *What do you imagine when you hear the word* snow? *What sights, sounds, smells, textures, and tastes come to mind?* Have students fill in the web, and then invite volunteers to share their responses.

Key to the Poem
Read aloud the first two lines from the poem, emphasizing the regular rhythm. Remind students what stressed and unstressed syllables are, and have them clap on the stressed syllables while you read the lines aloud again. Then have students read the directions and complete the activity. Suggest that they read the line aloud to themselves quietly to help identify the stressed words and syllables.

BUILD BACKGROUND Connect to Geography
Explain that Robert Frost is famous for his poetry about New England, a region in the northeast known for its thick forests, rugged landscape, and cold, snowy winters. You may wish to point out the New England states of Maine, Vermont, New Hampshire, Massachusetts, Connecticut, and Rhode Island on a map. Frost, who was born in San Francisco, came to love the New England countryside. His collection titled *New Hampshire* won the Pulitzer Prize in 1923, the first of four such awards for Frost.

Strategies for Reading Poetry

- Notice the form of the poem: the number of lines and their shape on the page.
- Read the poem aloud a few times. Listen for rhymes and rhythms.
- Visualize the images and comparisons.
- Think about the poet's choice of words.
- Ask yourself what message the poet is trying to send.
- Think about what the poem is saying to you.

FOCUS ON POETRY

The activities below and the tips shown at the left will help prepare students for reading "Stopping by Woods on a Snowy Evening." If your students need more detailed instruction on how to read and interpret poems, have them read "Poetry" on pages 187–191 of *The Language of Literature.*

- **Theme** Have students read the Preview on page 163. Then work with them to list some of the things that people often enjoy and admire about nature, such as beauty, wildness, and peacefulness. Also have students share their thoughts about solitude. Ask: *Do you think solitude can be enjoyable or valuable? Why or why not?* As they read the poem, have them pay attention to how the speaker seems to feel about solitude.

- **Sound** Read aloud the first stanza of the poem. Work with students to identify its slow, steady rhythmic pattern. Ask: *How does the rhythm of a poem affect the way you react to it?* Students may respond that a poem with a slow, steady beat makes them feel calm, while a poem with a rapid or irregular beat makes them more alert.

VOCABULARY FOCUS: Using Words with Multiple Meanings

Teacher Modeling Mention that many words have more than one meaning and that students can often use context clues as they read to help them figure out which meaning is intended. Model the strategy using the word **sweep** (page 164, line 11).

You could say Sweep *can mean "to clear or clean with a broom" or "a surging or flowing movement." The word here seems to tell about the movement and sound made by wind and falling snow. I think* sweep *means "a surging or flowing movement" in this poem.*

Student Modeling Ask a student volunteer to model using context clues to figure out the meaning of **easy** (page 164, line 12).

A student might say *I know the word* easy *has several meanings, including "simple" and "mild." In this line, the word describes the wind in the woods, which are "lovely, dark and deep." Since this scene is peaceful, I think the easy wind is probably one that is moderate or mild.*

Mini-Lesson See pages 108–109 of this Guide for additional work on **Using Words with Multiple Meanings.**

During Reading

COMPREHENSION FOCUS

Key Points	Strategies for Success
Target Skill ➡ Making Inferences To make sense of this poem, students must be able to read between the lines, making inferences about the speaker and the suggested inner conflict.	**Mini-Lesson** Before students read the poem, you may wish to teach or review the **Making Inferences** lesson on pages 138–140 of this Guide. • Read aloud lines 1–4 and ask: *How long do you think the speaker intends to stay in the woods?* Then read aloud lines 13–16 and ask: *What conflict does the speaker have at the end of the poem?*
Syntax and Pronouns The syntax of the first line and the pronouns *His* in line 2 and *He* in line 9 may confuse students.	After you read the poem aloud, ask a volunteer to paraphrase the first line. (I think I know whose woods these are.) If necessary, point out that the pronoun *His* in line 2 refers to the owner of the woods and that the pronoun *He* in line 9 refers to the speaker's horse.
Reading Poetry Students may not know that the end of a line does not always signal the end of a complete thought.	Remind students that the end of a line does not necessarily signal the end of a complete thought. Point out that paying attention to the punctuation will help them figure out where a particular idea begins and ends.

Suggested Reading Options

• An oral reading of "Stopping by Woods on a Snowy Evening" is available in *The Language of Literature* Audio Library. ◠
• Oral Reading (see page 8 of this Guide).
• Additional options are described on page 8 of this Guide.

RECIPROCAL TEACHING SUGGESTION ➡ Visualizing

Teacher Modeling *Pause & Reflect, page 165* Model for students how to visualize the scene described in lines 1–4.

You could say In the first stanza, the speaker pauses to watch the "woods fill up with snow." This phrase helps me picture a forest covered by a thick blanket of snow that piles up higher and higher as the snow continues to fall. This covering would give the woods a soft, peaceful, beautiful appearance. I can understand why the speaker stops to look at the scene.

Student Modeling *Pause & Reflect, page 165* Have several students model visualizing other images in the poem. Offer these prompts: *How light or dark is the setting? What movements does the horse make? What two sounds does the narrator hear?*

Encourage students to use the other five reading strategies when appropriate as they proceed through the rest of the poem. (See page 10 of this Guide.)

ENGLISH LEARNERS

1. Before reading, show students a photo or illustration of a peaceful, snowy forest scene, such as the one on page 163 of *The InterActive Reader.*™ Encourage them to recall this image as you read the poem.

2. Students might benefit from reading along with the recording of "Stopping by Woods on a Snowy Evening" provided in *The Language of Literature* Audio Library. ◯

After Reading

Recommended Follow-Up

- Thinking Through the Literature, page 392, *The Language of Literature*
- Choices & Challenges, page 393, *The Language of Literature*
- SkillBuilders, pages 166–167, *The InterActive Reader*™

Informal Assessment Options

Retell Have students imagine that the owner of the woods *did* see the speaker pause on his journey. Have them work in pairs to retell the main ideas and images in the poem as a conversation between the speaker and the owner the following day.

Spot Check Look at the notes students made in the margins. Pay particular attention to question 3 on page 165, which helps students describe the mood of the poem.

Formal Assessment Options in *The Language of Literature*

Selection Test, pages 57–58, Formal Assessment Book

For more teaching options, see pages 390–393 in *The Language of Literature* Teacher's Edition.

Additional Challenge

1. **Examine Repetition**
   Ask: *Why do you think Frost repeats the last line? How does it affect the mood of the poem?*

2. **Explore Contrast**
   Have students identify the contrasts that this poem suggests. To get students started, ask them how the speaker and the owner of the woods are different and what the speaker's horse might represent.

3. [||| MARK IT UP ⟩] **Identify Images**
   Have students underline words and phrases in the poem that help convey images of stillness and beauty. Ask: *Why do you think Frost used mostly short, simple words to set this scene instead of complex vocabulary?*

Before Reading

Direct students' attention to the **Connect to Your Life** and **Key to the Poems** activities on page 168 of *The InterActive Reader.*™ Use the following suggestions to prepare students to read the poems.

Connect to Your Life
Read aloud the first two questions from the activity, and allow students to respond to each one. Then read the directions and have students complete the activity. Invite them to share their lists in small groups.

Key to the Poems
Ask: *What is a symbol?* Elicit from students that it is something that stands for or represents something else—for example, a dove is sometimes used as a symbol for peace. Also discuss what *independence* means. Then read aloud the explanation and the excerpt from "the drum" on page 168. Have students work in pairs to complete the activity, and then invite them to share their ideas.

BUILD BACKGROUND Explain to students that many of Nikki Giovanni's poems show the independent spirit that characterizes her personality. For example, after completing her first book of poetry, *Black Feeling, Black Talk,* she talked a jazz club manager into letting her throw a book party at his club. She also convinced several radio talk show hosts to let her tell about her book on the air. These acts attracted the attention of major publishers. "If this sounds like a Cinderella story, remember I made my own slipper," she told an interviewer years later. "I believe people always have to make their own breaks." Have students look for other signs of Giovanni's creativity and determination in these poems as they read.

Strategies for Reading Poetry

- Notice the form of the poem: the number of lines and their shape on the page.
- Read the poem aloud a few times. Listen for rhymes and rhythms.
- Visualize the images and comparisons.
- Mark words and phrases that appeal to you.
- Ask yourself what message the poet is trying to send.
- Think about what the poem is saying to you.

FOCUS ON POETRY

The activities below and the tips shown at the left will help prepare students for reading "Legacies," "the drum," and "Choices." If your students need more detailed instruction on how to read and interpret poems, have them read "Poetry" on pages 187–191 of *The Language of Literature.*

- **Imagery** Remind students that *imagery* refers to words and phrases that appeal to the five senses. Poets often use vivid imagery to creature pictures in the reader's mind. Read aloud the excerpt on page 168 and ask students what image they picture when they hear the words. Many will say they imagine the beating of a drum. Encourage students to pay attention to the poet's imagery in all three poems as they read.

- **Speaker** Remind students that the *speaker* is the voice that the reader hears relating the ideas or story of the poem. Sometimes the speaker is the poet; at other times, the speaker is a character whom the poet creates. Discuss with students what they can tell about the speaker in the excerpt on page 168. As they read, encourage students to describe what the speaker is like in each of Giovanni's poems.

VOCABULARY FOCUS: Using Context Clues

Teacher Modeling Remind students that they can often figure out the meaning of an unfamiliar word by looking for clues in the surrounding sentences. Model using the word *dependent* (page 170, line 10).

You could say *I'm not sure what* dependent *means, so I look for context clues. The speaker says the little girl refuses to let her grandmother teach her how to make rolls. She wants to stay* dependent *on her grandmother's spirit instead. If she can't make rolls, she'll have to rely on her grandmother's help.* Dependent *must mean "relying on another person."*

Student Modeling Have a student volunteer model using context clues to figure out the meaning of *express* (page 173, lines 24 and 27).

A student might say *I'm not sure what* express *means here. The speaker seems to be describing feelings that she can and can't* express. *When I have strong feelings, I sometimes want to share them, but it's not always easy to do so.* Express *must mean "share" or "talk about."*

Mini-Lesson See pages 96–99 of this Guide for additional work on **Using Context Clues.**

During Reading

COMPREHENSION FOCUS

Key Points	Strategies for Success
Target Skill ➡ Making Inferences To understand these poems, the reader must make inferences about the speaker's situation and emotions.	**Mini-Lesson** Before students read "Legacies," "the drum," and "Choices," teach or review the **Making Inferences** lesson on pages 138–140 of this Guide. • After reading each poem, have students discuss their answers to the *Pause & Reflect* questions. Also ask: *How does the speaker in each poem seem to feel about life? about relationships? How can you tell?* • Have students complete the **Inference Chart** on page 139 of this Guide.
Author's Style Giovanni does not use capital letters or punctuation marks to indicate complete sentences. Students must rely on other clues to figure out where units of meaning begin and end.	Read each poem aloud, using the inflections of your voice to indicate where the speaker's sentences and ideas begin and end. Point out that the end of a line does not always signal the completion of a thought.

Suggested Reading Options

- Oral readings of "Legacies," "the drum," and "Choices" are available in *The Language of Literature* Audio Library. ◯
- Oral Reading (see page 8 of this Guide).
- Additional options are described on page 8 of this Guide.

RECIPROCAL TEACHING SUGGESTION ➡ Clarifying

Teacher Modeling *Pause & Reflect, page 170* Model using the clarifying strategy to help students understand what the little girl and her grandmother leave unspoken.

You could say *In lines 17 and 18, the speaker says that neither character "ever said what they meant." What couldn't they say to each other? I reread and find that the grandmother wants to share her skill with her granddaughter. This shows her love, but she doesn't put it into words. The girl resists because by learning the skill she will gain independence, which means greater separation from her grandmother. The girl wants to be close to her grandmother forever, but she doesn't say so.*

Student Modeling *Pause & Reflect, page 173* Have several student volunteers model using the clarifying strategy to help students understand the speaker's feelings in "Choices." Offer these prompts: *What is this speaker's attitude toward disappointment? What advice would she give to a friend who couldn't have something he or she wanted?*

Encourage students to use the other five reading strategies when appropriate as they proceed through these poems. (See page 10 of this Guide.)

ENGLISH LEARNERS

1. Have students work with English-proficient partners to mark where complete thoughts begin and end in each poem. Ask students to summarize the message of each poem and tell what emotions each one expresses.

2. Students might benefit from reading along with the recordings of "Legacies," "the drum," and "Choices" provided in *The Language of Literature* Audio Library. ◯

After Reading

Recommended Follow-Up

- Thinking Through the Literature, page 421, *The Language of Literature*
- Choices & Challenges, page 429, *The Language of Literature*
- SkillBuilders, pages 174–175, *The InterActive Reader*™

Informal Assessment Options

Retell Have pairs of students work together to role-play the conversation in "Legacies" and "the drum." Have partners take turns paraphrasing each stanza of "Choices."

Spot Check Review the notes students made in the margins to check for understanding. Answer any questions students still have about the poems.

Formal Assessment Options in *The Language of Literature*

Selection Test, pages 61–62, Formal Assessment Book

For more teaching options, see pages 417–421 and page 429 in *The Language of Literature* Teacher's Edition.

Additional Challenge

1. **Evaluate the Speaker's Viewpoint**
   Have each student choose one of the following three quotations and write a paragraph explaining what the statement means and why they agree or disagree with it: ". . . neither of them ever / said what they meant / and I guess nobody ever does" (page 170); "the world is / a drum tight and hard" (page 171); "if I can't have what I want then / my job is to want / what I've got" (page 172).

2. **║║MARK IT UP⟫ Compare and Contrast**
   Ask students to analyze the speaker's voice in each of the poems. Then have students briefly compare and contrast the speakers in the three poems. Ask: *How are they similar? How are they different?* Have students mark lines in the poem to explain their views.

Before Reading

Direct students' attention to the Connect to Your Life, Key to the Drama, and Preview activities on pages 176–179 of *The InterActive Reader.™* Use the following suggestions to prepare students to read the drama.

Connect to Your Life
Ask students what problems they face today that their parents didn't have to deal with. To get students started, you might mention increased crime and drug use. Then have students complete their lists and share their responses.

Key to the Drama
Read aloud the Key to the Drama on page 176 and have students study the map. Ask them to locate Germany and the Netherlands. Explain that Anne Frank was born in Germany and later moved to the Netherlands (formerly Holland) with her family. Tell students that this play excerpt takes place in Amsterdam, Holland's capital city.

BUILD BACKGROUND Who Was Anne Frank? Have students get together in small groups to discuss what they already know about Anne Frank. Then direct students to pages 178–179, and have them take turns reading the sections of the Preview aloud. After they read each section, ask volunteers to answer the questions. Finally, discuss any questions students still may have about Anne Frank or World War II.

WORDS TO KNOW

conspicuous

indignantly

insufferable

loathe

vile

Additional Words to Know

compassionate
   page 182, line 62

peculiar
   page 196, line 329

absurd
   page 205, line 182

meticulous
   page 218, line 619

characteristic
   page 221, line 703

VOCABULARY PREVIEW: Words to Know in Context

You can help students learn the Words to Know by reading aloud the following sentences or writing them on the board. Then show students how to use context clues to help them figure out the meaning.

conspicuous: I didn't think my new orange hat would be so *conspicuous,* but everyone seemed to notice it.

indignantly: Angered by the unfair treatment, he walked *indignantly* out of the room.

insufferable: When the child screams and pulls my hair, her behavior is *insufferable.*

loathe: Jessica loves the taste of fried liver, but I *loathe* it.

vile: The movie had such *vile,* disgusting characters that I didn't want to watch it any longer.

---

compassionate: Terri is a *compassionate* person who always feels sympathy for people in trouble.

peculiar: We thought the neighbors were very *peculiar,* but everyone else seemed to think they were perfectly normal.

absurd: How *absurd* of you to wear shorts when it's snowing out!

meticulous: My *meticulous* sister always keeps her side of the room clean, with everything in its proper place.

characteristic: It is *characteristic* of Joanie to be late. She is never on time for anything.

VOCABULARY FOCUS Word Parts: Roots

Teacher Modeling Remind students that they can sometimes figure out the meaning of an unfamiliar word if they recognize its root from other, familiar words. Then use the following modeling suggestions for the word *emigrated* (page 183, line 112).

You could say *I don't know the meaning of* emigrated, *but part of it looks like* migrate, *which means "to move from one country or region to another." Maybe* emigrated *and* migrate *come from the same root word and are related in meaning. In this sentence,* emigrated *could mean "to leave one country to live in another" because Anne's family left Germany to go to Holland.*

Student Modeling Now have a volunteer model the strategy to figure out the meaning of *studiously* (page 210, line 339).

A student might say *I don't know what* studiously *means, but the first part looks like* study, *which can be a verb meaning "to pay careful attention to something." Maybe* study *and* studiously *have similar meanings. Since Mrs. Frank and Margot try to avoid watching the Van Daans as they argue,* studiously *could mean "in a careful manner."*

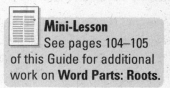

Mini-Lesson See pages 104–105 of this Guide for additional work on **Word Parts: Roots.**

During Reading

COMPREHENSION FOCUS

Key Points	Strategies for Success
Target Skill ➡ Narrative Elements This excerpt contains many characters and events and an unusual setting. Students must keep track of these elements in order to follow the plot.	**Mini-Lesson** Before students read the excerpt from *The Diary of Anne Frank,* teach or review the **Narrative Elements** lesson on pages 147–150 of this Guide. • Read aloud lines 21–57 on pages 199–200. Ask students to identify the characters, setting, and events in this passage. • As they read, have students complete the **Active Reading SkillBuilder** on page 227 of *The InterActive Reader.*™
Stage Directions Stage directions play a crucial role in students' understanding of the characters' emotions and behavior. Students must be able to distinguish between stage directions and dialogue and use the directions to help visualize the action and understand the emotions.	• Draw students' attention to the Reading Tip on page 181 and read it aloud. • Read aloud lines 37–57 on pages 181–182. Discuss the action and emotions it describes. Ask: *What does Mr. Frank find on the floor of the annex? How does he react when he picks it up? Why do you think he cries?*

Suggested Reading Options

• An oral reading of the excerpt from *The Diary of Anne Frank* is available in *The Language of Literature* Audio Library. 🎧
• Oral Reading (see page 8 of this Guide).
• Additional options are described on page 8 of this Guide.

RECIPROCAL TEACHING SUGGESTION ➡ Evaluating

Teacher Modeling *Pause & Reflect, page 190* Model using the evaluating strategy to help students form opinions about the living conditions in the Secret Annex.

You could say *The rules for living in the Secret Annex sound very restrictive. There are many things the characters can't do during daytime hours—make noise, run water, throw out trash. I think it would be stressful to live under such conditions, especially when the characters already live in fear for their lives.*

Student Modeling *Pause & Reflect, page 212* Have students model the evaluating strategy to form opinions about why Mrs. Van Daan is so upset when Anne spills milk on the fur coat. Offer this prompt: *Who gave the coat to Mrs. Van Daan? How many belongings was she allowed to bring to the Annex? What might the fur coat remind her of?*

Encourage students to use the other five reading strategies when appropriate as they proceed through the rest of the drama. (See page 10 of this Guide.)

ENGLISH LEARNERS

1. Students might have trouble visualizing the Secret Annex. Have them use the description in lines 1–30 on pages 180–181 to draw a diagram of the Annex rooms. As they read the drama, students can use this illustration to track the movement of characters.

2. Students might benefit from reading along with the excerpt from *The Diary of Anne Frank* provided in *The Language of Literature* Audio Library. ◠

After Reading

Recommended Follow-Up

- Thinking Through the Literature, page 475, *The Language of Literature*
- Choices & Challenges, pages 532–533, *The Language of Literature*
- SkillBuilders, pages 227–229, *The InterActive Reader™*

Informal Assessment Options

Retell Have students choose one of the characters in the play and retell the story from that person's perspective. Use the following prompts:
- *How did you feel when you first arrived in the Secret Annex?*
- *What did you think of the other inhabitants?*
- *What was hardest about life in the Annex?*
- *How did you feel when Mr. Dussel moved in?*

Spot Check Look at the notes students made in the margins. Invite them to explain their answers and discuss any questions they still have about the drama.

Formal Assessment Options in *The Language of Literature*

Selection Quiz, page 59, Unit Three Resource Book

For more teaching options, see pages 447–533 in *The Language of Literature* Teacher's Edition.

Additional Challenge

1. **Compare and Contrast**
   Have students compare Anne's relationship with her mother to her relationship with her father. Ask: *What does Anne call her father? What does she call her mother? How does Anne speak to her mother? How does she speak to her father?* Then ask students what generalizations they can make about how Anne feels about each parent.

2. **⫿ MARK IT UP ⟩ Write a Character Sketch**
   Point out to students that the characters' good and bad qualities are revealed in the drama. For instance, Anne appears to be generous when she offers to share her room with Mr. Dussel. However, she is also shown to be thoughtless when she teases Peter. Have students select a character and underline details that reveal his or her personality. Then have students use the details to write a character sketch.

Before Reading

Direct students' attention to the **Connect to Your Life** and **Key to the Story** activities on page 230 of *The InterActive Reader.*™ Use the following suggestions to prepare students to read the story.

Connect to Your Life Explain to students that this story revolves around a character faced with a difficult decision. Read aloud the directions for the activity on page 230. You may wish to model the activity by describing a difficult decision you yourself had to make. Have students fill out the chart, and invite volunteers to share their examples.

Key to the Story Read aloud the paragraph on page 230. If necessary, explain that gladiators were often prisoners of war, slaves, or condemned criminals who were forced to fight to the death in front of crowds of spectators. Tell students that in this story the author gives a new twist to this barbaric practice in ancient Rome.

BUILD BACKGROUND **Connect to History** Tell students that author Frank Stockton included realistic details in even his most fantastic stories. For example, the setting of "The Lady, or the Tiger?" is an imaginary kingdom, but Stockton mentions the country's "distant Latin neighbors"—probably a reference to the Latin-speaking Roman Empire. Also, the king's system of justice used in Stockton's imaginary "semibarbaric" kingdom resembles a very real and cruel Roman practice: the gladiator games in the Colosseum.

WORDS TO KNOW

assert

decree

destiny

doleful

exuberant

imperious

procure

retribution

subordinate

valor

Additional Words to Know

barbaric
    page 232, line 9

ardor
    page 236, line 136

novel
    page 237, line 150

VOCABULARY PREVIEW: Words to Know in Context

You can help students learn the Words to Know by reading aloud the following sentences or writing them on the board. Then show students how to use context clues to help them figure out the meaning.

assert: You *assert* that the rent was paid on time, but I know this is not true.

decree: The king's *decree* of a new tax was posted throughout the land.

destiny: I don't believe in *destiny;* it seems ridiculous to think that fate or a higher force makes things happen the way they do.

doleful: My sister's *doleful* look changed to a smile when I told her that we could go to the beach.

exuberant: After the prize was announced, the *exuberant* winner jumped for joy.

imperious: When the beggar pulled at the queen's robe, she froze him with an *imperious* look. "Guard!" she said. "Throw the poor dog a piece of bread."

procure: I was unable to *procure* tickets for the concert, so we won't be going.

retribution: The army set fire to their enemies' crops in *retribution* for the murder of their captain.

subordinate: The young prince is *subordinate* to the king.

valor: The firefighter saved three people from a burning building. Her *valor* earned her a medal from the governor.

---

barbaric: The invading army commited *barbaric* acts such as torture and murder.

ardor: Tamara has great *ardor,* or passion, for ballet; she practices constantly.

novel: You're inventing a solar-powered car? What a *novel* idea; I've never seen such a thing.

VOCABULARY FOCUS Word Parts: Prefixes

Teacher Modeling Remind students that they can sometimes figure out the meaning of an unfamiliar word if it contains a prefix they recognize. Model using the word *impartial* (page 233, line 39).

You could say I'm not sure what the word impartial *means, but I recognize the prefix* im- *from words such as* impatient. I know it often means "not." The word partial *can mean "biased," so* impartial *must mean "not biased" or "fair." This meaning makes sense in the sentence.*

Student Modeling Now have students follow your example. Call on a volunteer to model the strategy to figure out the word *unsurpassed* (page 236, line 135).

A student might say I recognize the prefix un- *in* unsurpassed *from words such as* unhappy. I know that un- *means "not." Since* surpassed *means "went beyond" or "exceeded," I think* unsurpassed *must mean "not exceeded." This makes sense here; the courtier's bravery was greater than anyone else's in the kingdom.*

> **Mini-Lesson**
> See pages 100–101 of this Guide for additional work on **Word Parts: Prefixes**.

During Reading

COMPREHENSION FOCUS

Key Points	Strategies for Success
Target Skill ➡ Making Inferences This story presents students with a kind of puzzle to answer. Students must be able to use story clues and their own experiences to make inferences about the characters and events in this story.	**Mini-Lesson** Before students read "The Lady, or the Tiger?" teach or review the **Making Inferences** lesson on pages 138–140 of this Guide. • At the *Pause & Reflect* on page 240, ask students what they can infer about the princess's state of mind as she sits and watches her lover enter the arena. • After reading, students can complete the **Active Reading SkillBuilder** and the **Literary Analysis SkillBuilder** on pages 243 and 244 of *The InterActive Reader.*™
Formal Language The author uses a formal style and ornate language, characteristic of 19th-century writing. Students may be confused by words and phrases in the story and need assistance with reading comprehension.	Read aloud the Reading Tip on page 232. Then read aloud the story's first paragraph and paraphrase it. Help students identify the story setting and the details that reveal the king's personality. As students continue to read, encourage them to paraphrase difficult passages.

Suggested Reading Options

- An oral reading of "The Lady, or the Tiger?" is available in *The Language of Literature* Audio Library. 🎧
- Shared Reading (see page 8 of this Guide).
- Additional options are described on page 8 of this Guide.

RECIPROCAL TEACHING SUGGESTION ➡ Evaluating

Teacher Modeling *Pause & Reflect, page 232* Model using the evaluating strategy to help students form opinions about the king.

You could say *I see that the king is cruel, tyrannical, and self-important—he enjoys crushing anything that gets in his way. I'm not sure I like or trust this character. However, he is dynamic and entertaining in a strange way. I'm curious about what he will do next in the story.*

Student Modeling *Pause & Reflect, page 238* Have several students model using the evaluating strategy to form opinions about the king's reaction to his daughter's love affair. Offer this prompt: *Do the king's actions seem like those of a man who loves his daughter "above all humanity?" What do you think of the king's response to his daughter's love affair?*

Encourage students to use the other five reading strategies when appropriate as they proceed through the rest of the story. (See page 10 of this Guide.)

ENGLISH LEARNERS

1. Have students work with English-proficient partners to read and paraphrase the difficult parts of the story.
2. Students might benefit from reading along with the recording of the story provided in *The Language of Literature* Audio Library. ◯

After Reading

Recommended Follow-Up

- Thinking Through the Literature, page 601, *The Language of Literature*
- Choices & Challenges, pages 602–603, *The Language of Literature*
- SkillBuilders, pages 243–245, *The InterActive Reader*™

Informal Assessment Options

Retell Have pairs of students work together to retell the story as a conversation between the king and the princess after the courtier has made his decision. Point out that partners should select an ending to the story before scripting the characters' dialogue.

Spot Check Look at the notes students made in the margins of the story. Ask students who used the **?** notation if they were able to clear up their confusion, and if so, how.

Formal Assessment Options in *The Language of Literature*

Selection Quiz, page 33, Unit Four Resource Book

Selection Test, pages 93–94, Formal Assessment Book

For more teaching options, see pages 592–603 in *The Language of Literature* Teacher's Edition.

Additional Challenge

1. **Write an Editorial**
   Have students write an editorial from the perspective of one of the king's subjects—or one of his prisoners—that supports an opinion about the king's criminal justice system.

2. **[‖ MARK IT UP ⟩ Evaluate Character**
   Have students mark words and phrases that describe the princess's jealousy and her love for the courtier. Then have students discuss which force is stronger. Students should use the marked details to support their responses.

Before Reading

Direct students' attention to the Connect to Your Life and Key to the Story activities on page 246 of *The InterActive Reader.*™ Use the following suggestions to prepare students to read the story.

Connect to Your Life
Invite students to name good horror stories they have read. Ask: *What qualities do these stories have that make them appealing and effective?* Then have students read the directions and complete the list on page 246. Ask them to share their ideas in small groups, and discuss why they think some people enjoy being frightened by scary stories.

Key to the Story
Read aloud the story excerpt on page 246. Use your voice to convey the feverish, jittery quality of the words. Ask students what impressions they have of the narrator, based on these lines. Then have them read the directions, complete the sentence, and share their responses with a partner. Encourage students to watch for other clues that reveal the narrator's state of mind as they read.

BUILD BACKGROUND Horror Tales Explain to students that the best horror-story writers are experts at frightening us. Edgar Allan Poe (1809–1849) was one of the first American authors to do this. Oddly enough, his work owes much to his own feverish dreams, as well as his rare talent for shaping believable tales. Poe's characters face mysterious forces both within and outside themselves. Underneath the bizarre and frightening details of his stories, Poe explored conflict in the human soul.

WORDS TO KNOW

acute
audacity
conceived
crevice
derision
hypocritical
stealthy
stifled
vehemently
vex

Additional Words to Know

cunningly
    page 249, line 40
enveloped
    page 251, line 104
stimulates
    page 252, line 129

VOCABULARY PREVIEW: Words to Know in Context

You can help students learn the Words to Know by reading aloud the following sentences or writing them on the board. Then show students how to use context clues to help them figure out the meaning.

acute: A bat's vision is not *acute*—perhaps that is why we often say, "blind as a bat."

audacity: Mark had the *audacity*, or boldness, to start a fight with a pro wrestler.

conceived: Sometimes, I try to act on the ideas *conceived* when I take a walk by myself.

crevice: Laura opened the door slightly, creating a *crevice*, or narrow crack, to look through.

derision: The *derision*, or ridicule, made his face turn red with anger.

hypocritical: You are being *hypocritical*; you seem friendly but you really want to hurt me.

stealthily: We walked *stealthily* and kept very quiet so that we would not spoil the surprise.

stifled: The infant's mother *stifled* his cry to keep him from disturbing others at the service.

vehemently: Filled with emotion, the coach spoke *vehemently* to the players.

vex: I was *vexed* at my brother for making me late for the party.

cunningly: The magician *cunningly* used tricks to fool everyone.

enveloped: A thick fog *enveloped* the city, covering everything from tall buildings and trees to streets and cars.

stimulates: The caffeine in coffee *stimulates* people, making them feel more alert.

VOCABULARY FOCUS: Using Words with Multiple Meanings

Teacher Modeling Remind students that some words have more than one meaning, and that they can often use context clues to figure out which meaning is intended in a sentence. Then use the following modeling suggestion for the word *film* (page 248, line 19).

You could say *I'm not sure which meaning of the word* film *is used here. I know it can mean "a movie" or "a thin strip used to make photographs." It can also mean "a thin layer covering the cornea in a person's eye." In this sentence the narrator describes a* film *that lies over the old man's "pale blue eye." The word* film *must mean "a thin layer that covers the cornea."*

Student Modeling Have a volunteer model the same strategy using the word *fairly* (page 250, line 67).

A student might say *I'm not sure which meaning the word* fairly *has here. I know it can mean "in a fair or just manner," "reasonably," or "clearly or distinctly." In this sentence, the narrator thought the old man might have heard him when he "fairly chuckled" because the old man moved suddenly, "as if startled." Fairly must mean "clearly."*

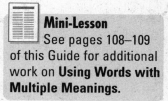

Mini-Lesson See pages 108–109 of this Guide for additional work on **Using Words with Multiple Meanings**.

During Reading

COMPREHENSION FOCUS

Key Points	Strategies for Success
Target Skill ➡ Predicting Horror story writers use foreshadowing and other clues to build suspense and a sense of dread in their readers. Recognizing specific clues will help students predict and understand the narrator's actions throughout the story.	**Mini-Lesson** Before students read "The Tell-Tale Heart," you may want to teach or review the **Predicting** lesson on pages 141–143 of this Guide. At each *Pause & Reflect,* ask students to make predictions about what they think will happen next, based on story clues and their familiarity with other horror stories.
Unreliable Narrator Poe gives clues throughout this story that the narrator is insane. Students must understand the narrator's state of mind in order to make appropriate judgments about his actions.	Read aloud lines 1–28. Then ask students to discuss what impressions they've formed about the narrator. Have them continue this process as they read. At the *Pause & Reflect* on page 256, ask: *How does the narrator's state of mind reveal his guilt to the police?*

Suggested Reading Options

- An oral reading of "The Tell-Tale Heart" is available in *The Language of Literature* Audio Library. ◯
- Partner Reading (see page 8 of this Guide).
- Additional options are described on page 8 of this Guide.

RECIPROCAL TEACHING SUGGESTION ➡ Visualizing

Teacher Modeling *Pause & Reflect, page 248* Model using the visualizing strategy to help students make mental pictures of details of the old man.

You could say *As I read, I picture certain images in my mind. The line "He had the eye of a vulture—a pale blue eye, with a film over it" helps me imagine a blue and filmy eye with an inhuman quality to it. This spooky image adds to my sense of horror as I read.*

Student Modeling *Pause & Reflect, page 253* Have several students model visualizing the setting, characters, and events in the story. Offer this prompt: *What details tell you what the narrator heard, how he felt, and how he acted? What details add to the story's scary atmosphere?*

Students may also complete the **Active Reading SkillBuilder** on page 257 of *The InterActive Reader.*™

Encourage students to use the other five reading strategies when appropriate as they proceed through the rest of the story. (See page 10 of this Guide.)

After Reading

Recommended Follow-Up

- Thinking Through the Literature, page 631, *The Language of Literature*
- Choices & Challenges, pages 632–633, *The Language of Literature*
- SkillBuilders, pages 257–259, *The InterActive Reader*™

Informal Assessment Options

Retell Have students work in small groups to present imaginary news broadcasts about the events in the story. Group members can role-play news anchors, on-the-scene reporters, and characters from the story who are interviewed for the broadcast.

Spot Check Look at the notes students made in the margins of the story. Invite them to explain their answers and discuss any questions they still have about the story.

Formal Assessment Options in *The Language of Literature*

Selection Quiz, page 50, Unit Four Resource Book

Selection Test, pages 97–98, Formal Assessment Book

For more teaching options, see pages 624–633 in *The Language of Literature* Teacher's Edition.

Additional Challenge

1. **Examine Point of View**
   Have students rewrite the scene in lines 60–107 from the old man's point of view or the scene in lines 172–235 from a police officer's perspective.

2. ‖ MARK IT UP ⟩ **Explore Conflict**
   Tell students that *conflict* is a struggle between opposing forces. In an external conflict, a character struggles against another person or some outside force. An internal conflict, on the other hand, involves a struggle within a character. Ask students to describe one external and one internal conflict in the story. Have them mark passages in the story to support their views.

Before Reading

Direct students' attention to the Connect to Your Life and Key to the Story activities on page 260 of *The InterActive Reader.*™ Use the following suggestions to prepare students to read the story.

Connect to Your Life
Encourage students to discuss events or situations in their lives that they would like to change. You might begin by naming an event or situation in your own life that you would change if you could, such as where you live or how much money you have. Then ask students what effects these changes might have on their lives. Ask: *How might your life change? Do you think all the effects would be positive?* Finally, have students fill out the chart and share their examples.

Key to the Story
Ask students to discuss some of the horror movies they have seen. To get students started, you might mention movies such as *Dracula, Nightmare on Elm Street,* and *Scream.* Ask students what made these movies so scary. Then have them fill in the chart on page 260.

BUILD BACKGROUND
Connect to Culture Tell students that many folktales and horror stories involve magic or magic objects. In this story, the magic object is a monkey's paw, which gives unusual powers to anyone who owns it. Point out that in many parts of the world, certain objects—especially those associated with animals—are believed to have special powers. For example, in Western culture, a rabbit's foot was once believed to bring luck, and lucky horseshoes still hang on the doors of many barns and farmhouses.

WORDS TO KNOW

credulity

fate

grimace

peril

surveying

Additional Words to Know

hospitable
  page 263, line 37

presumptuous
  page 265, line 98

wont
  page 272, line 312

VOCABULARY PREVIEW: Words to Know in Context

You can help students learn the Words to Know by reading aloud the following sentences or writing them on the board. Then show students how to use context clues to help them figure out the meaning.

credulity: His extreme *credulity* sometimes gets him into trouble because he believes anything people tell him.

fate: She thinks that *fate,* or a higher power, brought us together, but I think we met by chance.

grimace: When I saw the bug in my soup, I made a *grimace,* or a look of disgust.

peril: A firefighter faces all kinds of *perils,* including out-of-control fires, thick smoke, and collapsing buildings.

surveying: I was *surveying* the groceries when Dad said, "Stop looking at the food and start putting it in the cupboards."

hospitable: Our *hospitable* hosts always offer their guests plenty of good food.

presumptuous: It was *presumptuous* of me to offer you advice without being asked.

wont: Every morning my aunt was *wont* to take a walk, but now her illness has forced her to give up this habit.

VOCABULARY FOCUS Word Parts: Suffixes

Teacher Modeling Remind students that they can sometimes figure out the meaning of an unfamiliar word by thinking about the word parts it contains. Then use the following modeling suggestions for the word **placidly** (page 262, line 12).

You could say I'm not sure what the word placidly *means, but I recognize the suffix -ly from words such as* neatly. *I know that –ly means "in a particular way or manner." I also see the base word* placid, *which means "calm or peaceful." From these word parts, I can figure out that* placidly *is an adverb that must mean "in a calm or peaceful manner."*

Student Modeling Now have students follow your lead. Ask a volunteer to model using the base word and suffix to figure out the meaning of **senseless** (page 273, line 336).

A student might say I'm not familiar with the word senseless. *However, I do know that the base word* sense *means "feeling" or "sensation," and the suffix –less means "without." So* senseless *must mean "without feeling" or "unconscious."*

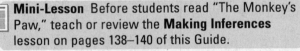

Mini-Lesson See pages 100 and 102 of this Guide for additional work on **Word Parts: Suffixes.**

During Reading

COMPREHENSION FOCUS

Key Points	Strategies for Success
Target Skill → Making Inferences It is crucial that students be able to make inferences in order to understand the story's key events and its conclusion.	**Mini-Lesson** Before students read "The Monkey's Paw," teach or review the **Making Inferences** lesson on pages 138–140 of this Guide. • Read aloud lines 95–99 on page 265. Then ask students what Morris's reaction suggests about his experience with the paw. • As students read, have them fill in the **Inference Chart** on page 139 of this guide.
Theme An important theme in "The Monkey's Paw" is that attempting to interfere with fate can have terrible results. It is essential that students understand this theme in order to appreciate the story on a deeper level.	Before reading, discuss the definition of *fate* at the bottom of page 265. At the *Pause & Reflect* on page 266, ask: *What did the first owner ask for with his third wish? What does this suggest about his first two wishes? Why do you think the sergeant-major doubts whether he would accept another three wishes?* After reading, ask students what they think the elderly couple came to realize as the result of their experience with the monkey's paw.

Suggested Reading Options

• An oral reading of "The Monkey's Paw" is available in *The Language of Literature* Audio Library. ◯
• Partner/Cooperative Reading (see page 8 of this Guide).
• Additional options are described on page 8 of this Guide.

RECIPROCAL TEACHING SUGGESTION ➡ Clarifying

Teacher Modeling *Pause & Reflect, page 263* Model for students how to use the clarifying strategy to understand Mr. White's changing moods.

You could say *When I reread lines 13–20 on page 262, I see that Mr. White has lost the chess match. The loss makes him angry, and he begins shouting. However, in lines 30–31 on page 263, Mr. White sees his wife and son exchange a glance; they know why he is so angry. Mr. White's "guilty grin" reveals his realization that he has overreacted. The interaction between the three characters also suggests that they have a very close and loving relationship.*

Student Modeling *Pause & Reflect, page 273* Ask several students to model using the clarifying strategy to understand Mr. and Mrs. White's horror at the news that they will receive two hundred pounds. Offer this prompt: *What has happened to Herbert? What did Mr. White wish for? How has the wish come true?* Have students use the **Active Reading Skillbuilder** on page 279 to clarify other passages in the story.

Encourage students to use the other five reading strategies when appropriate as they proceed through the rest of the story. (See page 10 of this Guide.)

ENGLISH LEARNERS

1. Direct students to the many selection footnotes as an aid to understanding unfamiliar words and idioms. You might review these footnotes with students before they begin reading.

2. Students might benefit from reading along with the recording of "The Monkey's Paw" provided in *The Language of Literature* Audio Library. ◯

After Reading

Recommended Follow-Up

• Thinking Through the Literature, page 691, *The Language of Literature*

• Choices & Challenges, page 692, *The Language of Literature*

• SkillBuilders, pages 279–281, *The InterActive Reader*™

Informal Assessment Options

Retell Write each of the following phrases on cards: Morris's visit; *Mr. White's first wish; the messenger's news; Mr. White's second wish; Herbert's pounding on the door; Mr. White's third wish.* Distribute the cards in random order to a small group of students. Have them place the cards in the correct order. Then have them use the cards as prompts to retell the story. Encourage students to add a few details to explain each phrase.

Spot Check Look at the notes students made in the margins of the story. Invite them to explain their answers and discuss any questions they still have about the story.

Formal Assessment Options in *The Language of Literature*

Selection Quiz, page 81, Unit Four Resource Book

Selection Test, pages 107–108, Formal Assessment Book

For more teaching options, see pages 680–692 in *The Language of Literature* Teacher's Edition.

Additional Challenge

1. **Make a Judgment**
   Have students write a paragraph to answer this question: *Is it possible that the events of this story—for example, Herbert's death or the mysterious knocking—are caused by something other than the monkey's paw?* Explain.

2. **MARK IT UP ➤ Examine Suspense**
   Tell students that suspense is a feeling of growing tension and excitement felt by the reader. Have students underline passages in "The Monkey's Paw" that build suspense. Then have students discuss the passages they have identified. Ask: *Why is the passage suspenseful? How does the author build suspense throughout the story?*

Before Reading

Direct students' attention to the Connect to Your Life and Key to the Poem activities on page 282 of *The InterActive Reader.*™ Use the following suggestions to prepare students to read the poem.

Connect to Your Life
Write the word *patriotism* on the board. Make sure that students understand that it means devotion to one's country. Then read aloud the Connect to Your Life question and invite students to respond. Finally, read aloud the directions for the activity, have students fill in the web, and ask them to share their ideas in small groups.

Key to the Poem
Discuss with students what they know about the reasons for and the events leading up to the American Revolution. Then ask volunteers to read aloud the Key to the Poem paragraphs. Point out that the colonists believed that British imposition of military rule violated their rights. Acts such as this one eventually prompted the colonists to fight for independence from Britain.

BUILD BACKGROUND
Connect to History Have students locate Boston, Concord, and Lexington on a map of Massachusetts or the United States. Tell students that the battles of Lexington and Concord marked the beginning of the Revolutionary War in 1775. "Paul Revere's Ride" describes the events that took place the night before these battles. Then have a volunteer read aloud the Preview on page 283. Ask: *Why do you think it was important for colonists to know how the British planned to advance on these towns? How do you think Paul Revere might have felt on the night of April 18, 1775?* Discuss students' responses.

Strategies for Reading Poetry

- Notice the form of the poem: the number of lines and their shape on the page.
- Read the poem aloud a few times. Listen for rhymes and rhythms.
- Visualize the images and comparisons.
- Mark words and phrases that appeal to you.
- Ask yourself what message the poet is trying to send.
- Think about what the poem is saying to you.

FOCUS ON POETRY

The discussion points below and the tips shown at the left will help prepare students for reading "Paul Revere's Ride." If your students need more detailed instruction on how to read and interpret poems, have them read "Poetry" on pages 187–191 of *The Language of Literature.*

- **Form** Have students look at the form of the poem on page 284 of *The InterActive Reader.*™ Help them to identify the stanzas, and point out that they have differing numbers of lines. Explain that each stanza in this poem focuses on a different image, event, or main idea, and that breaks between stanzas often signal a shift in the poem's mood. Encourage students to identify each stanza's central idea and mood as they read the poem.

- **Rhythm** Read aloud the first stanza of the poem twice. The first time, have students listen quietly; the second time, have them identify the stressed syllables by clapping on these beats. Discuss some of the possible associations the poet may have hoped to create with the regular rhythm. Students may say that the rhythmic pattern resembles a military march or a horse's gait. Encourage students to pay attention to the effect the steady rhythm has on the mood of the poem as they read.

VOCABULARY FOCUS Word Parts: Compound Words

Teacher Modeling Remind students that they can often determine the meaning of an unfamiliar compound word by looking at the smaller words it contains. Model the strategy using the word *churchyard* (page 286, line 42).

Mini-Lesson See pages 100 and 103 of this Guide for additional work on **Word Parts: Compound Words.**

You could say I don't recognize this word, but I see that it contains two shorter words I know, church and yard. I know that a church is "a building for public (especially Christian) worship" and that a yard can mean "an area of ground." A churchyard must be an area of ground next to a church. The churchyard in the poem seems to be a cemetery, since "the dead" lie there.

Student Modeling Ask a student volunteer to use this strategy to determine the meaning of *musket-ball* (page 292, line 110).

A student might say I don't know what this word means, but I recognize the words it contains. I know a musket is a type of gun used in colonial times and ball can mean "a solid object shot from a cannon or gun." A musket-ball must be an object that is shot from a musket, similar to a bullet. That makes sense in the poem.

During Reading

COMPREHENSION FOCUS

Key Points	Strategies for Success
Target Skill → Narrative Elements This narrative poem tells a suspenseful story based on historical events. To understand the poem, students must keep track of the characters and events described.	**Mini-Lesson** Before students read the poem, teach or review the **Narrative Elements** lesson on pages 147–150 of this Guide. • Read aloud lines 1–23 on page 284. Then work with students to identify the setting, main character, and main problem described in these lines. • After reading, have students complete the **Literary Analysis SkillBuilder** on page 297 of *The InterActive Reader.*™
Unusual Syntax/Antiquated Language Longfellow's use of unusual syntax and formal, antiquated language may confuse students.	Read aloud the entire poem at least once and use your voice and gestures to help convey its meaning. Pause at difficult lines or passages and briefly restate them or explain their meaning in simple terms. Have students restate difficult lines, such as "Hardly a man is now alive / Who remembers that famous day and year," in a more familiar word order. After students listen to the poem once, discuss any questions they have about its meaning. Then have them paraphrase challenging parts of the poem, using the **Active Reading SkillBuilder** on page 296 of *The InterActive Reader.*™

Suggested Reading Options

• An oral reading of "Paul Revere's Ride" is available in *The Language of Literature* Audio Library. ◯
• Oral Reading (see page 8 of this Guide).
• Additional options are described on page 8 of this Guide.

RECIPROCAL TEACHING SUGGESTION ➡ Visualizing

Teacher Modeling *Pause & Reflect, page 284* Model for students how to visualize details in the setting of "Paul Revere's Ride."

You could say *As I read lines 15–23, I try to picture what Paul Revere might have seen on that important night. When I read the lines "a huge black hulk, that was magnified / By its own reflection in the tide," I imagine a large, menacing shape in the water. This helps me appreciate the tense, suspenseful mood of the poem.*

Student Modeling *Pause & Reflect, page 288* Have several students model visualizing what Revere's friend observes that night. Offer these prompts: *What does Revere's friend see in and from the belfry chamber? What does he hear? What mood do these images help create?*

Encourage students to use the other five reading strategies when appropriate as they proceed through the rest of the poem. (See page 10 of this Guide.)

ENGLISH LEARNERS

1. Before reading, summarize the main events of the poem for students. After reading, have them work with English-proficient partners to paraphrase the main events in each stanza.

2. Students might benefit from reading along with the recording of "Paul Revere's Ride" provided in *The Language of Literature* Audio Library. ☊

After Reading

Recommended Follow-Up

- Thinking Through the Literature, page 721, *The Language of Literature*
- Choices & Challenges, page 722, *The Language of Literature*
- SkillBuilders, pages 296–297, *The InterActive Reader*™

Informal Assessment Options

Retell Have students work in small groups to stage oral retellings of the poem. Explain that retellings should include paraphrased narration, invented dialogue, and role-played action.

Spot Check Look at the notes students made in the margins. Make sure their answers show an understanding of what they have read. Pay particular attention to the questions on page 291, as these check students' understanding of the order and meaning of events in the poem.

Formal Assessment Options in *The Language of Literature*

Selection Test, pages 111–112, Formal Assessment Book

For more teaching options, see pages 713–722 in *The Language of Literature* Teacher's Edition.

Additional Challenge

1. **Create a Storyboard**
   Have students imagine they are making the movie version of this poem and prepare storyboards that include illustrations and captions for one or more scenes. Encourage them to think about what visuals, voice-over narration, dialogue, sound effects, and music would make the scene or scenes effective.

2. **⫿⫿⫿ MARK IT UP ⟩ Examine a Character**
   Ask: *Based on this poem, how would you describe Paul Revere's character and personality?* Have students mark words and phrases in the poem that support their answers.

Before Reading

Direct students' attention to the **Connect to Your Life** and **Key to the Biography** activities on page 298 of *The InterActive Reader.*™ Use the following suggestions to prepare students to read the biography.

Connect to Your Life
Ask students what they know about Harriet Tubman. If necessary, explain that she was an African-American woman who helped many slaves escape to freedom during the mid-1800s. Read aloud the directions and the example on page 298. Have students fill in their web and share their responses with the class.

Key to the Biography
Ask students to share what they know about the Civil War and the history of slavery in the United States. Then read aloud the Key to the Biography. Discuss with students why they think the escape network was called the "Underground Railroad," and ask what dangers they think conductors and runaways might have faced. You may also wish to show students the route Tubman took to Canada on a class map or the map on page 756 of *The Language of Literature.*

BUILD BACKGROUND Connect To History Explain to students that Harriet Tubman (1820?–1913) was herself an escaped slave who led nineteen trips along the Underground Railroad. She was known by enslaved people as Moses, in reference to the Biblical figure who led enslaved Jews from Egypt. Have students speculate about what might have motivated Tubman to risk her life to help others.

WORDS TO KNOW

- borne
- cajoling
- disheveled
- dispel
- eloquence
- fastidious
- indomitable
- instill
- mutinous
- sullen

VOCABULARY PREVIEW: Words to Know in Context

You can help students learn the Words to Know by reading aloud the following sentences or writing them on the board. Then show students how to use context clues to help them figure out the meaning.

borne: The balloons were *borne,* or carried, by the heavy winds.

cajoling: My little sister's voice can be *cajoling,* gently urging our parents to buy what she wants.

disheveled: The doll in the attic looked *disheveled:* its dress was torn, and its hair was dirty.

dispel: Instead of spreading rumors, we should *dispel* them before they hurt other people.

eloquence: Dr. King spoke with an *eloquence* that moved people to do good.

fastidious: As a child I was very *fastidious* about cleaning my room, but now I am extremely messy.

indomitable: The *indomitable* hero was fearless and brave in front of his enemies.

instill: Parents try to *instill* good values in their children so that they, in turn, can pass these values on to others.

mutinous: Pirate ships were not peaceful; often, sailors would grow *mutinous,* turning against their leader.

sullen: After losing the game, the players looked *sullen* and gloomy.

VOCABULARY FOCUS: Using Context Clues

Teacher Modeling Remind students that they can often figure out the meaning of an unfamiliar word by looking for context clues. Then use the following modeling suggestion for the word *vicinity* (page 301, line 52).

You could say *I'm not familiar with the word* vicinity, *so I'll look for context clues to help me. The phrases "of the plantation" and "carefully selecting the slaves" show me that Tubman had spent time near the plantation where the slaves worked.* Vicinity *probably means "a nearby place or region."*

Student Modeling Ask a student volunteer how to use context clues to determine the meaning of *reluctance* (page 307, line 220).

A student might say *I'm not sure what* reluctance *means, so I'll look for context clues to help me. The phrases "slept, all that night" and "had all been warm and safe and well-fed" tell me that the slaves were finally resting after their long journey. They would probably be unwilling to leave a warm, secure place for the cold and dangerous escape routes.* Reluctance *probably means "unwillingness."*

Mini-Lesson See pages 96–99 of this Guide for additional work on **Using Context Clues.**

During Reading

COMPREHENSION FOCUS

Key Points	Strategies for Success
Target Skill ➡ Sequence Students must keep track of the sequence of events in order to understand the biography and appreciate the magnitude of Tubman's efforts.	**Mini-Lesson** Before students read, teach or review the **Sequence** lesson on pages 127–129 of this Guide. • Read aloud lines 1–47 on pages 300 and 301. Help students recognize that the author begins the biography by describing the reactions of slave masters to Tubman's activities. Point out that in the next section beginning with line 48 the author describes a particular journey when Tubman helped a group of runaway slaves escape to Canada. • At each subsequent *Pause & Reflect* have students identify the major events in the correct order and then fill in the **Sequence/Flow Chart** on page 128 of this Guide.
Cause and Effect Students must be able to recognize cause-and-effect relationships to understand Tubman's actions and motives.	At the *Pause & Reflect* on page 301, ask: *Why did Tubman arrange it so that the slaves were discovered missing on a Sunday? Why did she wait for a night when the North Star was visible?* At each subsequent *Pause & Reflect,* draw students' attention to other key cause-and-effect relationships.

Suggested Reading Options

• An oral reading of this excerpt from *Harriet Tubman: Conductor on the Underground Railroad* is available in *The Language of Literature* Audio Library. ◯
• Independent Reading (see page 8 of this Guide).
• Additional options are described on page 8 of this Guide.

RECIPROCAL TEACHING SUGGESTION ➡ Questioning

Teacher Modeling *Pause & Reflect, page 301* To help students make connections between Moses and Harriet Tubman, model using the questioning strategy.

You could say *In line 11, the author states that the slave masters "never saw him." I ask myself: To whom is the author referring? I reread and see that the masters thought a man named Moses was responsible for running off slaves. Since they never saw Tubman and probably didn't expect a woman to do such dangerous work, they assumed "Moses" was a man.*

Student Modeling *Pause & Reflect, page 304* Have several students model using the questioning strategy to understand the biography better. Offer this prompt: *What questions do you have about the Fugitive Slave Law, or about the special challenges Tubman faced on this journey?*

Have students complete the **Active Reading SkillBuilder** on page 315 of *The InterActive Reader™* as they read.

Encourage students to use the other five reading strategies when appropriate as they proceed through the rest of the selection. (See page 10 of this Guide.)

ENGLISH LEARNERS

1. Help students understand these words and expressions:
   plantation, page 300, line 16
   overseer, page 300, line 17
   machinery of pursuit, page 301, line 34
   flight, page 302, line 89
   vain effort, page 308, line 264
   turn traitor, page 309, lines 290 and 291
   crystallized, page 314, line 442

2. Students might benefit from reading along with the excerpt from *Harriet Tubman: Conductor on the Underground Railroad* provided in *The Language of Literature* Audio Library. ○

After Reading

Recommended Follow-Up

- Thinking Through the Literature, page 766, *The Language of Literature*
- Choices & Challenges, pages 767–768, *The Language of Literature*
- SkillBuilders, pages 315–317, *The InterActive Reader™*

Informal Assessment Options

Retell Have students work in small groups to retell the events in this biography. Explain that each group member should role-play the operator of a "safe house" along Tubman's route. They should describe portions of Tubman's journey as if they had heard these details from her.

Spot Check Look at the notes students made in the margins. Make sure their answers show an understanding of what they read.

Formal Assessment Options in *The Language of Literature*

Selection Quiz, page 26, Unit Five Resource Book

Selection Test, pages 117–118, Formal Assessment Book

For more teaching options, see pages 756–768 in *The Language of Literature* Teacher's Edition.

Additional Challenge

1. **Evaluate Character**
   Ask: *What qualities of a leader does Harriet Tubman show in this excerpt?* Have students write a paragraph or two to explain their ideas.

2. **▏▎MARK IT UP ⟩ Word Pictures**
   Tubman creates "word pictures" to instill hope and courage in the runaways. Have students highlight or underline the word pictures she "paints." Then have them discuss what makes each word picture so appealing.

Before Reading

Direct students' attention to the Connect to Your Life and Key to the Essay activities on page 318 of *The InterActive Reader.*™ Use the following suggestions to prepare students to read the essay.

Connect to Your Life
Tell students about a job or chore you enjoy and one you don't enjoy. Then read aloud the Connect to Your Life directions and have students fill out the chart. Afterwards, invite volunteers to share their examples. Explain that this essay describes the narrator's attempts to find a job he likes and can do well.

Key to the Essay
Explain that Mark Twain uses humor and exaggeration in this essay to make many of his job experiences seem amusing or adventurous. With students, read the Key to the Essay and look at the example in the web. Have students work in pairs to add other unusual jobs to the web, and ask them to share their responses with the class.

BUILD BACKGROUND
Connect to History Tell students that Mark Twain, the author of this essay, lived from 1835 to 1910. Explain that in the early 1800s, advances in printing technology made it possible to produce newspapers more quickly and cheaply. Until this time, only the wealthy could afford newspapers, but now they became widely available to people throughout the United States. In this essay, Twain describes how he became the city editor of a newspaper.

WORDS TO KNOW

- affluent
- barren
- board
- contrive
- emigrant
- endow
- lavish
- legitimate
- proprietor
- vocation

Additional Words to Know

momentous
  page 320, line 2
diffidence
  page 326, line 111

VOCABULARY PREVIEW: Words to Know in Context

You can help students learn the Words to Know by reading aloud the following sentences or writing them on the board. Then show students how to use context clues to help them figure out the meaning.

affluent: You can tell it's an *affluent* neighborhood because the houses are so grand and beautiful.

barren: This field is *barren* in the winter, but crops will grow here next spring.

board: Exchange students who live in our home don't pay rent, but they do pay *board*—$50 a week for food and other expenses.

contrive: I *contrived,* or invented, a new way to entertain my little brother when I made hand puppets out of socks.

emigrant: The *emigrants* left their homeland to find a better way of life.

endow: Cody is *endowed* with artistic talent; he can paint and draw very well.

lavish: The *lavish* display of flowers contained many colorful, expensive plants.

legitimate: Are you making a *legitimate* attempt to learn to play the piano, or are you just fooling around?

proprietor: The *proprietor* of this bakery has owned the store for many years.

vocation: Celia doesn't know which *vocation* to choose; she wants to be either a singer or an architect.

---

momentous: Aaron faced a very important, even *momentous,* decision: whether to stay in the woods with his injured friend or to go in search of help.

diffidence: Sharon has tried to overcome her *diffidence,* but she is still one of the shyest people I know.

VOCABULARY FOCUS: Understanding Idioms

Teacher Modeling Remind students that they can sometimes figure out the meaning of an idiom by looking for context clues. Model using the idiom *take pains* (page 328, line 145).

You could say I'm not sure what this expression means, so I'll look for context clues. Twain says his editor taught him to get the facts and report them with certainty. Twain seems to think, therefore, that reporters who don't describe events with certainty must not have made the effort to get all the facts. To take pains *must mean "to make an effort."*

Student Modeling Call on a volunteer to model figuring out the meaning of the expression *get the upper hand* (page 328, lines 147–148).

A student might say I don't recognize this expression. The narrator admits that on a slow newsday—one without many facts to report—he might let fancy (imagination) get the upper hand *of fact. Without facts to report, he might have let his imagination take over.* Get the upper hand *must mean "gain control over."*

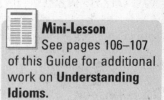 **Mini-Lesson** See pages 106–107 of this Guide for additional work on **Understanding Idioms.**

During Reading

COMPREHENSION FOCUS

Key Points	Strategies for Success

Target Skill ➡ Main Idea and Details

In this essay, Mark Twain explains how he became a journalist, what he enjoys about the job, and what he learned about himself along the way. Students must be able to identify his stated or implied main ideas and the supporting details to understand this humorous essay.

Mini-Lesson Before students read the excerpt from "Roughing It," you may want to teach the **Main Idea and Details** lesson on pages 123–126 of this Guide.

- Read the lines 17–59 on pages 320 and 322. Then work with students to identify the implied main idea—Twain has had several jobs and failed at all of them—and the key details of the paragraph. At each subsequent *Pause & Reflect,* have students identify the main points and supporting details.

Difficult Language

This essay contains many lengthy and complex sentences. Students may need help breaking the sentences down into meaningful parts in order to understand them. They also may need help with the selection's difficult vocabulary.

- At the *Pause & Reflect* on page 322, review with students the sentence on lines 36–39 ("I had made . . . thus far."). Walk them through the sentence, breaking it down into clauses and phrases. Help them see how the different word groups (in this case, separated by commas) relate to each other. Finally, paraphrase the sentence for students. Repeat this exercise with the remaining three sentences on the page.
- Remind students to use the sidenotes for help with difficult or dated vocabulary and idioms.

Suggested Reading Options

- An oral reading of the excerpt from "Roughing It" is available in *The Language of Literature* Audio Library. ◯
- Shared Reading (see page 8 of this Guide).
- Additional options are described on page 8 of this Guide.

RECIPROCAL TEACHING SUGGESTION ➡ Questioning

Teacher Modeling *Pause & Reflect, page 322* Model using the questioning strategy to help students figure out why Twain was fired from his job in a bookstore.

You could say When I read lines 29–33, I don't understand why Twain lost his job as a bookseller's clerk. I ask myself: What did he do wrong? I reread and find that the customers "bothered" him because they kept him from reading at work. I think this is Twain's humorous way of saying he was not a good clerk because he preferred reading for pleasure to doing his job.

Student Modeling *Pause & Reflect, page 322* Have students model using the strategy to understand why the narrator couldn't keep his other jobs. Offer this prompt: *What jobs has the narrator had? What questions do you have about why he got fired from each one?*

Encourage students to use the other five reading strategies when appropriate as they proceed through the rest of the essay. (See page 10 of this Guide.)

ENGLISH LEARNERS

1. The elaborate language and the use of exaggeration in this essay will challenge students. As students read, have them work with English-proficient partners to paraphrase Twain's descriptions of his jobs and activities.
2. Students might benefit from reading along with the recording of the essay provided in *The Language of Literature* Audio Library. ◠

After Reading

Recommended Follow-Up

- Thinking Through the Literature, page 802, *The Language of Literature*
- Choices & Challenges, page 803, *The Language of Literature*
- SkillBuilders, pages 335–337, *The InterActive Reader*™

Informal Assessment Options

Retell Have students work in groups of three to retell the essay. One group member should tell about Mark Twain's unsuccessful attempts at work. The second should describe his early introduction to journalism, before he learns to fill a page. The third should describe his experience of learning to write newspaper stories, and his feelings about journalism.

Spot Check Look at the notes students made in the margins of the essay. Ask students who used the ? notation if they were able to clear up their confusion, and if so, how.

Formal Assessment Options in *The Language of Literature*

Selection Quiz, page 43, Unit Five Resource Book

Selection Test, pages 123–124, Formal Assessment Book

For more teaching options, see pages 794–803 in *The Language of Literature* Teacher's Edition.

Additional Challenge

1. Support an Opinion
Have students write a paragraph explaining why they would or would not hire Mark Twain to work as a newspaper reporter. Have students cite details from the essay to support their opinions. Remind them that Twain uses a great deal of hyperbole, or exaggeration, in discussing his experiences as a journalist.

2. ▌▌▌**MARK IT UP** ⟩ **Examine the Narrator**
Have students select passages in the essay that they find especially funny. Ask: *What do you think these passages suggest about Mark Twain as a writer and a man?* To get students started, refer them to the **Active Reading SkillBuilder** on page 335 of *The InterActive Reader.*™ Have students mark details in the essay to support their views

Before Reading

Direct students' attention to the Connect to Your Life and Key to the Speech activities on page 338 of *The InterActive Reader.*™ Use the following suggestions to prepare students to read the speech.

Connect to Your Life Explain to students that in this speech Rudolfo Anaya tells his audience why he loves to read and how his love of reading began. Read aloud the Connect to Your Life directions and have students fill out the web. Afterwards, invite students to share their entries with the class.

Key to the Speech Ask students to share what they know about New Mexico, and explain that the author of this speech was born and raised there. Then have students read the paragraphs on page 338, study the maps, and complete the activity. You may wish to invite students to speculate about what types of Spanish influence still remain in New Mexico.

BUILD BACKGROUND **Connect to Social Studies** Ask a volunteer to read aloud the Preview on page 339. Explain that Rudolfo Anaya, a life-long resident of New Mexico, has been both a student and a professor at the University of New Mexico. His Hispanic-American roots and culture are very important to him, and he often writes about these themes in his books.

Spanish-speaking Mexicans began to settle in the Southwest when it was part of Mexico from 1598 to 1898. When this territory was ceded to the United States in 1848, after the Mexican-American War, English-speaking settlers arrived from other parts of the United States. Today many Hispanic Americans speak both English and Spanish. This blend of languages is also visible in many of Anaya's writings. Encourage students to look for examples of this blend as they read "One Million Volumes."

WORDS TO KNOW

- censorship
- ignite
- induce
- litany
- paradox

Additional Words to Know

inherent
page 341, line 41

imbedded
page 342, line 71

tattered
page 343, line 115

bewilderment
page 344, line 123

VOCABULARY PREVIEW: Words to Know in Context

You can help students learn the Words to Know by reading aloud the following sentences or writing them on the board. Then show students how to use context clues to help them figure out the meaning.

censorship: *Censorship* laws do not allow people to read certain books.

ignite: His message *ignited* feelings of hope and inspiration.

induce: My grandmother's exciting stories *induced* in me a love for adventure.

litany: The *litanies* spoken by the priest were also printed in the book of prayers.

paradox: When I get grounded and my mother says, "This hurts me more than it hurts you," she is stating a *paradox* I just can't understand.

---

inherent: A love of freedom is *inherent* in our nature.

imbedded: The memory of meeting the president is *imbedded* in my mind for as long as I live.

tattered: The old, *tattered* curtains looked like rags torn to pieces.

bewilderment: Greg was in a state of *bewilderment* when he lost his way down the winding streets.

VOCABULARY FOCUS: Using Context Clues

Teacher Modeling Remind students that they can often use context clues to figure out the meaning of an unfamiliar word. Then use the following modeling suggestion for the word *direst* (page 343, line 101).

You might say I don't recognize the word direst, *so I'll look for context clues. The author says the town's fire truck was dilapidated, or in bad condition, and was used only in the* direst *emergencies. I think if the truck didn't run well, the firemen would probably use it only when they needed it most. Direst* must mean *"most urgent."*

Student Modeling Call on a volunteer to model how to use context clues to determine the meaning of the word *nurture* (page 343, line 109).

A student might say I don't know what nurture *means, so I'll try using context clues to figure it out. The author compares the way Miss Pansy "fed" him books to the way a "mother would* nurture *her child." Nurture* must mean *"to feed or nourish."*

Mini-Lesson
See pages 96–99 of this Guide for additional work on **Using Context Clues.**

During Reading

COMPREHENSION FOCUS

Key Points	Strategies for Success

Target Skill ➡ Distinguishing Fact from Opinion
Rudolfo Anaya expresses strong opinions about the importance of reading in this speech. Students' ability to recognize the author's opinions and to note how he supports his opinions with facts and anecdotes is important to their understanding and enjoyment of this piece.

Mini-Lesson Before students read "One Million Volumes," you may want to teach the **Fact and Opinion** lesson on pages 144–146 of this Guide.

- Have students read aloud lines 1–42 on pages 340 and 341. Then help students identify the author's opinions as well as the facts and personal reflections he provides to support them. At each subsequent *Pause & Reflect,* repeat this process.

- After reading, have students record facts and opinions from this selection by using the **Two-Column Chart** on page 145 of this Guide.

Time Shifts
In the speech, the author shifts back and forth between present and past events. Students will need to recognize each time shift, understand which events happened long ago, and figure out how to connect to the occasion that the speech celebrates.

At the *Pause & Reflect* on page 342, have students identify the key events described so far and arrange them on a simple time line. Remind students that they can use clues in the text to determine roughly when the events took place. Have students add events to their time lines as they read, and then discuss the relevance of these events to the occasion celebrated by the speech.

Suggested Reading Options

- An oral reading of "One Million Volumes" is available in *The Language of Literature* Audio Library. ◯
- Oral Reading (see page 8 of this Guide).
- Additional options are described on page 8 of this Guide.

RECIPROCAL TEACHING SUGGESTION ➡ Connecting

Teacher Modeling *Pause & Reflect, page 341* Model for students how to make personal connections to the events described in "One Million Volumes."

You could say *When I read the line "all the children . . . listened to the stories of the old ones," (lines 9–12) I remember listening to my own grandparents' stories. They captivated me and made me hungry to hear more. This connection helps me see why these stories were important to the author.*

Student Modeling *Pause & Reflect, page 342* Have students identify with Anaya by asking volunteers to model how they might connect personally with what they are reading. Offer this prompt: *What memories do you have of learning to read, or of learning a new language? How did your family encourage you to learn?*

Encourage students to use the other five reading strategies when appropriate as they proceed through the rest of the speech. (See page 10 of this Guide.)

ENGLISH LEARNERS

1. Anaya writes metaphorically about the power of words and books. Before reading, discuss with students why a writer might describe a book as a "world." As you read the speech aloud, briefly paraphrase any passages that might confuse students.

2. Students might benefit from reading along with the recording of "One Million Volumes" provided in *The Language of Literature* Audio Library. ○

After Reading

Recommended Follow-Up

- Thinking Through the Literature, page 858, *The Language of Literature*
- Choices & Challenges, pages 859–860, *The Language of Literature*
- SkillBuilders, pages 345–347, *The InterActive Reader™*

Informal Assessment Options

Retell Write the following sentences and phrases on slips of paper. Have students work in groups of five to take turns selecting a slip of paper and explaining how the phrase is important in the essay.
- "a million books to read, . . . to learn, to dream"
- "The stories of the old people taught us to wonder and imagine."
- "thirst for knowledge"
- "magic in words"
- "In that small room [the library] I found my shelter and retreat."

Spot Check Look at the notes students made in the margins of the speech. Make sure their answers show an understanding of what they read.

Formal Assessment Options in *The Language of Literature*

Selection Quiz, page 80, Unit Five Resource Book

Selection Test, pages 133–134, Formal Assessment Book

For more teaching options, see pages 851–860 in *The Language of Literature* Teacher's Edition.

Additional Challenge

1. **Interpret a Statement**
   Write the phrase "room full of power" on the board. Ask students to write a paragraph explaining why Anaya describes a library this way, whether they agree, and why.

2. **MARK IT UP ⟩ Identify Figurative Language**
   "One Million Volumes" is rich with figurative language. Have students underline or highlight the similes and metaphors they find.

End Unit
Lesson Plans

Reading a Magazine Article

Introducing the Concept

Some students may be bewildered by the confusing assortment of headings, text, and visuals in some magazine articles. Tell students that using these strategies will help them read magazine articles.

Teaching Tips for the Magazine Article

A **Title and Headings:** Have students identify the title and the two smaller subheadings in this article. Then demonstrate the relation between the title and subheadings by combining them: Modern Cowboys at Work; Modern Cowboys at Play.

B **Different Typeface:** Point out that the introductory paragraph in this article is set in italic type and is separated from the rest of the text. The paragraph is meant to grab the reader's attention as it introduces the main topic.

C **Visuals:** Suggest that students preview the visuals in a magazine article before they begin reading. Have students note that the first photo is tied to the first subheading; the second photo is tied to the second subheading.

D **Special Features:** Tell students that the chart in this article describes some typical rodeo events. Point out that the chart is tied to the main topic but provides information that is specifically related to cowboys at play.

E **Italics and Boldface:** Remind students that boldface type is heavier than regular type. The boldfaced terms name the rodeo events discussed in the chart. You might ask students to use the terms to identify the rodeo event pictured in the photo above the chart.

Additional Questions

1. Which of the following captions might appear with the photo showing cowboys at work: "Helicopters help round up strays" or "A cowboy struggles to stay on a bucking bronc"? **(Helicopters help round up strays.)**

2. Which boldfaced term in the chart describes a rodeo event involving a bull? **(bull riding)**

3. Which boldfaced term describes a team event? **(team roping)**

Additional Tips for Reading a Magazine Article

- **Read items in any order:** Tell students that they can read the items in a magazine article in any order they choose. After they preview the article, students can study the charts or read the introductory text first—whatever catches their interest.

- **Ignore advertising:** Encourage students to mentally screen out the ads that appear in some articles. Sometimes these ads are made to appear as if they were part of the article. However, in most cases, the ads are only there to entice readers to buy.

- **Understand slang terms:** Point out that magazines aimed at teenagers often use informal language and popular slang. Students whose first language isn't English may have trouble understanding such slang as *stylin'* (meaning "fashionable") and *chillin'* (meaning "relaxing"). You might suggest that students jot down any words and terms they don't understand and ask a friend to translate.

Reading a Textbook

Introducing the Concept

Many students are overwhelmed by the titles, subheadings, and features on a textbook page. They may become discouraged if they have trouble finding their way through these items. Tell students that these skills and strategies will help them learn to read textbooks.

Teaching Tips for the Textbook Page

A **Title and Headings:** Have students identify the title of the lesson and the headings that indicate related subtopics. Point out the different sizes and typefaces of the heads. Students should note that subheadings are usually smaller than the lesson title.

B **Vocabulary Terms:** Encourage students to scan the vocabulary terms before they begin reading the lesson. You might ask students to find the vocabulary terms that are defined on this page.

C **Main Idea:** Tell students that the main idea introduces the topic and tells them what they will learn about in the lesson. The sentence under "Why It Matters Now" explains the relevance of the lesson to today's world.

D **Primary Source:** Make sure students understand that a primary source provides firsthand knowledge by an eyewitness or participant about a specific event or period of time. Point out that primary sources are often included in textbooks because they help make a topic come alive.

E **Visuals and Captions:** Tell students that the visual on this page presents a photo of Nat Love, an African-American cowhand. Explain that Nat Love is also the author of the primary source paragraph on the page.

F **Boldface and Parentheses:** Suggest that students highlight or write down the definitions of the boldfaced vocabulary terms as they read a lesson. Help students locate the parenthetical reference to a map on another page. Explain that when they encounter such a reference, they can interrupt their reading and turn to the map or other visual.

Additional Questions

1. Who is the lesson about? (miners, ranchers, and cowhands)
2. What is the name of the primary source? (The Life and Adventures of Nat Love)
3. What did people call the unsettled or sparsely settled area of the country occupied largely by Native Americans? (frontier)

Additional Tips for Reading a Textbook

- **Take notes before reading:** Before students begin reading, have them write down what they know and what they want to find out about the topic.
- **Follow the PACER method:** When students read a lesson in a textbook, encourage them to follow the PACER method: preview the entire lesson, use section subheadings to analyze the purpose of a passage, carefully read the text, evaluate the material, and, finally, review their notes.
- **Use a graphic organizer:** As students read, suggest that they use a graphic organizer to help make sense of the material. For example, they might use a concept web to record a lesson's main ideas and supporting details.

Reading Graphs

Introducing the Concept

Graphs can present numerical information in a way that is quick and easy to grasp. Learning how graphs function can make them easier to understand. You might want to tell students that circle graphs are also called pie charts or pie graphs and that each pie in the circle represents a percentage.

Teaching Tips for the Graph

A **Title:** A graph's title usually contains key phrases that let the reader know what kind of information the graph shows. Before reading a graph, students should read the title and headings to get a quick overview.

B **Horizontal and vertical lines:** Point out the horizontal lines to students and explain that each line represents a rounded dollar amount. In addition, the bars show the average allowance for each age group.

C **Headings:** Tell students that the heading in the bar graph shows a relationship between the amount of weekly allowance children get and the ages of children. In the circle graph, the headings indicate what percentage of children get either spending money, allowance, or no allowance and no spending money.

D **Relationship:** In the example, the bar graph and the circle graph show different information. Have students explain how the two graphs relate. In this case, the circle graph shows additional information about allowances. Be sure to explain to students that both graphs are important in understanding the survey.

E **Credit:** Remind students that the credit is very important because it shows that a source is reliable.

Additional Questions

1. What information does the credit give? (It shows that the source is *Zillions* Jan/Feb 1999)
2. Add the percentages of children who get allowance and spending money only. (69%)

Other Types of Charts and Graphs

Reproduce the following charts and graphs to show students the variety of visuals they will come across in their reading. When reading a line graph remind them to read the labels on the horizontal and vertical axes before trying to understand the graph's content. In a flow chart, remind them to follow the arrows and for a diagram emphasize reading the labels.

Line Graph shows change over time

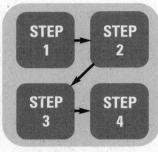

Flow Chart explains the step of a process

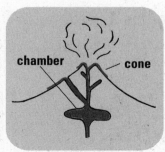

Diagram explains a process

Reading a Transit Map

Introducing the Concept

Some maps represent geographical information like lakes, oceans, and mountains. Other maps show streets, highways, and landmarks in a particular city. Still other maps illustrate the losses or victories of a battle. You might want to show students examples of the different types of maps (see list below) and then explain to them that most maps share similar features.

Teaching Tips for the Map

A **Title:** Map titles tell the reader the type of information represented on the map. Many titles have dates reflecting a time period; others have names of geographical regions; and some have names of political or economic activity.

B **Key or Legend:** Most keys and legends include a combination of arrows, symbols, colors, letters, numbers, and lines to represent an item or activity on the map. This legend on this map shows symbols for the elevated/subway train.

C **Geographic labels:** Tell students to watch for different type styles on geographic labels. On complicated political maps, for example, recognizing the type style (italic, all caps, boldface) and size will help students distinguish capital cities, state names, highways, routes etc.

D **Scale and Pointer:** A pointer, or compass rose, shows which way the directions north (N), south (S), east (E), and west (W), point on the map. Some maps will also include a scale used to measure the distance between certain areas in miles and kilometers.

Additional Questions

1. Which two lines will get passengers to the downtown Springfield area? (red and blue lines)

2. How many stops does the Yellow Line make? (six)

3. Which line closes on Sundays and holidays? (Yellow Line)

4. In which direction is Green Park? (west)

Basic Types of Maps

- **Physical maps** show mountains, hills, rivers, lakes, gulfs, oceans, and other physical features of an area.

- **Political maps** show political units, such as countries, states, counties, districts, and towns. Each unit is typically shaded a different color, represented by a symbol, or shown with a different typeface.

- **Historical maps** illustrate such things as economic activity, migrations, battles, and changing national boundaries.

Reading a Diagram

Introducing the Concept

While diagrams can be an important aid in illustrating and understanding written texts, they pose their own set of challenges for readers. After the first glance, many diagrams require close study and interpretation. Explain to students that although diagrams may look easy because of the pictures, they sometimes contain complex information. These strategies should help them sort through many different kinds of diagrams.

Teaching Tips for the Diagram

A **Title:** A diagram's title is not necessarily at the top. Remind students that it might be at the bottom or on the side, and that some diagrams don't even have titles.

B **Images:** Explain to students that the images in this diagram are a visual explanation of concepts explained in the text at left. They should glance at the images, read the text at left, and then study the images more closely. It is this second look at the images that will really help them understand the text.

C **Caption and Labels:** Remind students that they should not overlook the text to the left of the images because it contains the key concepts of the diagram.

D **Arrows and Other Markers:** Point out to students that these markers often illustrate the diagram's most important concept. For example, in this diagram, the arrows show the force of gravity and the force of the crane. The size of each arrow represents the degree of the force. The arrows in the second picture make it easier to see that the force of the crane is greater than the force of gravity.

More Practice with Diagrams

Reproduce the diagram and caption below for your students, asking them the following questions.

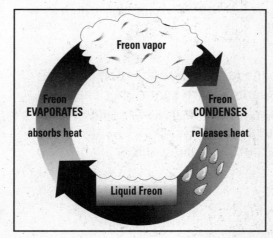

Freon vapor

Freon EVAPORATES

absorbs heat

Freon CONDENSES

releases heat

Liquid Freon

In a refrigerator, a liquid carries heat from one place to another.

Additional Questions

1. What does the cloud at the top of the circle represent? (**Freon vapor**)

2. What does the rectangle at the bottom of the circle represent? (**liquid freon**)

3. What happens to the freon after it evaporates? (**It condenses.**)

4. Why are the arrows in a continuous circle? (**They represent phases that repeat themselves in a cycle.**)

Main Idea and Supporting Details

Introducing the Concept

Students may have trouble identifying the main idea in a paragraph. They may not be able to distinguish the main point of a paragraph from the details that support it. Tell students that these strategies can help.

Teaching Tips for Main Idea and Support

- **Main Idea:** Tell students that the main idea of a paragraph is presented in a general statement. Specific details in the other sentences in the paragraph support this general statement.
- **Summary:** Encourage students to summarize the paragraph by restating a main idea as a headline or title.
- **Supporting Details:** Introduce different types of supporting details, such as sensory details, specific examples, facts and statistics, reasons, and anecdotes.

Additional Questions

1. How would you use the main idea to summarize the first paragraph? (Scientists are searching for extraterrestrials.)

2. How might you restate the main idea in the second paragraph as a headline? (Nothing Can Escape a Black Hole)

Additional Tips

Tell students that not all main ideas are stated in the first sentence. Some main ideas appear in the middle of a paragraph; some are stated in the last sentence. Sometimes, especially in narrative or descriptive writing, a main idea is implied rather than stated. When the main idea is implied, students must figure out the major point that ties all the sentences together. In the following paragraph, for example, all of the sentences are tied together by the following implied main idea: Anna is frightened.

> Anna's hands shook as she opened the door to the room. As she peeked inside, she felt her heart beating hard against her chest. "Is anyone there?" she tried to say, but the words only came out in a soft whisper. Suddenly, something rubbed against Anna's leg, making her jump. She turned and ran, screaming, down the hall.

Problem and Solution

Introducing the Concept

Familiarity with common text structures, such as problem and solution, can improve students' comprehension and mental organization of what they read. Explain to students that a text describing a problem and solution can often be broken down into recognizable parts.

Teaching Tips for the Problem and Solution Text

- **Statement of Problem:** Point out to students that the statement of the problem appears in the second sentence rather than the first sentence.
- **Explanation of Problem:** Explain to students that a writer will often write persuasively in order to convince the reader why the problem is important. The rhetorical question and exclamation are persuasive devices.
- **Proposed Solution:** Remind students that while the proposed solution here is stated clearly, it may be phrased as a question in some cases.
- **Support for Proposal:** Tell students that the support for a proposal is another place where writers will often use persuasive language.
- **Evaluating the Solution:** Encourage students to form their own opinions about every proposed solution they read, whether in their school work or independent reading.

Additional Example

The following paragraph contains another problem and proposed solution. Share it with students. Ask them to identify its different elements and evaluate the proposed solution.

Bring Back Caps and Gowns at Graduation

It's graduation time again. In just a few weeks the eighth-graders of Percy Julian Junior High will walk across the auditorium stage to receive their diplomas. It's a proud day for students, parents, and teachers alike. However, as the day approaches, people are beginning to grumble again about what the students are going to wear.

Some parents and teachers feel that graduation dress has gotten too casual, and that informal clothing takes away from the dignity of the occasion. Graduates at Percy Julian dress up for graduation. The boys wear dark suits and the girls wear white dresses or pants-suits. In the past few years, however, students have begun to "dress down": the boys have shown up in worn dark jeans, and the girls have worn casual, everyday outfits.

Perhaps it's time to bring back the cap and gown—this traditional uniform brings dignity to a very special occasion. It also sets students apart; isn't that what we want to do on graduation day?

Answers

Statement of problem: *"People are beginning to grumble again about what the students are going to wear"*

Explanation of problem: second paragraph

Proposed solution: *"Perhaps it's time to bring back the cap and gown"*

Support for proposal: third paragraph

Sequence

Introducing the Concept

Ask students to give examples of when they need to use correct sequence in their reading, writing, and speaking. Answers may include writing a report (introduction, body, and conclusion), following instructions in a manual, telling a story, and creating a comic strip. Explain that many reading assignments contain clues that help readers determine the sequence of events. When students recognize sequence, they understand material better and take clearer notes.

Teaching Tips for Sequence

- **Main steps:** Students may want to number or write down the main steps or stages as they read. For complicated or especially important sequences, advise students to create time lines or flow charts.
- **Time words:** Have students suggest other words and phrases that can signal time, such as *last Thursday, eventually, in a few minutes, simultaneously,* and *an hour later.*
- **Order words:** Ask students to think of more words and phrases that signal order, such as *first, the next step is,* and *last.*

Additional Questions

1. How long did Nicole's day as an extra last? (almost seven hours—from 6:45 A.M. until sometime after 1:30 P.M.)

2. What is the first thing Nicole did in this sequence, and when did she do it? (reported to the set at 6:45 A.M.)

3. What was the last thing Nicole did before she left with her friends? (stood in line to get paid)

4. Nicole told the events in the order in which they happened, so the sequence is very clear. If she wanted to tell the events out of order to build suspense or increase reader interest, what events could she begin with and why? (possible answers: her big scene, since that is the most important event; the end of shooting, so she could describe feeling tired, wet, and grouchy and then explain why she felt that way)

Additional Tips for Recognizing Sequence

- **Sequence Outside the Classroom** Challenge students to think of written materials outside the classroom that often use sequence. Answers may include recipes, directions to a friend's home, posted instructions at campgrounds and other public places, the rules of most board games, and some magazine articles.
- **Sequence in the Content Areas** Explain that understanding sequence is especially important when reading science and social studies materials. Encourage students to look for dates, times, and numbered steps when reading social studies and science books.
- **Events Out of Sequence** When students notice that a writer has presented events out of sequence, they may wish to write down the events in their actual order to make sure they understand the material.
- **Numbered or Lettered Items** Encourage students to look for numbered or lettered items as well as signal words. In some cases, bulleted lists are used to indicate sequence.

Cause and Effect

Writing organized by causes and effects shows that one event took place as a result of another event. However, tell students that events that follow one another do not necessarily have a cause-and-effect relationship. The events may be sequential. Students can use these strategies to determine whether events have a cause-and-effect relationship.

Teaching Tips for Cause and Effect

- **Effects:** Suggest that students look for effects in a piece of writing by posing a question based on the title of the piece, such as "What happened because the *Sultana* sank?"
- **Causes:** Tell students that they can also look for causes by posing a question, such as "Why did the *Sultana* sink?"
- **Signal Words:** Point out that when cause-and-effect writing does not contain signal words, students can use the "because test" to determine whether two events have a cause-and-effect relationship. Have students link the events with the word *because*. If the sentence still makes sense, the relationship is causal.

Additional Questions

1. What signal word introduces the phrase that explains why the *Sultana* was going slowly? (because)
2. What happened because the newspapers were covering the death of Abraham Lincoln? (The sinking of the *Sultana* was barely reported.)

Additional Tips

Tell students that not all events are linked by a series of causes and effects. Sometimes a single cause can have more than one effect. Also, several causes can result in a single effect. You might use the following chart to demonstrate a single cause with multiple effects.

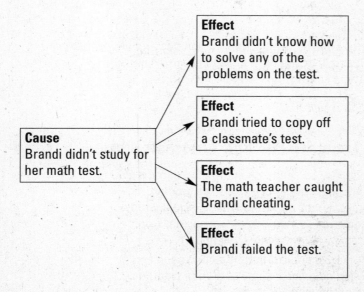

Cause
Brandi didn't study for her math test.

Effect
Brandi didn't know how to solve any of the problems on the test.

Effect
Brandi tried to copy off a classmate's test.

Effect
The math teacher caught Brandi cheating.

Effect
Brandi failed the test.

Comparison and Contrast

Introducing the Concept

Explain that, although comparisons and contrasts can appear in all types of writing, they are especially common in the following types of materials:

- social studies texts (for example, comparing the North and the South before the Civil War)
- science texts (for example, contrasting Earth with other planets)
- charts, graphs, and tables in texts, newspapers, and magazines
- reviews of films, television programs, albums, and Web sites

Teaching Tips for Comparison and Contrast

- **Direct statements:** Ask students to find the direct statement of similarity in the article ("... the dress code in my new school is almost the same as in Bosnia") and the two direct statements of difference ("Another big difference is the school system" and "... all the rules were different"). Point out that in each case, the author alerts her readers to a similarity or difference that she is going to discuss. Then she gives details about that similarity or difference, so her readers will understand what she is describing.

- **Comparison signal words:** Give students examples of other comparison signal words and phrases, such as *additionally, neither, on the one hand, as well as,* and *likewise.*

- **Contrast signal words:** Mention some other words and phrases that signal a contrast, such as *yet, in contrast,* and *instead.*

Additional Questions

1. Reread the first paragraph of the essay. What does the word *Still* signal about the author's upcoming description of her birthplace? (**Her birthplace is very different from Chicago.**)

2. In the third paragraph, Pandzic describes her school in Bosnia. How is this school similar to or different from your school? (**Answers will vary. Students may discuss grading systems, uniforms, and talking in class.**)

3. In her conclusion, the author says, "Wherever I end up, I will celebrate the best of both worlds." What are some aspects of life in Bosnia that she would like to retain? What parts of life in the United States would she try to keep? (**She likes the fast pace of Chicago and the freedom of expression in her American school, but she misses the landscape of Bosnia.**)

Additional Tips for Recognizing Comparisons and Contrasts

- **Lack of Signal Words** Direct students' attention to the sentence in the third paragraph that reads, "Another thing that has taken some time getting used to is the grading system." Point out that this sentence introduces a contrast without using signal words. Warn students to be alert for comparisons and contrasts that do not use signal words, such as, "At my old school, we wore uniforms. At my new school, we don't."

- **Multiple Items** If students are reading a text that compares more than two people or things, suggest making a chart with side-by-side columns instead of a Venn diagram. A chart can help students clarify and remember the multiple elements.

Argument

Introducing the Concept

Remind students that an argument is a form of persuasive writing. An effective argument states an opinion clearly and supports the opinion with various kinds of evidence ranging from facts to personal examples to expert opinions. Students need to identify the opinion in an argument and determine if the supporting details are reasonable and accurate.

Teaching Tips for the Argument

- **Signal Words:** Tell students that not all arguments will contain signal words, but looking for such words can help them determine the writer's position or opinion. Some additional examples include *accept, believe, agree, propose, reject,* and *oppose.*

- **Support:** A well-supported argument will use a combination of facts, statistics, examples, observations, narratives, or expert opinions. In the example, the writer gives both sides of an issue *(whether television is good or bad)* and presents personal observations and examples.

- **Errors in Reasoning:** Have students evaluate the argument by asking them to look closely at the evidence the author provides to back up the conclusions. Ask: *Does the argument make sense? Is it reasonable and clearly supported with evidence?* Then ask students to look for errors in reasoning in the argument.

Additional Questions

1. What kind of error in reasoning is the statement, "People were not violent because they did not watch violent programs." (an overgeneralization)

2. Are you for or against television? Give reasons to back up your opinion. (Students who are against television may feel that it takes time away from after-school activities and from homework. They may also feel that watching too much television results in a lack of exercise and few social contacts. Students who are in favor of television may feel that well-written programs provide informative news and entertainment. They may also feel that television helps them relax.)

Avoiding Errors in Reasoning

Fallacious reasoning can weaken an argument and show that the writer has not given careful thought about the points he or she wants to make. Read the following examples aloud or write them on the board, and then ask students to volunteer additional examples for each error in reasoning.

- **Overgeneralizations** are statements that are too broad to be valid. *(Everyone thinks that New York City is a great place for a vacation.)* Using words such as *some, many, few, almost,* and *sometimes* can help one avoid overgeneralization. Caution students that although they may agree with an overgeneralization, agreeing with the statement does not make it true.

- **Circular Reasoning** repeats a statement in different words rather than giving reasons to support it. *(Ice-skating is difficult to learn because it is hard.)*

- **Either/or statements** suggest that there are only two choices available in a situation. *(Either we start using the Internet, or we will lose touch with the world.)* Remind students that there might be other possibilities to consider in either/or statements.

Social Studies

Introducing the Concept

Explain that when students understand the special features of a social studies page, it becomes easier to find, understand, and remember key information.

Teaching Tips for the Social Studies Page

A **Subheads:** Encourage students to pay attention to headlines and subheads as they preview the chapter as well as during reading.

B **Organizational patterns:** Point out the word *Effects* in the first subhead. Mention that this section gives many causes and effects related to the Civil War. For example, the income tax and a new currency (causes) led to the Union being able to pay its war-related expenses (effect). Other chapters may use organizational patterns such as sequence or comparison and contrast.

C **Vocabulary terms:** Tell students that after reading, they should be able to define these boldfaced, italicized, or underlined terms in their own words.

D **Sidebar articles and graphic:** The graphic on this page includes specific details to give students a clearer understanding of concepts in the main text.

E **Study tips:** Many social studies books include tips and questions that assess not only students' understanding but also their thinking and map-reading skills. Study questions and tips are also found in some science and math textbooks.

Additional Questions

1. What happens during a period of inflation? (prices go up)
2. What did many slaves do that hurt the Southern economy? (slowed their pace of work, stopped working, or destroyed crops or farm equipment)

Additional Tips for Reading in Social Studies

- **Read and review objectives** Many textbooks include objectives or goals for each lesson. Students can check their understanding by making sure they can answer what the goal or objective asks of them.

- **Find relationships to prior reading** Encourage students to think about how the material relates to subjects they have covered before. For instance, how was the period after the Civil War similar to or different from the period before it?

- **Overcome lack of prior knowledge** Students will have no prior knowledge of many historical events. Suggest that students create word webs, charts, cause-and-effect charts, Venn diagrams, and other graphic organizers as they read. Knowing how facts are related makes them easier to remember.

- **Use textbook aids** Remind students to use the aids in their social studies textbook:

  - sections on how to read maps, charts, and time lines
  - tips on interpreting political cartoons
  - explanations on how to recognize text structures such as sequence or comparison and contrast
  - a glossary with definitions of difficult words and concepts
  - a Spanish-language glossary

Science

Introducing the Concept

Many textbooks present special reading challenges for students. Science textbooks, for example, use highly specialized vocabulary and difficult, often unfamiliar concepts. They sometimes rely heavily on diagrams and illustrations. Let students know that these strategies will help them develop the special skills required for reading a science page.

Teaching Tips for the Science Page

A **Title and Headings:** Point out to students that the heading "Star Distances" is probably a subhead within a lesson, since the type is fairly small, and it is not accompanied by any objectives or other pre-lesson apparatus.

B **Boldfaced and Italicized Words:** Remind students that the boldfaced words on this page are vocabulary words. Urge students to note definitions as they read.

C **Scientific Concepts:** Point out to students that although they may have no prior knowledge of science concepts in a lesson, the comparison of flashlight distance to star distance can be very useful. After they finish reading the complete explanation of the concept, encourage them to go back and evaluate the comparison. Do they feel it is accurate?

D **Figure References:** Let students know that in some cases, figure references point them to diagrams or illustrations that are critical to their understanding of the text. For this reason, they should be sure to look at the figure in the margin right away, rather than wait until the end of the paragraph or the end of the page.

E **Diagrams, Photos, and Illustrations:** Remind students that the diagram on the page shows the Earth at two points on its orbit around the Sun; it is not suggesting that there is more than one Earth, or more than one planet on the same orbital path.

Additional Tips for Reading in Science

• **Keep track of references to diagrams or illustrations.** Some pages will contain several diagrams, photographs, or illustrations. Readers should keep track of the figure numbers when going back and forth between the text and the pictures, so as not to confuse the pictures with one another.

• **Don't assume knowledge of familiar vocabulary terms; be sure to read definitions carefully.** Some science terms are familiar, everyday words that have a more specific meaning in science. (For example, the word *heat* is generally used to describe a feeling of warmth or hotness. In science, however, *heat* refers to a form of energy associated with the motion of atoms or molecules.) When they encounter familiar words among science vocabulary terms, readers should take care to read each term's definition, and not assume that they already know it.

• **Be alert to surprising information, or information that contradicts prior knowledge.** Readers may find that what they read in a science lesson contradicts what they think they know about the concept. (For example, the fact that falling objects accelerate at the same rate, no matter what their weight, is often surprising to people.) Readers should be alert to startling information or corrections of their prior knowledge, and be ready to consciously revise their understanding of the material.

Mathematics

Introducing the Concept

Although student textbooks are the primary reading material for many students—especially in math and science classes—they pose some special challenges for readers. In addition to scanning titles and headings, students must make sense of very specific vocabulary and symbols. Let them know that reading a math page takes some special skills, and share these helpful strategies with them.

Teaching Tips for the Math Page

A **Title and Subheads:** Point out to students that the subhead "How hot is Earth's crust?" poses a question that can be solved mathematically. Since the lesson head is "Solving Multi-Step Equations," they should assume that the problem described in the subhead can be solved with a multi-step equation.

B **Objectives:** Have students rewrite the lesson objectives in the form of questions. For example, "How do you use two or more steps to solve a linear equation?" Seeing these goals as questions may help them see the point of the lesson.

C **Explanations:** Remind students that some explanations of mathematical concepts are complex and abstract, and they require extra concentration.

D **Special Features:** Boxed or highlighted text can contain special tips, strategies, or short summaries of important concepts. They are designed to make the material easier to understand and remember.

E **Worked-out Solutions to Problems:** Walk students through each step of these sample problems, making sure that they understand how the problems work and how the answer has been arrived at. Sample problems are their key to solving the other problems in the set.

Additional Tips for Reading in Mathematics

- **Reread previous material:** When the text refers to material you have read earlier, be sure to reread the previous material.

- **Watch for special vocabulary:** Keep in mind that some everyday words have different meanings in mathematics. For example, the words *product, base,* and *power* have special meanings in math.

- **Read directions carefully:** Carefully read directions for each exercise or problem set. In some cases, the directions may not ask you to solve a problem, but to answer questions about it.

- **Watch for boldface words:** Look out for boldface vocabulary words; be sure that you understand their definitions.

- **Read math in special ways:** One does not always read left to right in math. For example, fractions are to be read from top to bottom.

- **Watch for special words and symbols:** Read every word and symbol very carefully to avoid mistaking words such as *hundred* for *hundredth* or *1.0* for *.10.*

Reading an Application

Introducing the Concept

People generally think of applications as something to fill out rather than something to read. But an application must be read carefully in order to be filled out correctly. Remind students that many applications have numerous features in common, and a few strategies can help them read the applications accurately.

Teaching Tips for the Application

A **Sections:** Encourage students to always scan something before reading it. This will give them a general idea of the application as a whole, and will help them put the different sections in context once they begin to read carefully.

B **Special Instructions:** Caution students not to skip over the fine print on applications; it may contain important instructions or other information.

C **Other Materials:** Remind students that while it's very easy to overlook requests for supplementary materials, the application will not be considered complete without those materials.

D **Spaces To Be Left Blank:** Point out to students that many applications have such a section for the people receiving the completed application. It is often labeled "For Office Use Only." This section frequently appears at the bottom of the application; students should take care to notice this label and avoid writing in these sections.

E **Difficult Words or Abbreviations:** Tell students that certain abbreviations are standard on applications, such as *NA* (not applicable), *ph.* (phone), *H. phone* (home phone), *W. phone* (work phone), or *SSN* (Social Security Number).

More Practice with Applications

Here is another form that students might read and fill out. Reproduce it for your students and ask them the following questions.

Interlibrary Loan Request

Library card number _____

Fill out this form for a book not owned by this library. We will inform you by mail of the status of your interlibrary loan request.

Name _____ Phone _____

Address _____

Book title _____ Author _____

Publisher _____ Date of publication _____

Needed by what date? _____

FOR OFFICE USE ONLY

Lending Library _____

Book found _____ Date due _____

Additional Questions

1. What is the purpose of this form? (To request a book from another library)

2. What does the library need to know about the book you are looking for? (title, author, publisher, and date of publication)

3. Circle the part of the form that you are *not* supposed to fill out. (Students should circle the section marked "For Office Use Only.")

Reading a Public Notice

Introducing the Concept

Explain that public notices can appear on billboards, flyers, and even the Internet. The sample notice is a Web page from a public library, but the tips given for reading it can be applied to all kinds of notices.

Teaching Tips for the Public Notice

A **Title:** Point out that the title of the sample notice, like most titles, appears near the top of the page.

B **Audience and relevance:** Encourage students to think about whether the notice applies to them or to someone they know. Students can then concentrate on relevant messages and filter out irrelevant ones.

C **Instructions:** The instructions in this notice are clearly spelled out—as is the penalty for disobeying them.

D **Credit:** The sample gives the e-mail address for the library's "Webmaster," the employee or volunteer who maintains the page. Point out that it also includes the name of the library as well as its street address and main telephone number.

E **Details:** Explain that the menu of options on the left side of the Web page gives much more information about the library. Specific questions about the library's Internet use policy could be answered by e-mailing the Webmaster or calling the main number.

F **Special features:** This site includes a Spanish-language version of each page. Other notices students encounter may have information in languages other than English or Spanish, Braille sections for the visually impaired, or references to TDD (Telephone Device for the Deaf) numbers.

Additional Questions

1. Why is it important to follow the library's Internet use rules? Give two reasons. (for safety; so that others are treated politely; failure to observe the rules means loss of library Internet privileges)

2. How long may people use the library's Internet hookups during busy periods? (20 minutes at most)

3. What are "flames" in Internet slang? (rude or hateful messages sent to individuals or computer bulletin boards)

4. What does "spam" mean to Internet users? (advertisements, chain letters, or pointless messages sent to large groups)

Other Types of Public Notices

Other public notices that students should watch for include:

• **rules and warnings for public areas** such as parks, pools, and community centers;

• **health and safety information,** such as road signs;

• **announcements** of community events, classes, meetings, and elections; and

• **instructions from the federal, state, or local government** describing how to register to vote, obtain a driver's license, or participate in a census.

Mention that some of these notices will use symbols or incomplete sentences, but students can examine them using many of the same techniques they used on the sample notice.

Reading a Web Page

Introducing the Concept

Explain that reading a Web page is different from reading a book or a newspaper. In general, a Web page has smaller "chunks" of text, that allows users to read those text chunks in almost any order, and provides ways to interact with the people who created or maintain the material.

Teaching Tips for the Web Page

A **Web address:** Tell students that a Web address can give clues about the site. For instance, *http://www.lookquick.com* is probably a commercial site—it contains the abbreviation *.com*. The Oakland Museum of California site, *http://www.museumca.org,* contains the abbreviation *.org,* which usually indicates a not-for-profit company. Other abbreviations include *.edu* (educational), *.gov* (government), and *.mil* (military).

B **Title:** Point out that both of the sample Web pages use large type to draw the reader's eye to the title.

C **Menu bars:** The "Gold Fever" site has menu bars at the top and bottom of the page and on the left side. Explain that, with this many choices, it is easy for a user to get lost in the site. Have students use the Back button in their browsers or click on the Home link if they feel they have wandered into pages that are irrelevant to the information they are seeking.

D **Links:** Links let users jump from page to page on one site or to a different site altogether. Remind students that links are not always checked for accuracy and timeliness by the person posting the link.

E **Interactive areas:** Call students' attention to the Guest Book link at the bottom of the "Gold Fever" page. Remind students that if they choose to send comments about a site, they should be just as polite as they would be in a letter.

Glossary of Web-Related Terms

bookmark: a saved link to a Web page. If you bookmark a site, you can call it up again without having to type in the Web address.

browser: a computer program that lets you look at and interact with material on the World Wide Web. Some commonly used browsers are Netscape Navigator and Internet Explorer.

download: to copy a file from another computer. Text files, video clips, audio clips, and image files can all be downloaded.

http: Hypertext Transfer Protocol, the computer rules for exchanging information on the Web. Web addresses include the *http* coding, a colon, and two slashes (http://).

hypertext: information organized through different associations, or links, rather than chapters or articles. Hypertext gives users more freedom in choosing information, but it can cause users to miss important details or get bogged down in irrelevant material.

netiquette: etiquette on the Internet. One rule of netiquette is that users should not e-mail or post rude, abusive comments, sometimes called "flames."

search engine: a program that reviews millions of Web pages for keywords entered by a user.

spam: unsolicited or bulk e-mail. Such mailings often offer products for sale or ask users to visit the sender's Web site.

URL: a Uniform Resource Locator, or Web address, such as http://www.mcdougallittell.com.

Reading Technical Directions

Introducing the Concept

Examples of technical directions can be found with products such as cameras, CD players, calculators, DVD players, and VCRs. Reading such directions can be challenging because of difficult vocabulary and complex instructions; however, most directions can be broken into easily recognizable parts.

Teaching Tips for the Microwave Instructions

A Encourage students to read the directions from beginning to end at least once. Tell students that this is one of the most important steps in reading technical directions because it provides an overall picture of what they must do.

B Some technical directions will separate sections by using headings. Most headings will indicate the type of procedure involved in each section. Tell students that they should understand each section before moving on to the next.

C Directions will usually provide letters or numbers to show the order in which the steps occur. If no numbers or letters are given, tell students they may find it helpful to insert the numbers themselves.

D Warnings or notes are very important because they often refer the reader to another page for more information, or they may tell the reader to take certain precautions before attempting a step.

Additional Practice Using Technical Directions

Reproduce the directions below for your students and ask them the questions that follow.

Patching the Inner Tube of a Bike

Before patching an inner tube, you should purchase a patch kit. Your patch kit will include the following: patches, sandpaper or a scraper, and glue. Use the directions on your patch kit, or follow these simple steps to patch your inner tube.

1. Make sure the damaged area is clean and dry.
2. Gently roughen the damaged area with sandpaper or a scraper.
3. Apply glue to the patch and then place the patch over damaged area. Press the patch firmly for ten seconds so that it adheres to the tube.
4. If the patch does not stick to the surface, apply a thin layer of glue over the hole. Then place the patch over the damaged area and press firmly.
5. Once the patch has set (about two minutes), inflate the tube to make sure the patch is holding properly.

Warning Be careful not to overinflate the tube because it can blow up like a balloon if the surrounding tire does not contain the tube.

Mark it Up

1. What items does a patch kit include? (patches, sandpaper or a scraper, and glue)
2. If the patch does not stick to the damaged area, what should you do? (Apply a thin layer of glue over the hole.)
3. Circle the time it takes for the patch to set. (two minutes)

Reading Product Information: Warranties

Introducing the Concept

Warranties appear on many appliances and electronic goods. You might tell students that learning how to read a warranty will help them understand their rights and responsibilities if a product they buy is not satisfactory.

Teaching Tips for the Warranty

A **Services:** Tell students that "Labor" refers to the work of the employee who repairs a product. "Parts" are the pieces of the product, such as a picture tube in a television set or a switch on an appliance.

B **Conditions:** Point out that "cosmetic damage" refers to imperfections in the product's appearance, such as small scratches or dents. This type of damage does not affect how the product functions.

C **Proof of Purchase:** Explain that many manufacturers require consumers to produce their receipts in order to obtain warranty service. Some manufacturers may also ask consumers to place the product in its original packaging.

D **Service Center:** Point out that the warranty on this page provides a free 800 number for consumers to call. Customers can send products that need to be repaired to the service center.

Additional Questions

1. For what period will the manufacturer supply new or rebuilt replacement parts at no charge? (one year)

2. What will you have to pay for if you have the manufacturer replace a picture tube 91 days after you purchase the product? (labor for removal and installation)

3. For how long will the manufacturer cover parts and labor on all accessories? (one year)

Other Types of Product Information

Students encounter many different types of product information in their daily life. For example:

- **Labels on food products** provide consumers with nutritional information. This information lists the amount of fat, carbohydrates, and other nutrients in a single serving of a particular food.

- **Medicine labels** on over-the-counter pain relievers tell how to take these preparations safely and effectively.

- **Clothing labels** provide cleaning instructions for the item. Failure to read and follow these instructions carefully can result in discolored, shrunken clothing.

Reading a Train Schedule

Introducing the Concept

Students may have difficulty reading a train schedule because of the confusing lists of names and numbers. Tell students that using these strategies will help them read most train schedules.

Teaching Tips for the Train Schedule

A **Title:** Remind students to make sure that they are reading the correct schedule. Tell students to check the title carefully. Confusion can easily arise when students look at the schedule for trains running from Turner City to Kenwood, for instance, instead of from Kenwood to Turner City.

B **Date or Day Labels:** Tell students that many local trains have several different operating schedules. These trains may publish schedules for weekdays, weekends, and holidays.

C **Place Labels:** Point out that *LV* following the first station name stands for *leaves*; *AR* following the last station name stands for *arrives*. Make sure students understand, however, that they can depart from and get off at any of the stations listed. When students consult a train schedule, you might suggest that they circle and label their departure and arrival points.

D **Expressions of Time:** Before they consult a train schedule, students should know their approximate departure time. They should then find their departure time under the correct station heading and use their finger or a ruler to trace along the row and find their arrival time under the appropriate station label. Tell students that a horizontal line indicates that a train does not leave from or go to a particular station. A vertical arrow indicates that a train goes through a station without stopping there.

E **Train Numbers** Help students understand that trains 308 and 312 do not provide service on this route in the early morning hours.

Additional Questions

1. At what time does the first morning train leave from Kenwood? (5:55)
2. Which train station does not provide early morning service to Turner City? (Santa Ana)
3. If you board train 318 in River Falls, when will you arrive in Erie Falls? (7:52)

Other Types of Schedules

Students encounter many different kinds of schedules in their daily lives. For example:
- Bus schedules and schedules for other modes of transportation
- Class schedules for schools, parks, and sports centers
- Rehearsal and practice schedules for extracurricular activities
- TV scheduling and movie listings

Vocabulary
Mini-Lessons
with Graphic Organizers

1 Explain to students that sometimes they can figure out the meaning of an unfamiliar word or term by thinking about the context, or the surrounding words of the sentence or passage.

2 Write the following paragraph on the board and read it aloud:

> There is a serious *scarcity* of books in our school. Many of the bookcases in our library are bare, forcing students to look elsewhere for print resources. School administrators plan to order more books. Until the books arrive, however, students will have to deal with the shortage.

3 Then model how to use context to figure out the meaning of *scarcity:*

MODEL
I'm not sure what scarcity *means. I can look for context clues in the sentence this word is in and in the surrounding sentences. The phrases "bookcases are bare," "plan to order more books," and "deal with the shortage" help me figure out that* scarcity *means "lack or shortage."*

4 Now write the following paragraph on the board and read it aloud. Have a volunteer underline the context clues that could be used to help determine the meaning of the word *drought.*

> No rain had fallen in the area for months. For miles around, the land was dry and cracked. Hot winds blew dust around the dying crops. Unfortunately, according to weather experts, the *drought* would continue for months.

Point out to students that in the example above, a type of clue known as **details from general context** helped them figure out the meaning of *drought.* Encourage students to use this strategy throughout the year, along with other common types of context clues:

Definition and Restatement
The **epidermis**—that is, the outer layer of skin—protects the nerves and sensitive tissue below.

(The phrase introduced by *that is* helps define *epidermis* as "the outer layer of skin.")

Example
I am frightened of **arachnids,** such as spiders and scorpions.

(*Spiders* and *scorpions* are examples of arachnids.)

Comparison and Contrast
Like the overjoyed crowd in the audience, I was **ecstatic** when I heard he had won.

(The word *like* helps you understand that *overjoyed* has the same or similar meaning as *ecstatic.*)

Here's How
See the next three pages for useful lessons on context clues that you can duplicate for students.

Context Clues (Example)

A good way to make sense of an unfamiliar word is to look at the **context**: the other words in the sentence and other sentences in the paragraph that might give clues to the meaning of the word. There are a number of ways you can use context clues to help you determine a word's meaning.

Sometimes a sentence will provide an **example** that will help you understand the meaning of the word. Examples are often signaled by words or phrases such as

like	for instance	this	such as	especially
these	for example	other	includes	

Here's How   Using Examples in Context to Figure Out an Unfamiliar Word

The governor asked that farmers make use of all *arable* land, such as corn and wheat fields.

1. Identify the unfamiliar word.
   (I'm not sure what the word *arable* means.)

2. Read to see if there is a word that signals that an example may follow.
   (I see the phrase *such as.* Those words could lead to an example.)

3. Find the example or examples.
   (The phrase *corn and wheat fields* follows the phrase *such as.* These must be examples of arable land.)

4. Ask yourself how the example or examples relate to the unfamiliar word.
   (Corn and wheat are crops.)

5. Use this information to figure out what the word means.
   (Since the examples are fields of crops, *arable* land must be land on which crops are grown, and *arable* must mean "capable of growing crops.")

6. Now, look the unfamiliar word up in the dictionary and jot the word and definition down in your personal word list.
   arable *adj.* Fit for cultivation (planting and growing crops)

Context Clues (Comparison or Contrast)

A good way to make sense of an unfamiliar word is to look at the **context**: the other words in the sentence and other sentences in the paragraph that might give clues to the meaning of the word. There are a number of ways you can use context clues to help you determine a word's meaning.

Sometimes a sentence will provide a **comparison** or a **contrast** that will help you understand the meaning of the word. Certain words or phrases signal comparison or contrast.

Some Comparison Signals		**Some Contrast Signals**	
like	similar to	but	although
as	also	unlike	however
related	resembling	rather than	on the other hand

Here's How   Using Comparison or Contrast to Figure Out an Unfamiliar Word

Our small shop is nearly as *prosperous* as that fancy department store, although we made very little money when we first opened.

1. Identify the unfamiliar word.

(I'm not sure what the word *prosperous* means.)

2. Read to see if there is a word or phrase that signals that a comparison or a contrast may follow.

(I see the words *as* and *although*. *As* could signal a comparison, and *although* could signal a contrast.)

3. Identify the comparison or contrast.

(The sentence compares the prosperous shop with a big, fancy store, while it also sets up a contrast, stating that the shop didn't make much money at first.)

4. Use this information to figure out what the unfamiliar word means.

(The contrast to the way the shop used to be and the comparison to the department store suggest that the shop is doing well. *Prosperous* must mean "doing well.")

5. Find the word in the dictionary and record it in your personal word list.

prosperous *adj.* Having success; well-off

6. A sentence may contain only comparison or only contrast as a context clue. You can still use the strategy above to find the meaning.

Context Clues (Restatement)

A good way to make sense of an unfamiliar word is to look at the **context**: the other words in the sentence and other sentences in the paragraph that might give clues to the meaning of the word. There are a number of ways you can use context clues to help you determine a word's meaning.

Sometimes a writer will **restate** the meaning of a difficult word within a sentence, defining it for you. Restatements or definitions are often signaled by words or phrases such as

| or | which is | that is |
| also called | also known as | in other words |

Here's How Using Restatement in Context to Figure Out an Unfamiliar Word

Our teacher received a small *stipend,* or payment, for giving travel lectures to local clubs.

1. Identify the unfamiliar word.

(I'm not sure what the word *stipend* means.)

2. Read to see if there is a word that signals that a restatement may follow.

(I see the word *or.* What follows may include a restatement or definition.)

3. Find the restated information.

(The word *or* points to the word *payment.*)

4. Use this information to figure out what the unfamiliar word means.

(Because the words *or payment* follow *stipend,* I think *stipend* must mean "payment.")

5. Now, look the unfamiliar word up in the dictionary and jot the word and definition down in your personal word list.

stipend *n.* A regular payment, such as a salary or allowance

1 Explain to students that sometimes they can figure out the meaning of an unfamiliar word by thinking about the meaning of the word parts it contains.

2 Write the word *depopulated* on the board and read it aloud. Model how to use the base word and affixes to figure out the meaning of the word.

You could say: I'm not sure what depopulated *means. I can try breaking the word into parts. I see the prefix* de-, *which means "opposite," and which I have seen in other words, such as* deactivate *and* defrost. *I see the base word* populate, *which means "to supply with people; to live in or inhabit." I also see the suffix* -ated, *which means "made or acted." By combining the meanings of these word parts, I can figure out that* depopulated *must mean the opposite of "supplied with people." Maybe it means "took people out of an area." When I look in the dictionary to see if I am right, I find that the definition is "having a greatly reduced number of people or animals, often because of disease, war, or forced relocation."*

3 Explain to students that they can also break down compound words, which are made up of two words put together. Tell students that they can sometimes tell the meaning of a compound word by looking at the meaning of each word part.

4 Write the word *arrowhead* on the board and read it aloud. Model how to break it into parts and figure out the meaning.

You could say: I've never seen the word arrowhead *before. I can try to figure out its meaning by breaking it into two words,* arrow *and* head. *I know that an arrow is a weapon that is shot out of a bow, and a head is often the top or most important part of something. I think an arrowhead must be the top or most important part of an arrow— the part that sticks into the target.*

5 Share with students the following lists of commonly used prefixes, suffixes, and compound words.

Prefixes	Suffixes	Compound Words
ab- (away or apart from)	*-like* (similar to)	beadwork
chron- (time)	*-ful* (full of, resembling)	headache
tri- (three)	*-less* (without)	field trip
hyper- (excessively)	*-er* (person who does)	daydream
inter- (among or between)	*-ery* (job or skill)	sandpaper
micro- (small)	*-ation* (action or process)	fishpond
tele- (far)	*-arium* (place for)	lightheaded
trans- (across, beyond, or through)	*-hood* (state or quality of)	skateboard
uni- (one)	*-ate* (to make)	downturn

6 The following list provides additional words for you and your students to model. Have volunteers explain how to use word parts to figure out the meaning of each word.

abnormal   childlike   adulthood   scarecrow   hyperactive   chronology

planetarium   telemarketer   interconnect   schoolwork   machination   sweatshirt

microscope   unicycle   hailstorm   transaction   broadcast

Here's How

See the next three pages for useful lessons on working with prefixes, suffixes, and compound words. You can duplicate these lessons for students.

Prefixes

A **prefix** is a word part attached to the beginning of a base word or root. The meaning of a prefix combines with the meaning of the base word or root. For example, the prefix *in-* often means "not," as in *indirect,* which means "not direct."

Here's How **Using Prefixes to Determine Word Meaning**

1. When you encounter an unfamiliar word, try to determine whether the word contains a prefix.

> **malnutrition**

(*Mal-* may be a prefix. The rest of the word is *nutrition,* which can stand on its own, so I think *mal-* is a prefix.)

....

2. Try to think of other words containing the same prefix. Think about what these words mean.

> **maltreat, malfunction, malnourish, malpractice**

(I know that *maltreat* means "to treat badly," and the meanings of the other words also involve something bad, so *mal-* must mean "bad or badly.")

....

3. Look at the way the word was used in the sentence. On the basis of the context and on the meaning of the prefix, make an educated guess about the word's meaning.

(*Nutrition* means "the process by which a living being takes in and uses nutrients or food," and *mal-* means "bad or badly," so I think *malnutrition* means "bad nutrition.")

....

4. Look up the word's definition in the dictionary and compare it with your guess.

> **malnutrition** *n.* Poor nutrition because of an imbalanced diet or faulty digestion.

(*Malnutrition* does have to do with bad nutrition; my guess was correct.)

Suffixes

A **suffix** is a word part attached to the end of a base word or root. Most suffixes determine a word's part of speech. Familiarity with common suffixes can help you determine the meaning of some unfamiliar words.

Here's How Using Suffixes to Determine Meaning

1. When you encounter an unfamiliar word, try to determine whether the word contains a suffix.

> **perishable**

(I think –*able* must be a suffix added to the word *perish*. I also recognize –*able* as a suffix because I've seen it in other words.)

2. Try to think of other words containing the same suffix. Think about what these words mean.

> **avoidable, acceptable, believable, comfortable**

(I know that *avoidable* means "able to be avoided." The other words all have to do with being able to do something, so –*able* probably means "capable of."

3. Look at how the word was used in the sentence. On the basis of its context and the meaning of the suffix, make an educated guess about the word's meaning.

(I know that *perish* means "to be destroyed," so *perishable* may mean "able to be destroyed."

4. Look up the word's definition in a dictionary and compare it with your guess. If the word isn't listed on its own, you may need to look for it within the entry for its base word.

> **perishable** *adj.* Subject to decay, spoilage, or destruction, especially relating to food

(*Perishable* means "able to be destroyed;" my guess was correct.)

Compound Words

A **compound word** is a word made up of two words put together. The meanings of the two word parts combine to form a new meaning. Sometimes the meaning of a compound word is obvious when you look at the meaning of each word part. For example, the word *doghouse* is made up of the words *dog* and *house*. It simply means a small building where a dog can live. Other times, the meaning is not as clear, but it is usually still related to the meaning of the two word parts.

Here's How   Understanding Compound Words

1. When you see an unfamiliar compound word, look first for its two word parts.

downpour

(The word parts of *downpour* are *down* and *pour*.)

2. Look at the meanings of the two parts and think of how they might be related.

(*Downpour* probably has something to do with both *down* and *pour*. I know that *down* means "from a higher place to a lower place," and I know that to *pour* something means to make it flow or empty out. How are these two words connected? I've heard people say "It's pouring out" or "It's pouring down" when it rains, so maybe the word *downpour* is related to rain.)

3. Look up the word's definition in the dictionary and compare it with your guess.

downpour *n.* a severe rainstorm; a heavy fall of rain.

(My guess was correct.)

4. Some compound words have a meaning that doesn't make obvious sense. When you encounter such a word, break it into its word parts and see what sense you can make of it.

far-flung

(The word parts of *far-flung* are *far* and *flung*. Does it have something to do with throwing things?)

5. Look up the word's definition in the dictionary and compare it with your thoughts.

far-flung *adj.* Distant, wide-ranging, or widely distributed: *a far-flung family.*

(Although *far-flung* doesn't literally mean "thrown a long distance," it does mean "found over a wide area." I can imagine someone throwing a handful of seeds or rocks and watching them spread out as they fall, and the same idea could be used to describe things that aren't thrown. So there is at least a loose connection between *far-flung* and throwing something a long way.)

1 Explain to students that sometimes they can figure out the meaning of an unfamiliar word if they recognize its root from other, familiar words. You may want to explain that a **root** is a word part that contains the most important element of that word's meaning. A root must be combined with other word parts, such as prefixes or suffixes, to form a word.

2 Write the word *humidifier* on the board and read it aloud. Model how to use the root to help determine the word's meaning.

You could say: *I've never seen the word* humidifier *before. I've seen the root* humid- *in other words, such as* humidity. *I know that* humidity *refers to how much water is in the air, so I think* humid- *means "moisture" or "water." I've seen the word part* -ifier *in words such as* amplifier *and* purifier, *and I'm pretty sure it means "a person or machine that does something." Does* humidifier *mean "someone or something that puts water in the air"? When I look up the word in the dictionary to confirm my guess, I see that it means "a device for increasing the amount of moisture in the air of an enclosed space, such as a room or greenhouse."*

3 Now write the following chart on the board:

Root	Meaning
arithm-	number
auto-	self
dic- or *dict-*	speak
fin-	end *or* limit
mim-	imitate

Root	Meaning
mut-	change
nega-, negat-	deny
plac-	please
poli-	city

4 Have volunteers use the information in the chart as they try to define the words below. Make sure they explain the process they used to figure out the meaning of each word.

arithmetic   automated   automaton   dictator   diction   predict   finality
mimic   pantomime   immutable   mutation   negation   placid   metropolitan

5 As the year progresses, you may wish to review this strategy. The following chart provides you with additional words, roots, and meanings.

Root	Meaning	Examples
alter-	the other	alternate, alternative
credit-	believe *or* trust	discredit, incredible
dent-	tooth	dental, indent, trident
don-	give	donor, donation
geo-	earth	geography, geocentric, geopolitical
fac-	make *or* do	factory, manufacture
log-	word, speech, *or* idea	apology, monologue
neo-	new	neon, neoclassical, neologism
phys-	nature *or* growth	physician, physics
soph-	wise	philosopher, sophomore
vis-	see	visual, television, revise

Here's How

See the next page for useful lessons on using word roots to determine meaning. You can duplicate these lessons for students.

Roots

Many English words, especially long ones, can be broken into smaller parts. A **root** is the core of a word, or the part that contains the most important element of the word's meaning.

Many words in English have their roots in other languages, particularly Greek and Latin. Knowing the meaning of Greek and Latin roots can help you to understand unfamiliar words.

Here's How Using Word Roots to Determine Meaning

1. When you encounter an unfamiliar word, first look for any prefixes or suffixes and remove them to try to isolate the root.

> **audible**

(The word ends with *–ible,* which is a suffix meaning "capable of." After *–ible* is removed, what remains is *aud.* This part of the word must contain the root.)

2. Try to think of other words containing the same root. Think about what these words mean.

> **audition, auditorium, audience, audio, auditory**

(These words all refer to something involving sound or hearing.)

3. Look at the way the word was used in the sentence. On the basis of its context and its parts, make an educated guess about what the word means.

(I think that *audible* might mean have to do with sound. Since *–ible* means "capable of," maybe the word means something that is able to be heard.)

4. Look up the word's definition in a dictionary, and compare it with your guess.

> **audible** *adj.* Loud enough to be heard

(*Audible* means something that can be heard; my guess was correct.)

1 Tell students that an idiom is a phrase whose meaning is different from the meanings of its individual words put together. Explain to students that they can sometimes figure out the meaning of an unfamiliar idiom by thinking about its context, or the surrounding words of the sentence or passage.

2 Write the following sentences on the board and read them aloud:

> **Emily wasn't supposed to tell Fred that we're planning a surprise party for him, but she let the cat out of the bag. Now it won't be a surprise anymore.**

3 Then model how to use context to figure out the meaning of let the cat out of the bag.

MODEL

I've never seen the phrase let the cat out of the bag *before, and I have no idea what it means. To find out, I can look for context clues in the rest of the passage. Emily wasn't supposed to tell about the party, but then she did something, and now the party won't be a surprise. I think she must have told Fred the secret about the party. If I substitute* told a secret *for* let the cat out of the bag, *it makes sense in the passage. Therefore, I think that to* let the cat out of the bag *means "to tell a secret."*

4 The following boldface sentences contain commonly used idioms. Write these sentences on the chalkboard (but not the translations given in parentheses). Ask students to read the sentences and use context clues to figure out the meaning of the idioms.

> **Can we *count on* you to help us with the cooking? Are you sure you will be there?** (Can we depend on, rely on, or trust you?)

> **Last night's math homework sure was *a tough nut to crack*. I spent an hour working hard on it before I got the answers.** (The homework was difficult and time-consuming.)

> ***"Hold your horses!"* Tammi said. "I'm not ready, so you'll have to wait!"** (Slow down! Be more patient!)

> **Ed didn't know whether the plans were *in cement* or whether he could make some changes.** (He didn't know if the plans were firmly set.)

5 As the year progresses, you may wish to review this strategy. The following list provides you with more idioms to share with your students.

Idiom	Meaning
a bolt from the blue	a shocking, startling, unexpected event
give him (or her) the runaround	avoid a clear explanation
hit the books	study hard
ill at ease	uncomfortable
in a flash	very quickly
an iron hand	total control
just what the doctor ordered	precisely what is needed
knock our socks off	impress us, amaze us
knows his (or her) stuff	is an expert
make a bundle	earn a great deal of money
a mover and shaker	a powerful person
pull the wool over my eyes	fool me, deceive me
see red	become angry
the spitting image	exactly like
top dollar	an extremely high price
What's eating you?	What's upsetting or bothering you?

Here's How

See the next page for a useful lesson on understanding idioms. You can duplicate this lesson for students.

Understanding Idioms

An **idiom** is a set phrase whose meaning is different from the literal meaning of its individual words. For example, the idiom *all fired up* has nothing to do with fires; it simply means "very angry or wildly excited."

Most idioms are so common that people use them without thinking about them. However, unfamiliar idioms can be very confusing. If you didn't know that *he sees the world through rose-colored glasses* really means "he has an unrealistically positive opinion of every situation" or "he is an optimist," you might wonder what the color of a person's glasses has to do with anything!

When you see an unfamiliar idiom, you can sometimes find clues in the idiom's context, or surrounding words and paragraphs.

Here's How   Understanding Idioms

When Sandy saw the mess her little brothers had made in the kitchen, she knew they would all be *in hot water* with their mother. "Mom is going to be furious with us!" she said.

1. Identify the unfamiliar idiom.

   (I'm not sure what *in hot water* means. The first sentence mentions a kitchen, so does it have to do with cooking?)

2. Look for context clues, such as a restatement or explanation.

   (First, Sandy says that her little brothers have made a mess. Then there's the part about their mother and the hot water, and then Sandy says their mom will be very angry.)

3. Use this information to figure out what the idiom means.

   (If Sandy's brothers have done something to make their mom angry, they will probably get in trouble. Also, actually being in hot water would be awfully uncomfortable-maybe even dangerous. For these reasons, I think the expression *in hot water* means "in trouble.")

4. Some idioms appear in regular dictionaries under the definition of the phrase's main word. Look up this idiom in a regular dictionary or in a dictionary of idioms, under *hot* or *water*.

   hot water *n.* Trouble, difficulty, distress.

5. If you can't find the idiom in a dictionary, ask a teacher, another adult, or a classmate what it means.

1 Explain to students that many words have more than one meaning. They can figure out the intended meaning of a word in a sentence by looking for clues in the context.

2 Write the following sentence on the board and read it aloud:

> We didn't understand the *import* of her speech, but many of the other people in the audience grasped its meaning.

3 Then model how to use the context to figure out the meaning of the word *import*:

MODEL

I'm not sure which meaning of import *is being used in this sentence.* Import *can mean "something brought in from another country" and it can also mean "meaning or importance." I can look for context clues in the sentence. The phrases "didn't understand" and "grasped its meaning" help me figure out that, in this sentence,* import *means "meaning or importance."*

4 Now write the following sentence on the board and read it aloud. Have a volunteer underline the clues that help determine the meaning of the word *impression*.

> With his helpful attitude and good manners, the student made an excellent *impression* on the new teacher.

5 If students are not familiar with a word or its multiple meanings, encourage them to look up the word in a dictionary. Sometimes dictionaries provide sample contexts to show the different meanings of a word. Tell students to compare the sample contexts and figure out the one that best fits the sentence. As the year progresses, you may wish to review these strategies.

The following chart provides you with additional words and some of their multiple meanings. Have students create sentences that demonstrate their understanding of the words' multiple meanings.

Word	Meanings	Word	Meanings
character	1. person in a story 2. personality 3. symbol or letter	key	1. lock opener 2. important element or point 3. musical pitch
store	1. a shop 2. a supply 3. put away for future use	seal	1. stamp 2. secure or close 3. acquatic animal
volume	1. one book in a series 2. quantity or amount 3. control for adjusting loudness	cast	1. actors in a play 2. dressing used to cover injury 3. throw something
watch	1. timepiece 2. observe 3. guard or sentry	aim	1. goal 2. direct toward a target 3. try
branch	1. limb of a tree 2. division of a business 3. area of specialized knowledge	project	1. task or undertaking 2. throw forward 3. cause images to appear on screen

Here's How

See the next page for a useful lesson on words with multiple meanings that you can duplicate for students.

Words with Multiple Meanings

Because language constantly changes to meet the needs of those who use it, many words in English have more than one meaning. These multiple meanings may lead to confusion, causing readers to misinterpret a writer's message.

Here's How Selecting the Appropriate Meaning of a Word

1. When you are not sure which definition of a word applies in a particular sentence, look for clues in the surrounding context.

   I stopped at the roadside stand and bought several bags of farm-fresh *produce*, including corn, tomatoes, and peppers.

   (I know that *produce* is a verb meaning "to bring about or create," but in this sentence the word seems to be used as a noun. Maybe *produce* can be a different part of speech and have another meaning.)

2. If the meaning you know does not make sense in the context of the sentence and you don't have enough clues to help you figure out the meaning, look up the word in a dictionary. Look for the definition that makes sense in the sentence.

   (I see that there are several meanings for the word *produce,* including "to create," "to show," and "farm products.")

3. Decide which dictionary definition works best in the sentence you are examining.

   (In this sentence, *produce* refers to the items purchased at a farm stand, so in this case, *produce* probably is a noun meaning "farm crops or products.")

Teaching Decoding Strategies

Teaching Decoding Strategies

By middle school, your students should have had years of instruction in systematic, explicit phonics and decoding skills. Good readers have well developed decoding skills which enable them to quickly and automatically identify printed words so that attention can be focused on the more challenging task of understanding.

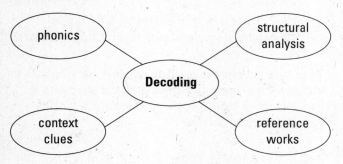

Phonics

Phonics is a system of teaching the basic sound-letter relationships in the English language. Phonics lays the foundation for young readers understanding the relationship between spoken and written words. Instruction is usually coupled with decodable text so students can apply skills to manageable reading and develop automaticity—the ability to recognize words in text automatically and effortlessly.

In the primary grades, phonics receives the main emphasis as a decoding strategy. The chart shows when phonics instruction usually occurs.

Phonics	Grade where taught
consonants (initial, medial, final)	through first half grade 1
consonant digraphs (/th/ *th*, etc.)	through grade 1
consonant clusters (*st, bl, br*, etc.)	through early grade 2
short vowels	first half grade 1
long vowels	through grade 1
r-controlled vowels (*er, ir, ar*, etc.)	through grade 2
diphthongs (*oi, oy*, etc.)	through grade 2
variant vowels (*ough, au, aw*, etc.)	through grade 2

As a result of phonics instruction, many young students can decode the vast majority of phonetically regular words they read. In the intermediate grades and beyond, the problem becomes how to decode irregular and multisyllabic words which appear increasingly in reading materials.

Structural Analysis

Structural analysis is a strategy used to figure out the meanings of multisyllabic words. When students encounter an unfamiliar multisyllabic word, they are taught to remove any prefixes, remove any suffixes, and look at the bases, roots or combining forms. Once they figure out the meanings of the parts of the word, they put the word back together again and check their understanding of the word within the context of the sentence and paragraph. You can help your students use structural analysis by teaching the procedure outlined below.

Example Sentence and Procedure

When Fred opened the old refrigerator the *malodorous* aroma convinced him to give the refrigerator a good cleaning.

1. If there is a prefix, take it off. (-*mal*)
2. If there is a suffix, take it off. (-*ous*)
3. Look at the base or root that is left, *odor*
4. Say to yourself, what do I know about the word *odor*? You might know it means *smell*.
5. Consider the meaning of the prefix, which you might recognize if you speak Spanish, because it is identical to the word for "bad" in Spanish. If you don't speak Spanish, think of other words that start with -*mal*, like *malformed, malnutrition, malpractice,* or *malcontent.* which would lead you to guess that -*mal* means "bad."
6. Consider the meaning of the suffix -*ous* which you might recognize from other words like *studious* and as a suffix that turns a noun into an adjective.
7. Put the meanings of the parts together, *bad* + *smell* in an adjective form.

8. Check your understanding in the context of the sentence, "When Fred opened the old refrigerator the bad smelling aroma convinced him to give the refrigerator a good cleaning." It fits!

9. If the sentence still does not make sense, look the word up in the dictionary.

You can help students recognize prefixes by making sure they know the four most common prefixes: *un-, re-, in-,* and *dis-,* which account for about 65% of all words with prefixes.

For additional suggestions on teaching structural analysis skills, see *The Language of Literature.*

Syllable patterns Instruction and practice in understanding the basic syllable patterns helps students break words into smaller parts and then use phonics skills to pronounce the word. The following pages contain lessons in understanding the **syllabication generalizations** that will support students' word attack skills. Although there are exceptions, we will use the word **rule** to help students remember them easily.

Rule 1: When there are two consonants between two vowels, divide between the two consonants, unless they are a blend or a digraph.

Rule 2: When there are three consonants between two vowels, divide between the blend or the digraph and the other consonant.

Rule 3: When there are two consonants between two vowels, divide between the two consonants between vowels unless they are a blend or a digraph. The first syllable is a closed syllable, and the vowel sound is short.

Rule 4: Do not split common vowel clusters, such as vowel digraphs, r-controlled vowels, and vowel diphthongs.

Rule 5: When you see a VCV pattern in the middle of a word, divide the word before or after the consonant. If you divide after the consonant, the first vowel sound is short. If you divide before the consonant, the vowel sound is long.

Rule 6: Always divide compound words between the individual words.

Rule 7: When a word includes an affix, divide between the base word and the affix (prefix or suffix).

When students use these syllabication generalizations to pronounce the word, they can match the word with a word already in their speaking vocabulary or look for meaningful word parts.

Quick Diagnostic Test

Use the list below to determine how well your students read multisyllabic words. The lists are organized by syllabication rule. If your students are unable to read some or all of these words, teaching them high-utility syllabication rules may help improve their decoding skills. Use the lessons on the following pages to assist you.

(Rules 1, 3)	(Rule 5)
picture	model
happen	robot
feather	crazy
follow	never
usher	final

(Rule 2)	(Rule 6)
angler	whirlwind
merchant	grasshopper
tumbler	grapevine
children	wastebasket
purchase	earring

(Rule 4)	(Rule 7)
party	readjustment
poison	rebound
feature	childish
royal	unavoidable
chowder	unselfish

Syllabication

LESSON 1: Consonant Blends and Digraphs in Multisyllabic Words

This lesson will help students chunk, or syllabicate, multisyllabic words that contain consonant blends and digraphs. Your students most likely recognize blends and digraphs when they see them in print; however, they may have problems decoding multisyllabic words if they attempt to syllabicate between the two letters in the blend or digraph. If you think your students would benefit from a review of blends and digraphs, begin with Parts 1 and 2. If not, you may go directly to Parts 3 and 4.

Part 1: Quick Review of Consonant Blends

Following are common consonant blends with examples of each. The two letters in each blend represent two sounds.

br	break, brand	sl	slick, slam
cr	crane, crack	-ld	field, hold
dr	drive, drip	-lk	milk
fr	free	-lp	help
gr	green	-lt	melt
pr	press	sc	scare
tr	true	sk	ski, risk
bl	blue	sm	smart
cl	clue, close	sn	snare, snack
fl	flame, flute	sp	spell, clasp
gl	glue, glide	st	state, twist
pl	please, plan	sw	switch, sway

DIRECT INSTRUCTION

To help your students focus on consonant blends, write the following sentences on the board.

> 1. Brown bears slide on the frost.
> 2. The grand prize was a silk scarf.
> 3. Flutes fly in blue skies.
> 4. Sly smelt swim in swift surf.

Ask a student to read aloud the first sentence. Call attention to the words *brown, slide,* and *frost.*

You could say: **What two letters do you see at the beginning of *brown (br),* at the beginning of *slide (sl),* at the beginning and end of *frost (fr, st)?* These are called consonant blends. The consonant blends are made up of two consonant letters and stand for two sounds. You will always say both sounds when you sound out a word.**

Follow the same procedure with the remaining sentences.

Answers: #2: grand (*gr*), prize (*pr*), silk (*lk*), scarf (*sc*); #3: Flutes (*fl*), fly (*fl*), blue (*bl*), skies (*sk*); #4: Sly (*sl*), smelt (*sm, -lt*), swim (*sw*), swift (*sw*)

Part 2: Quick Review of Consonant Digraphs

Following are consonant digraphs and examples of each. The two letters in each digraph represent one sound.

ch cheat, check, touch
sh shine, fish, push
th (voiced) that, the, this
th (voiceless) think, teeth, thumb, thank
wh (hw blend) where, whoops, when, white, wheel

DIRECT INSTRUCTION

Write these sentences on the chalkboard.

> 1. How much fish does a whale eat?
> 2. She will think the thing is cheap.
> 3. When will you change and wash the sheets?
> 4. Do white hens have teeth?

Ask a student to read aloud the first sentence.

You could say: **What two letters do you see at the end of *much (ch),* at the end of *fish (sh),* at the beginning of *whale (wh)?* The consonant digraphs are made up of two consonant letters but represent only one sound. You will say only one sound when you sound out a word.**

Follow the same procedure with the remaining sentences.

Answers: #2: She (*sh*), think (*th*), the (*th*), thing (*th*), cheap (*ch*); #3: When (*wh*), change (*ch*), wash (-*sh*), the (*the*), sheets (*sh*); #4: white (*wh*), teeth (*th*)

Part 3: Syllabication Strategy: Consonant Blends and Digraphs

In the following lesson, students will use their knowledge of consonant blends and digraphs to syllabicate words. You may find it helpful to review the most basic syllabication rule: *Each syllable has one and only one vowel sound.*

DIRECT INSTRUCTION

Write Rule 1 and the example words on the chalkboard. Remind students that V stands for vowel and C stands for consonant. Ask a student to give examples of vowel and consonant letters.

> **Rule 1: VCCV**
> **When there are two consonants between two vowels, divide between the two consonants, unless they are a blend or a digraph.**
>
> **picture   happen   abrupt   feather**

Have a student read Rule 1. Ask a student to explain the rule in his or her own words and then to read the first word. You could then say to students:

You could say: Find the VCCV pattern in the word *picture* (*ictu*). Do you see a blend or digraph? (no) Where would you divide this word according to Rule 1? (between the *c* and the *t*) Look at each syllable. Pronounce the word. Do you recognize the word?

Repeat the process with the remaining words.

Answers: hap/pen; a/brupt, feath/er

Write Rule 2 and the example words on the chalkboard.

> **Rule 2: VCCCV**
> **When there are three consonants between two vowels, divide between the blend or the digraph and the other consonant.**
>
> **angler   merchant   tumbler   children**

Have a student read Rule 2. Ask a student to explain the rule in his or her own words and then to read the first word. You could then say to students:

You could say: Find the VCCCV pattern in the word *angler.* (*angle*) Do you see a blend or digraph? (yes) Where would you divide this word according to Rule 2? (between the *n* and the *gl*) Look at each syllable. Pronounce the word. Do you recognize the word?

Repeat the process with the remaining words.

Answers: (mer/chant), (tum/bler), (chil/dren)

Part 4: Strategy Practice

Write the following words on the board. Have students divide the words according to the two rules, identify the rule, and pronounce the word.

Practice applying Rule 1

	Answers		Answers
scatter	scat/ter	whether	wheth/er
garden	gar/den	zipper	zip/per
crafty	craft/y	fashion	fash/ion
scarlet	scar/let	forget	for/get
traffic	traf/fic	respect	re/spect

Practice applying Rule 2

	Answers		Answers
hungry	hun/gry	nothing	noth/ing
concrete	con/crete	purchase	pur/chase
hundred	hun/dred	address	ad/dress
worship	wor/ship	supply	sup/ply
handsome	hand/some	employ	em/ploy

Cumulative practice

	Answers		Answers
written	writ/ten	toddler	tod/dler
constant	con/stant	lather	lath/er
secret	se/cret	sandal	san/dal
surplus	sur/plus	merchant	mer/chant
kindling	kin/dling	silver	sil/ver

LESSON 2: Short Vowels in Multisyllabic Words

When your students have trouble figuring out words unfamiliar in print, they are most likely having problems decoding the letters that stand for the vowel sound(s) in the word. Usually this is because the relationship between vowel sounds and letters that represent them isn't as predictable as the relationship between consonant sounds and the letters that represent them.

This lesson will help your students syllabicate words that contain short vowels. If you think your students would benefit from a review of short vowels, you may begin with Part 1. If not, you may skip directly to Parts 2 and 3.

Part 1: Quick Review of Short Vowels

Of the vowel sounds in English, the short vowels have the most predictable relationship between the sounds and the letters that represent them.

DIRECT INSTRUCTION

To help students focus on short vowels, write the list below on the board.

at	end	in	on	up
bat	bend	fin	odd	cup
and	vest	lick	mop	duck
fad	tell	drip	trot	lump

Have a student read the first column of words.

You could say: **What vowel sound do you hear in each of these words? (/a/ or short a) What letter represents that sound in each of these words? (the letter *a*)**

Follow the same procedure with the remaining lists.

Answers: column 2: /e/ or short e; column 3: /i/ or short i; column 4: /o/ or short o; column 5: /u/ or short u

Part 2: Syllabication Strategy: Short Vowels

Use the following syllabication strategy to help your students figure out some of the vowel sounds in multisyllabic words. You will note that Rule 3 expands upon Rule 1 introduced in Lesson 1.

DIRECT INSTRUCTION

Write Rule 3 and the example words on the board or use the copy master on page 49. Remind students that V stands for vowel and C stands for consonant.

> **Rule 3: VCCV**
> **When there are two consonants between two vowels, divide between the consonants, unless they are a blend or a digraph. The first syllable is a closed syllable, and the vowel sound is short.**
>
> | | | | |
> |---|---|---|---|
> | butter | lather | follow | usher |
> | summer | traffic | tender | invent |

Have a student read Rule 3 and explain the rule in his or her own words.

Have a student read the first word.

You could say: **Find the VCCV pattern in the first word. (*utte*) Do you see a blend or a digraph? (no) Where would you divide this word according to Rule 3? (between the two *t*'s) What vowel sound do you hear in the first syllable? (short) Look at each syllable and pronounce the word. Do you recognize the word?** Repeat this process with the remaining words.

Answers: but/ter, lath/er, fol/low, ush/er, sum/mer, traf/fic, ten/der, in/vent

Part 3: Strategy Practice

Write the following on the board. Have students divide the words according to the rule and pronounce the word.

	Answers		Answers
under	un/der	billow	bil/low
bother	both/er	enter	en/ter
bottom	bot/tom	number	num/ber
rather	rath/er	object	ob/ject
practice	prac/tice	dipper	dip/per
snapper	snap/per	silver	sil/ver
after	af/ter	grammar	gram/mar
cashew	cash/ew	sudden	sud/den
pulpit	pul/pit	vintage	vin/tage
pencil	pen/cil	member	mem/ber

LESSON 3: Vowel Clusters in Multisyllabic Words

This lesson will show students how to chunk, or syllabicate, multisyllabic words that contain vowel clusters: long vowel digraphs, r-controlled vowels, and vowel diphthongs. If your students aren't aware of vowel clusters, they might syllabicate between the two vowels in the cluster. In that case, they will syllabicate incorrectly and mispronounce the word when they attempt to sound it out. If you think your students would benefit from a review of vowel clusters, begin with Parts 1–3. If not, skip to Parts 4 and 5.

Part 1: Quick Review of Long Vowel Digraphs

In words with vowel digraphs, two vowel letters are represented by one vowel sound.

DIRECT INSTRUCTION

Write the list below on the board.

cream	play	boat
beast	gray	coal
bean	paint	goat
green	aim	row
peel	stain	slow

Have a student read the first column of words.

You could say: What vowel sound do you hear in each of these words? (long e) What letters stand for the long e sound in *beast*? (*ea*) What letters stand for the long e sound in *green*? (*ee*) These are called vowel digraphs. Vowel digraphs are made up of two vowel letters that stand for one sound.

Follow the same procedure with the remaining lists.

Answers: column 2: long a, *ay* in *gray*, *ai* in *paint;* column 3: long o, *oa* in *boat, ow* in *slow*

Part 2: Quick Review of R-controlled Vowels

In words with r-controlled vowels, the vowel sound is influenced by the *r* that follows it.

DIRECT INSTRUCTION

Write the list below on the board.

fern	car	born
dirt	star	cord
fur	arm	sort
her	yarn	more
birth	farm	horn

Have a student read the first column of words.

You could say: These words all have the "er" sound. What letters stand for the "er" sound in *fur*? *(ur)* in *her*? *(er)* in *birth*? *(ir)* These are called r-controlled vowels. The r-controlled vowels are made up of a vowel and the letter *r*. In words with r-controlled vowels, the vowel sound is influenced by the *r* that follows it.

Follow the same procedure with the remaining columns.

Answers: column 2: all words have the "ar" sound letters are *ar;* column 3: all words have the "or" sound letters are *or.*

Part 3: Quick Review of Vowel Diphthongs

DIRECT INSTRUCTION

To help students focus on vowel diphthongs write this list on the board.

oil	ouch
boil	cloud
boy	how
spoil	scout
toy	towel

Have a student read the first column of words.

You could say: These words all have the oi sound. What letters stand for the "oi" sound in *boil?* (oi) in *boy?* (oy) These are called vowel diphthongs. Vowel diphthongs are made up of two vowel letters that stand for two vowel sounds.

Follow the same procedure with the remaining column.

Answers: column 2: all words have the ow sound, letters are *ou* or *ow.*

Part 4: Syllabication Strategy: Vowel Clusters

Use the following syllabication strategy to help your students syllabicate words that contain vowel clusters.

DIRECT INSTRUCTION

Write Rule 4 and the example words on the board or use the copymaster on page 49.

> **Rule 4:**
> **Do not split common vowel clusters, such as long vowel digraphs, r-controlled vowels, and vowel diphthongs.**
>
> **party   poison   feature   royal   chowder   garden**

Have a student read Rule 4. Have a student explain the rule in his or her own words.

Have a student read the first word.

You could say: **Do you see a vowel cluster in this word? (yes) If you do, what is the cluster? (*ar*) Where would you avoid dividing this word according to Rule 4? (between the *a* and *r*) Where do you think you should divide the word? (after the cluster, between the *r* and *t*) Look at each syllable and pronounce the word. Do you recognize the word?**

Repeat this process with the remaining words. In the case of *poison, feature,* and *royal,* students will be asked to syllabicate words for which they haven't learned all of the syllabication rules. Encourage them to try out what they know and attempt a pronunciation based on what they've learned so far.

Answers:

poison: (*oi*) avoid dividing between cluster; divide after the cluster

royal: (*oy*) avoid dividing between cluster; divide after the cluster

feature: (*ea*) avoid dividing between cluster; divide after the cluster

chowder: (*ow*) avoid dividing between cluster; divide after the cluster

garden: (*ar*) avoid dividing between cluster; divide after the cluster

Part 5: Strategy Practice

Write the following on the board. Have students divide the words according to the rules they know, and pronounce the word.

	Answers		Answers
carton	car/ton	peanut	pea/nut
powder	pow/der	council	coun/cil
circus	cir/cus	purpose	pur/pose
mountain	moun/tain	moisture	mois/ture
maintain	main/tain	voyage	voy/age
fertile	fer/tile	mayor	may/or
darling	dar/ling	freedom	free/dom
coward	cow/ard	tailor	tai/lor
hornet	hor/net	eager	ea/ger
barter	bar/ter	order	or/der

LESSON 4: Short and Long Vowels in Multisyllabic Words

This lesson will help your students develop flexibility in applying syllabication strategies as they attempt to decode multisyllabic words.

Part 1: Quick Review

If you have skipped over Lessons 1–3, you may want to preview this lesson to be sure your students are prepared for a more complicated syllabication strategy.

Part 2: Syllabication Strategy: Is the vowel sound long or short?

Use the following syllabication strategy to help your students decide whether a vowel letter stands for a long or short vowel sound.

DIRECT INSTRUCTION

Write Rule 5 and the example words on the board. Remind students that V stands for vowel and C stands for consonant.

> **Rule 5: VCV**
>
> **When you see a VCV pattern in the middle of a word, divide the word either before or after the consonant. If you divide the word after the consonant, the first vowel sound will be short. If you divide the word before the consonant, the first vowel sound will be long.**
>
> **model   robot   crazy   never**

Have a student read Rule 5 and explain the rule in his or her own words.

Ask a student to read the first word.

You could say: **Find the VCV pattern in the first word. (*ode*) Where should you first divide the word? (after the *d*, the first consonant) What happens to the vowel sound in the first syllable? (The vowel sound is short) Say the word. Do you recognize it? (yes) When the consonant is part of the first syllable, the first syllable is called "closed."**

Ask a student to read the second word.

You could say: **Find the VCV pattern in the second word. (*obo*) Where should you first divide the word? (after the *b*, the first consonant) What happens to the vowel sound in the first syllable? (The vowel sound is short) Say the word. Do you recognize it? (no)**

Try the second part of the rule. Where should you divide the word? (before the consonant) What happens to the vowel sound in the first syllable? (The vowel sound is long) Say the word. Do you recognize it? (yes) When the consonant is part of the second syllable, the first syllable is called "open."

Repeat this process with the remaining words.

Answers: crazy: (*azy*) Divide after the *z,* the first consonant; vowel is short; no, do not recognize the word. Divide before the *z;* the vowel is long; yes, recognize the word.

never: (*eve*) Divide after the *v;* vowel sound is short; yes, recognize the word.

Part 3: Strategy Practice

Write the following words on the board. Have students divide the words and pronounce the words.

	Answers		Answers
legal	le/gal	final	fi/nal
gravel	grav/el	prefix	pre/fix
basic	ba/sic	level	lev/el
driven	driv/en	moment	mo/ment
minus	mi/nus	paper	pa/per
panic	pan/ic	soda	so/da
spider	spi/der	devil	dev/il
honor	hon/or	tiny	ti/ny
seven	sev/en		

LESSON 5: Compound Words

When students encounter multisyllabic words, they often don't try the obvious; i.e., to look for words or word parts they already know within the longer word. Lessons 5 and 6 will help students develop these skills.

Part 1: Syllabication Strategy: Compound Words

Use the following syllabication strategy to help your students determine where to divide a compound word.

DIRECT INSTRUCTION

Write Rule 6 and the example words on the board.

> **Rule 6:**
>
> **Divide compound words between the individual words.**
>
> | | | |
> |---|---|---|
> | **grapevine** | **lifeguard** | **whirlwind** |
> | **butterfly** | **grasshopper** | |

Have a student read Rule 6. Ask a student to explain the rule in his or her own words.

You could say: **When you see a multisyllabic word, stop and see if it is made up of one or more words that you already know.**

Have a student read the first word.

You could say: How many words do you see in the first word? (two) Where should you divide the word? (between *grape* and *vine*)

Repeat the process with the remaining words in the first row.

Answers: (life/guard), (whirl/wind)

Have a student read the first word in the second row.

You could say: **How many words do you see in the word? (two) Where should you divide the word? (between *butter* and *fly*) Where else should you divide the word? (between the two t's) How do you know? (Rule 1 says to divide two consonants between vowels.)**

Repeat the process with the remaining words. (grass/hop/per)

Part 2: Strategy Practice

Write the following words on the board. Have students divide the words, identify the rule(s) they use, and pronounce the word.

	Answers		Answers
shipwreck	ship/wreck	buttermilk	but/ter/milk
postcard	post/card	notebook	note/book
screwdriver	screw/dri/ver	volleyball	vol/ley/ball
oatmeal	oat/meal	washcloth	wash/cloth
windmill	wind/mill	wastebasket	waste/bas/ket
dragonfly	dra/gon/fly	peppermint	pep/per/mint
pancake	pan/cake	hardware	hard/ware
earthquake	earth/quake	handlebar	han/dle/bar
pigtail	pig/tail	earring	ear/ring
wristwatch	wrist/ watch	weekend	week/end

LESSON 6: Affixes

This lesson will give students help in dividing multisyllabic words that contain one or more affixes. These are the kinds of words that give students the most problems because they tend to be long and can look overwhelming. If you think your students would benefit from practice with identifying prefixes and suffixes, start with Parts 1 and 2. If not, go directly to Parts 3 and 4.

Part 1: Quick Review of Prefixes

Recognizing prefixes in multisyllabic words can help your students chunk words into manageable parts. You may use the following list of common prefixes and their meanings to expand upon the lesson described below.

auto-	self	by-	near, aside
mis-	bad	under-	below
pre-	before	un-	not
re-	again	de-	from, down
with-	back, away	dis-	opposite
bi-	two	uni-	one
on-	on	be-	make
tri-	three		

DIRECT INSTRUCTION

Write the following prefixes and their meanings on the board.

auto-	self	bi-	two	un-	not

You could say: **The word part on the left side of each pair is called a prefix. Prefixes can be added to root words or base words to change the meaning of the word. Think of a word that begins with this prefix.**

Write the word on the board.

Follow the same procedure with the remaining prefixes. If you wish, include additional prefixes. Save the words and use them for syllabication practice later.

Possible answers: *auto-* (autobiography); *bi-* (bicycle, bifold); *un-* (unhappy, unlikely)

Part 2: Quick Review of Suffixes

Recognizing suffixes in multisyllabic words can help your students chunk words into manageable parts. You may use the following list of common suffixes and their meanings to expand upon the lesson described below.

-ness	state or quality of	-less	without
-like	resembling	-ship	state or quality of
-ish	relating to	-ful	full of
-ways	manner	-er	one who
-ly	like, or resembling	-ous	full of
-ion	state or quality of	-ment	action or process

DIRECT INSTRUCTION

Write the following suffixes and their meanings on the board.

-ness	state or quality of	-ly	resembling
-ful	full of		

You could say: **The word part on the left side of each pair is called a suffix. When suffixes are added to root words or base words, they often change the part of speech of the root or base word. Think of a word that ends with this suffix.**

Write the word on the board.

Follow the same procedure with the remaining suffixes. If you wish, include additional suffixes. Save the words and use them for syllabication practice later.

Possible answers: *-ness* (happiness, sadness); *-ly* (quickly, lively); *-ful* (thankful, eventful)

Part 3: Syllabication Strategy: Affixes

Use the following syllabication strategy to help your students determine where to divide words that contain affixes.

DIRECT INSTRUCTION

Write Rule 7 and the examples on the board.

Rule 7:

When a word includes an affix, divide between the base word and the affix (prefix or suffix).

rebound	restless	unavoidable
preschool	childish	readjustment
disprove	joyous	unselfish

Ask a student to read Rule 7 and to explain the rule in his or her own words.

Have a student read the first word in column 1.

You could say: **What prefix do you see in** *rebound? (re)* **Where should you divide** *rebound* **according to Rule 7?** *(re/bound)* Continue with the remaining words in column 1. In each case, have students apply the rule, divide the word, pronounce the word, and then see if they recognize it.

Answers: pre/school; dis/prove

Have a student read the first word in column 2.

What suffix do you see in *restless? (less)* **Where should you divide** *restless? (rest/less)* Continue with the remaining words in column 2. In each case, have students apply the rule, divide the word, pronounce the word, and then see if they recognize it.

Answers: child/ish; joy/ous

Have a student read the first word in column 3.

What affixes do you see in this word? *(un, able)* **Where should you divide the word?** *(un/avoid/able)* Continue with the remaining words in column 3. In each case, have students apply the rule, divide the word, pronounce it, and then see if they recognize it. Note: In *avoid, a* is also considered a prefix, and *able* is considered a suffix. You can further divide the word as follows: un/a/void/a/ble.

Answers: re/adjust/ment and re/ad/just/ment; un/self/ish

If you wish to extend this lesson, have students analyze each word to see if they should apply additional syllabication rules.

Part 4: Strategy Practice

Write the following words on the board. Have students divide the words, identify the rule(s) they use, and pronounce the words.

	Answers
uniform	uni/form (or u/ni/form)
fairly	fair/ly
beautiful	beau/ti/ful
unlikely	un/like/ly
recall	re/call
misfit	mis/fit
rigorous	rigor/ous (or rig/or/ous)
hopelessness	hope/less/ness
childlike	child/like
unwind	un/wind
selfish	self/ish
opinion	opin/ion (and o/pin/ion)
hardship	hard/ship
sticker	stick/er
sideways	side/ways
department	de/part/ment
disbelieve	dis/believe (and dis/be/lieve)
withstand	with/stand
become	be/come
refreshment	re/fresh/ment

Comprehension Mini-Lessons
with Graphic Organizers

1 For students who have trouble grasping the main idea of a paragraph or passage, discuss these points.

- The main idea is the most important idea a writer makes in a paragraph or passage.
- The writer may state the main idea in a sentence. This sentence can appear at the beginning, middle, or end of a paragraph or passage.
- Sometimes the writer implies the main idea. The reader must then figure it out by thinking about the details and stating it in his or her own words.

2 Duplicate the following paragraph. A master is provided on page 125. Have students follow along as you read it aloud, using it to model **stated main idea.**

> **Every year teens spend billions of dollars. In 1999 American teens spent $153 billion! According to one research company, the average teenager spends about $35 every time he or she goes to the mall. Experts expect more sales as the population of teens increases by 4 million by the year 2010.**

You could say: *Writers often put the main idea in the first sentence.* Every year teens spend billions of dollars *seems like the main idea. The second and third sentences tell how teenagers spend billions of dollars each year. The last sentence makes an additional point about teenage spending. Each sentence gives a detail that supports the first sentence. It is, therefore, logical to conclude that the first sentence is the main idea.*

3 Duplicate the following paragraph. A master is provided on page 125. Have students follow along as you read it aloud, using it to model **implied main idea.**

> **Ballooning got its start in 1783 when two ballooning pioneers launched a duck, a sheep, and a rooster in the first historic balloon flight. Since then, many people have ballooned successfully across lakes, channels, and even oceans. Ballooning has become so popular that people now compete for the world record in time and distance.**

You could say: *Let's look at the first sentence for the main idea. It tells me something about the history of ballooning. The second sentence tells me how the popularity of ballooning has grown. The third sentence gives me an additional detail about ballooning. In this case the writer chose not to state the main idea. I'll have to figure it out by looking at all the details. Each sentence gives a detail about the history of ballooning. Therefore, the implied main idea is* ballooning throughout history.

4 Duplicate the following paragraphs and read them aloud. A master is provided on page 126.

> **Have you ever wondered if time travel is possible? If you have, you're not alone. Philosophers and scientists, including Albert Einstein, have studied the concept of time. Writers have written stories about time travel into the past and future. Movies like *Star Trek* and *The Terminator* explore the possibilities of time travel.**
>
> **Although time travel may not be possible in the near future, history has taught us that advanced technology is capable of the impossible. In the beginning of the 20th century, many people doubted that humans would ever fly. Today we can get from one ocean to another in a matter of hours. Likewise, the thought of flying to the moon seemed an impossibility, but today we have the spacecraft to get us there and back. Perhaps someday we'll have a machine capable of transporting people into the past or future.**

5 Duplicate and distribute the Main Idea Web on the next page. Correct responses are shown in the Answer Key on page 189.

6 Make additional copies of the Main Idea Web and have them available for students to use when necessary throughout the year.

Detail:

Detail:

Main Idea:

Detail:

Detail:

Main Idea

Every year teens spend billions of dollars. In 1999 American teens spent $153 billion! According to one research company, the average teenager spends about $35 every time he or she goes to the mall. Experts expect more sales as the population of teens increases by 4 million by the year 2010.

Ballooning got its start in 1783 when two ballooning pioneers launched a duck, a sheep, and a rooster in the first historic balloon flight. Since then, many people have ballooned successfully across lakes, channels, and even oceans. Ballooning has become so popular that people now compete for the world record in time and distance.

Main Idea

Have you ever wondered if time travel is possible? If you have, you're not alone. Philosophers and scientists, including Albert Einstein, have studied the concept of time. Writers have written stories about time travel into the past and future. Television shows and movies like *Star Trek* and *The Terminator* explore the possibilities of time travel.

Although time travel may not be possible in the near future, history has taught us that advanced technology is capable of the impossible. In the beginning of the century, many people doubted that humans would ever fly. Today we can get from one ocean to another in a matter of hours. Likewise, the thought of flying to the moon seemed an impossibility, but today we have the spacecraft to get us there and back. Perhaps someday we'll have a machine capable of transporting people into the past or future.

1 Ask students if they have ever told a friend a story with events that weren't in the exact order in which they occurred. If details were out of order, the friend could ask questions to clarify the sequence. Explain that it is important to keep track of the sequence of events in order to understand the meaning of the story or how the plot moves forward. The following points will be useful to students who need more help.

- Sequence is the order in which events happen. Sequence refers to the chronological order in a story or piece of nonfiction. It may also refer to steps in a process or in following directions.

- Writers sometimes use words such as *first, next, after, before, then,* and *later* to connect ideas and indicate the order in which events occur.

- Words, phrases, or dates that tell when something is happening can also help readers figure out the sequence of events.

- A paragraph or story may begin telling about an event that happens in the present. Other sentences may tell about events that happened in the past leading up to the present.

- When events are not clearly laid out, it may help the reader to visualize in his or her mind how the events happened.

2 Duplicate the following paragraph. A master is provided on page 129. Have students follow along as you read it aloud, using it to model **sequence.**

> **I discovered the best recipe for a strawberry milk shake. First you gather all the ingredients: vanilla ice cream, fresh strawberries, 1 cup of skim milk, 2 tablespoons of cream cheese, and granola or your favorite topping. Then you mix all the ingredients, except the granola, in a blender for one to two minutes. Once you pour the milk shake into a tall glass, sprinkle the granola on top and the shake is ready to serve.**

You could say: The first sentence tells me something about a recipe for a strawberry milk shake. Chances are that the first sentence is not the first step in the sequence. The second sentence gives me a list of ingredients to gather. The third and fourth sentences give me additional steps in the recipe. So if I were to list the order of steps in the recipe I would say that first you gather the ingredients. Then you blend the ingredients. Next, you pour the milk shake into a glass and add the topping; and finally you serve the milk shake.

3 Duplicate the following paragraph. A master is provided on page 129. Have students follow along as you read it aloud.

> **My babysitting days are over! Yesterday afternoon, I got an emergency call from the Smiths asking if I could take care of the twins for a few hours. After dinner, I walked over to the Smiths'. As soon as Mr. and Mrs. Smith left, the twins started to run around the house, playing hide and seek. While I was frantically searching for the twins, the doorbell rang and a pizza delivery boy appeared at the door. As soon as I saw the order slip, I knew the troublemakers who had called for pizza. As I walked towards the twins' room, the fire alarm went off in the kitchen. With all the commotion, I had forgotten to turn off the stove and had burnt the popcorn. By midnight the twins finally fell asleep.**

4 Duplicate and distribute the Sequence/Flow Chart on the next page. Work with students to fill in the first event. Then have them complete the chart. Tell students to highlight any words or phrases that helped them determine the order of events. Ask volunteers to share how they mapped out the events of the paragraph. Possible responses are shown in the Answer Key on page 189.

5 Make additional copies of the chart on page 128 and have it available for students to use throughout the year.

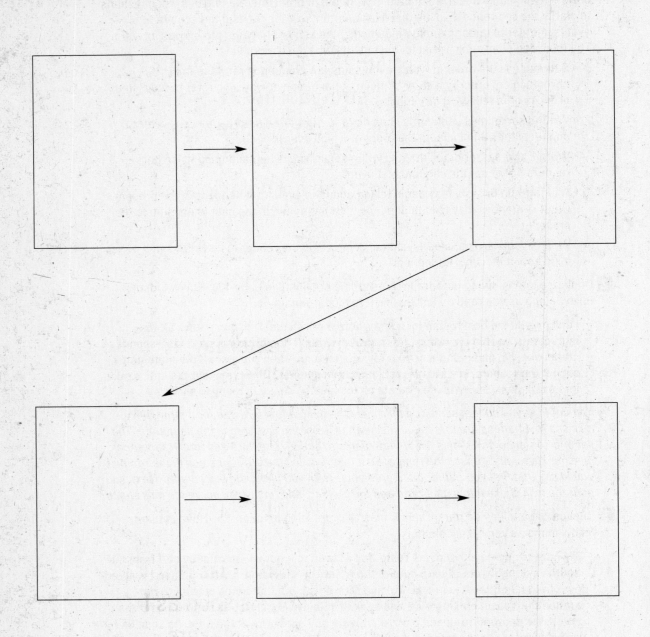

Sequence

I discovered the best recipe for a strawberry milk shake. First you gather all the ingredients: vanilla ice cream, fresh strawberries, 1 cup of skim milk, 2 tablespoons of cream cheese, and granola or your favorite topping. Then you mix all the ingredients, except the granola, in a blender for one to two minutes. Once you pour the milk shake into a tall glass, sprinkle the granola on top and the shake is ready to serve.

My babysitting days are over! Yesterday afternoon, I got an emergency call from the Smiths asking if I could take care of the twins for a few hours. After dinner, I walked over to the Smiths'. As soon as Mr. and Mrs. Smith left, the twins started to run around the house, playing hide and seek. While I was frantically searching for the twins, the doorbell rang and a pizza delivery boy appeared at the door. As soon as I saw the order slip, I knew the troublemakers who had called for pizza. As I walked towards the twins' room, the fire alarm went off in the kitchen. With all the commotion, I had forgotten to turn off the stove and had burnt the popcorn. By midnight the twins finally fell asleep.

1 Write the following sentence on the board and read it aloud.

Travis felt sick because he ate eight slices of pizza.

Ask students which event caused the other event to happen *(Travis ate eight slices of pizza, which caused him to feel sick)*. Discuss the following points.

- A **cause** is an action or event that makes something else happen.
- An **effect** is what happens because of a certain action or event.
- Writers use clue words or phrases *(because, since,* and *as a result)* to indicate causes and effects. However, clue words alone do not automatically indicate a cause-effect relationship. One event must make another event happen.
- A single cause can result in more than one effect *(Because Travis ate eight slices of pizza, he felt sick and went to the school nurse's office.)*. Also, several causes can lead to a single effect *(Since you are a talented artist and have some free time this weekend, you should help us paint a mural.)*.
- Sometimes a series of events are linked in a cause-and-effect chain in which one event causes another, which in turn causes another, and so on *(Because I didn't listen to the weather report, I didn't bring an umbrella with me. As a result, I got soaked when the rain started.)*.

Watch out for events that happen in sequence. Just because one event follows another doesn't mean the first event caused the second one. *Just as we got ready to go to the beach, it started to rain.* (The rain was not a result of us getting ready to go to the beach.)

2 Duplicate the following paragraph. A master is provided on page 134. Ask students to follow along as you read it aloud, using it to model **cause-effect.**

> Amanda worked hard to make this year's talent show a success. Because she put up so many posters, just about everyone in the area knew about the show. Lots of people bought tickets. More people attended than ever before, which meant that the show raised more money for charity than ever before.

You could say: *The first sentence tells what happened. The second sentence has a signal word,* because, *that may indicate a cause-effect relationship. If you look at sentences three and four, it is logical to say that Amanda's hard work also caused people to buy tickets and attend the show. These sentences show how one cause can result in more than one effect. Now look at the last sentence. It is an example of a cause-and-effect chain in which the first event* (hard work) *caused another event* (more people attending) *which in turn caused another event* (more money being raised).

3 Duplicate the following paragraph. A master is provided on page 134. Have students follow as you read it aloud.

> Last year, my mom decided that our family should learn more about nature. For this reason, we went on a camping trip—and had an awful time! We didn't have the right kinds of tents, and other supplies for the cool, damp weather at the campsite. As a result, we decided to do more research before planning this year's vacation.

4 Duplicate and distribute the Cause-and-Effect Chart on the next page. Work with students to fill in the first cause-and-effect relationship. Possible responses are shown in the Answer Key on page 189.

5 Make copies of the additional Cause-and-Effect Charts on pages 131–133 and have them available at appropriate times.

Cause	→	Effect(s)

Single Cause with Multiple Effects

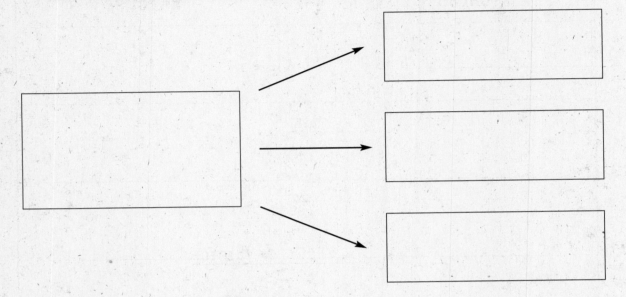

Multiple Causes with Single Effect

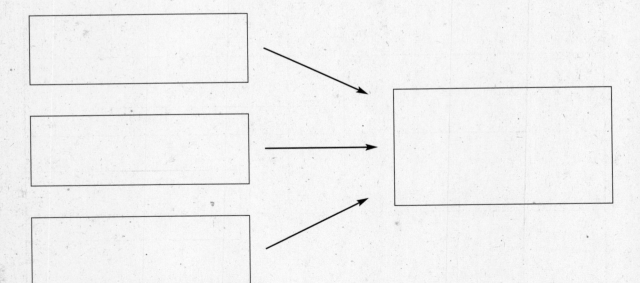

Cause-and-Effect Chain

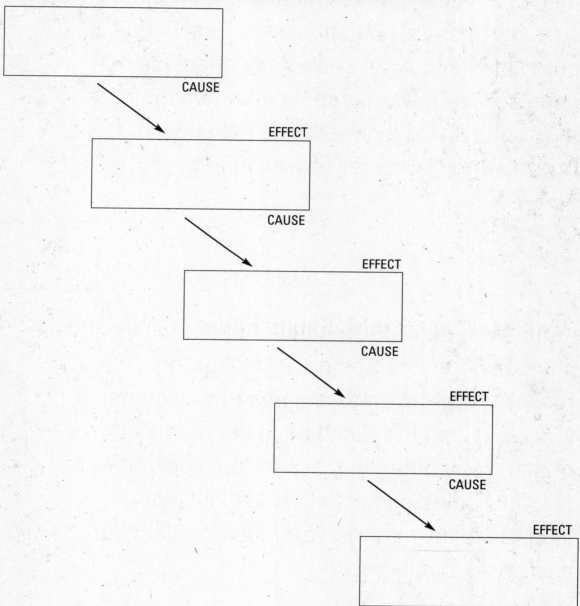

Cause and Effect

Amanda worked hard to make this year's talent show a success. Because she put up so many posters, just about everyone in the area knew about the show. Lots of people bought tickets. More people attended than ever before, which meant that the show raised more money for charity than ever before.

Last year, my mom decided that our family should learn more about nature. For this reason, we went on a camping trip—and had an awful time! We didn't have the right kinds of tents, and other supplies for the cool, damp weather at the campsite. As a result, we decided to do more research before planning this year's vacation.

1 The following points will be helpful to students who have trouble understanding the terms compare and contrast.

- **Comparing** means to think about the ways in which two or more people or two or more things are alike. *(Edgar Allan Poe and Agatha Christie wrote mysteries.)* Writers sometimes use words such as *both, same, alike, like, also, similarly,* and *too* to make comparisons. *(Both Edgar Allan Poe and Agatha Christie wrote mysteries.)*

- **Contrasting** means to think about ways in which two or more people or two or more things are different. *(Mike likes to read mysteries. Manuel likes to read science fiction.)* Writers sometimes use words or phrases such as *unlike, but, while, although, instead, yet, even though, however,* and *on the other hand* to contrast two or more things. *(Mike likes to read mysteries while Manuel likes to read science fiction.)*

- Sometimes there are no signal words. Readers must figure out what the writer is comparing and contrasting from the details given.

2 Duplicate the following paragraph. A master is provided on page 137. Have students follow along as you read it aloud, using it to model **compare and contrast.**

> **Ulysses S. Grant and Robert E. Lee were both admired for their leadership skills during the Civil War. Both were intelligent. Both were determined to win the war. However, General Grant took risks in his war tactics while General Lee was more cautious in his defense against the northerners.**

You could say: *The first sentence tells me that two people—Ulysses S. Grant and Robert E. Lee—are being compared. The second and third sentences contain the word* both, *which signals a way in which Grant and Lee are alike. The last sentence contains the phrase* however, *which signals a difference between Grant and Lee. Therefore, Grant and Lee were alike in that they were both intelligent and were both determined to win the war. The difference is that Grant took risks while Lee was more cautious.*

3 For reference, write on the board the signal words and phrases listed in the second bulleted item. Then duplicate the following paragraph and read it aloud. A master is provided on page 137.

> **While some people prefer to watch a movie at home, I prefer to go to a movie theater. Television and theater screens both present the same images; however, a theater screen is magnified and can, therefore, make each image feel more intense and real. In addition, the quality of television sound is weak in comparison to the sound in a movie theater. While watching television at home can be a quiet, personal experience, the moviegoer shares his or her emotions with the rest of the audience. From thrillers to action movies, the moviegoer can feel the anticipation of the audience begin to grow as something exciting is about to happen. Watching a film on television, on the other hand, gives little opportunity to feel the reactions of a large audience.**

4 Duplicate and distribute the Venn Diagram on the next page. Have students fill in the diagram, using information in the paragraph along with what they already know about television and movie theaters to compare and contrast the two.

5 Have volunteers share the information in their diagrams by first describing the similarities between television and movie theaters then describing their differences. Possible responses are shown in the Answer Key on page 190.

6 Make additional copies of the diagram on page 136 and have it available for students to use at appropriate times during the year.

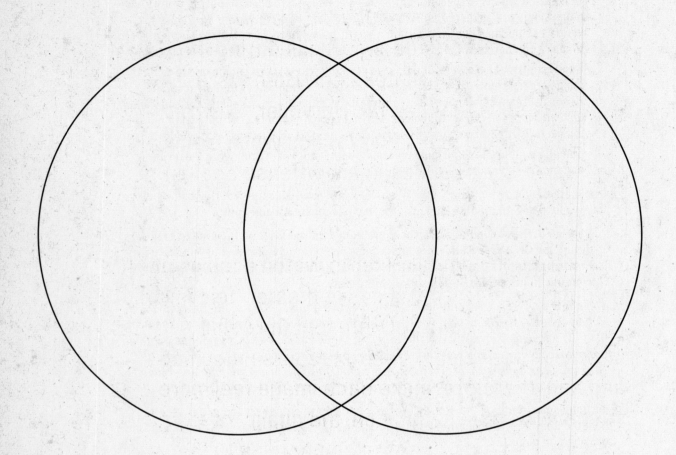

Comparison and Contrast

Ulysses S. Grant and Robert E. Lee were both admired for their leadership skills during the Civil War. Both were intelligent. Both were determined to win the war. However, General Grant took risks in his war tactics while General Lee was more cautious in his defense against the northerners.

While some people prefer to watch a movie at home, I prefer to go to a movie theater. Television and theater screens both present the same images; however, a theater screen is magnified and can, therefore, make each image feel more intense and real. In addition, the quality of television sound is weak in comparison to the sound in a movie theater. While watching television at home can be a quiet, personal experience, the moviegoer shares his or her emotions with the rest of the audience. From thrillers to action movies, the moviegoer can feel the anticipation of the audience begin to grow as something exciting is about to happen. Watching a film on television, on the other hand, gives little opportunity to feel the reactions of a large audience.

1 Present students with the following situation:

You look out the window of a high-rise building. You see people carrying umbrellas and cars running their windshield wipers. What inference can you make? (Students will most likely say that it's raining.) For students who need more help making inferences, discuss the following points.

- It is not possible for writers to include every detail about what is happening in a work of literature.

- Often writers purposely choose to hint at details rather than state them; this can add meaning and suspense for the reader.

- Inferences are logical guesses based on clues in the text and on the reader's own knowledge and common sense.

- To make inferences, readers must: look for details that the writer provides about character, setting, and events; think about what they already know about a topic; and connect the story to their own personal experiences.

2 Duplicate the following paragraph. A master is provided on page 140. Ask students to follow along as you read it aloud, using it to model the skill **making inferences**.

> **Donna paced up and down the room. When she heard footsteps outside, she ran to the window and looked outside. As her eyes searched up and down the street, her hopeful smile faded. She turned away from the window, glanced at her watch, and heaved a big sigh.**

You could say: *In the first sentence, I learn that Donna is pacing up and down a room. From her movements, I can infer that she is nervous or impatient about something. The second sentence tells me that Donna is probably waiting for someone because she looks out the window when she hears footsteps outside. In the third sentence, I learn that the person she is expecting has not arrived. Donna's smile fades as she scans the street. In the fourth sentence, Donna's sigh suggests that she is disappointed or sad. The glance at her watch tells me that the person she is waiting for is late.*

3 Duplicate the following passage. A master is provided on page 140. Have students follow along as you read it aloud.

> **Donna walked over to the kitchen phone and dialed a number. As she held the receiver to her ear, she drummed her fingers on the counter. She slammed the phone down when no one answered. With a sudden gesture, she picked up a magazine and leafed quickly through its pages. Then, just as quickly, she threw the magazine down on the table in front of her. She sat stiffly in her chair, her feet tapping rapidly. Finally, the sound of running footsteps pounding up the steps made Donna sit up. She grabbed her jacket and ran out the door.**

4 Duplicate and distribute the Inferences Chart on the next page. Work with students to fill in the first row. Then have them add to the chart any other inferences they make about the passage. Sample responses are shown in the Answer Key on page 190.

Selection Information	+	My Opinion/ What I Know	=	My Inference/ My Judgment
	+		=	
	+		=	
	+		=	
	+		=	

Making Inferences

Donna paced up and down the room. When she heard footsteps outside, she ran to the window and looked outside. As her eyes searched up and down the street, her hopeful smile faded. She turned away from the window, glanced at her watch, and heaved a big sigh.

Donna walked over to the kitchen phone and dialed a number. As she held the receiver to her ear, she drummed her fingers on the counter. She slammed the phone down when no one answered. With a sudden gesture, she picked up a magazine and leafed quickly through its pages. Then, just as quickly, she threw the magazine down on the table in front of her. She sat stiffly in her chair, her feet tapping rapidly. Finally, the sound of running footsteps pounding up the steps made Donna sit up. She grabbed her jacket and ran out the door.

1 To introduce the concept of predicting, ask students to make a guess about what they will study in their next class based on what they already know. Use the following points to explain how the strategy applies to reading a story.

- When you **predict,** you try to figure out what will happen next based upon what has already happened.

- To make a **prediction,** you must combine clues in a story with your own knowledge and experience to make a reasonable guess.

- Good readers make and revise predictions about characters, setting, and plot as they read. Sometimes, they don't even realize they're doing it.

- Sometimes you must first make a guess or inference about what is happening before you can predict what will happen next. *(Chan read his book as he walked down the street. A sleeping dog lay in his path.)* You might infer that Chan isn't looking where he is going. Since a sleeping dog lies in his path, you could then use the inference to predict that Chan is going to trip over it.

2 Duplicate the following paragraph. A master is provided on page 143. Have students follow along as you read it aloud, using it to model the skill of **predicting.**

> **Rachel walked into her room, sat down at her desk, and opened up her math book.**

You could say: *The first sentence tells me that Rachel is at home and sitting at her desk. Since she opens her math book, I think that Rachel is preparing to do some homework. I'll read further to see if my prediction is right.*

> **As she worked on some word problems, she felt her eyelids become heavy and she had trouble keeping her eyes open.**

You could say: *The second sentence tells me that Rachel is working on word problems. However, the description of her heavy eyelids suggests that she is very sleepy. Since she is having trouble keeping her eyes open, I predict that Rachel will fall asleep.*

> **With an effort, Rachel shook her head and sat up straighter. She had to be ready for the big math test tomorrow. Even as she told herself this, however, her head sank until it was resting on her arm and she fell fast asleep.**

You could say: *My predictions were right. Based on the fact that Rachel isn't going to be prepared for the math test, I can also predict that she won't do very well on it.*

3 Duplicate the following passage. A master is provided on page 143. Instruct students to follow along as you read it aloud. Afterwards, students should be ready to infer what has happened and to predict what will happen next.

> **Marcus grabbed the leash off the hook and whistled for his dog. "Come on, Max," Marcus said, attaching the leash to the dog's collar, "Let's go to the park."**
> **The park was full of people. Marcus led Max to a quiet area away from the crowds. He unleashed the dog and let Max roam freely on the grass.**
> **Marcus watched the dog, but after a while his mind began to wander. Then with a start, Marcus remembered the dog. He looked all around, but Max was nowhere in sight. As he neared the picnic area, Marcus heard loud, angry voices. Suddenly, Max appeared with a couple of hamburgers in his mouth. Marcus leashed his dog and made him drop the burgers. Marcus was holding the pieces of meat when the angry picnickers caught sight of him.**

4 Duplicate and distribute the Predicting Chart on the next page. Have students work in pairs to complete the chart. Possible responses are shown in the Answer Key on page 183.

Name **Date**

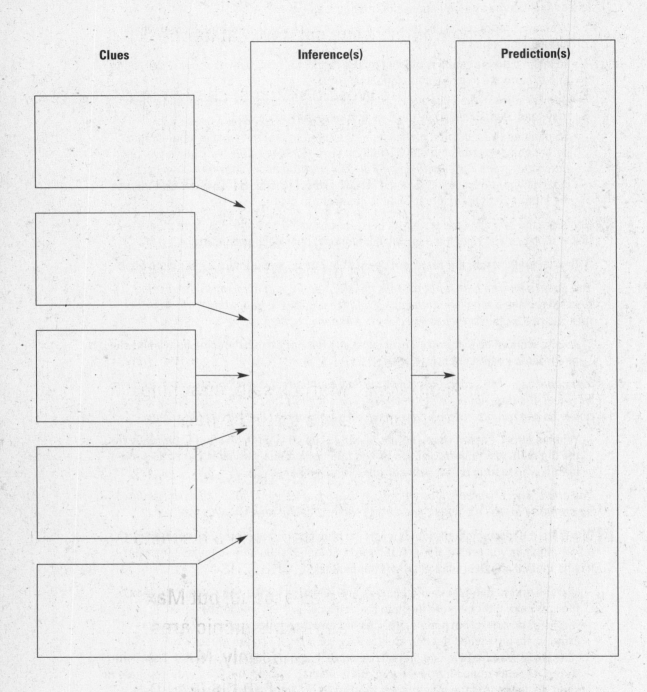

Clues

Inference(s)

Prediction(s)

Predicting

Rachel walked into her room, sat down at her desk, and opened up her math book.

As she worked on some word problems, she felt her eyelids become heavy and she had trouble keeping her eyes open.

With an effort, Rachel shook her head and sat up straighter. She had to be ready for the big math test tomorrow. Even as she told herself this, however, her head sank until it was resting on her arm and she fell fast asleep.

Marcus grabbed the leash off the hook and whistled for his dog. "Come on, Max," Marcus said, attaching the leash to the dog's collar, "Let's go to the park."

The park was full of people. Marcus led Max to a quiet area away from the crowds. He unleashed the dog and let Max roam freely on the grass.

Marcus watched the dog, but after a while his mind began to wander. Then with a start, Marcus remembered the dog. He looked all around, but Max was nowhere in sight. As he neared the picnic area, Marcus heard loud, angry voices. Suddenly, Max appeared with a couple of hamburgers in his mouth. Marcus leashed his dog and made him drop the burgers. Marcus was holding the pieces of meat when the angry picnickers caught sight of him.

1 Use examples from textbooks, newspapers, magazines, and pamphlets as you discuss the following points about distinguishing fact and opinion:

- A **fact** is a statement that can be proven or disproven through observation, experience, and research. A fact may include supporting evidence such as statistics or quotations from a recognized expert.
- An **opinion** is a statement that tells what a writer thinks, believes, or feels about a subject. It cannot be proven true or false.
- A writer may use words and phrases such as the following to signal an opinion: *according to, I think, in my opinion, perhaps, seem, should, bad, good, better, worse, terrible.* A writer may also use words that appeal to the reader's emotions.
- Sometimes a writer will use one or more facts to support an opinion.
- A single statement can contain both a fact and an opinion.
- A statement that you agree with is not necessarily a fact.

2 Duplicate the following paragraph. A master is provided on page 146. Have students follow along as you read it aloud, using it to model the skill of **distinguishing between fact and opinion.**

> **I believe that female politicians are such a powerful presence in politics that we may someday have a female president of the United States. Since the Women's Movement in the 1960s, the number of women in politics has increased dramatically. Women hold positions not only in state offices, but also in Congress and in the President's Cabinet. Female politicians have proven that they can be as politically intelligent as men. In fact, women already hold the presidency in other countries.**

You could say: First I look for numbers, statistics, or quotations from experts. If I don't find any, there's a good chance that the statements are the writer's opinion.

Next I look for words that might signal opinions. The first sentence contains the signal words I believe. These words tell me that the first sentence is an opinion. The second and third sentences do not contain any signal words, but I know that these statements are true. The fourth sentence does not contain any signal words that would tell me it is an opinion. In this case, we would have to see if we could prove the statement. The fifth sentence begins by stating that the statement is a fact; this could be proven by finding out which countries have female presidents.

3 For reference, write on the board the signal words and phrases listed in the third bulleted item. Then duplicate the following paragraph and read it aloud. A master is provided on page 146.

> **It seems that Mark Twain's popularity will never end. His work is still read by many people today. In addition, many of his short stories and novels have been made into movies. Recently, Disney Studios released *Tom and Huck,* a retelling based on two of Twain's popular novels. Twain's humor and memorable characters give his work long-lasting popularity. People will be enjoying his stories for years to come.**

4 Duplicate and distribute the Two-Column Chart on the next page and ask students to use it to list the facts and opinions in the paragraph. Suggest that they highlight any signal words that helped them distinguish between the two types of statements.

5 Have volunteers share their completed charts, explaining why they listed each statement where they did. Correct responses are shown in the Answer Key on page 191.

6 Make additional copies of the chart on page 145 and have them available for students to use at appropriate times during the year.

Name   **Date**

Fact and Opinion

I believe that female politicians are such a powerful presence in politics that we may someday have a female president of the United States. Since the Women's Movement in the 1960s, the number of women in politics has increased dramatically. Women hold positions not only in state offices, but also in Congress and the President's Cabinet. Female politicians have proven that they can be as politically intelligent as men. In fact, women already hold the presidency in other countries.

It seems that Mark Twain's popularity will never end. His work is still read by many people today. In addition, many of his short stories and novels have been made into movies. Recently, Disney Studios released *Tom and Huck,* a retelling based on two of Twain's popular novels. Twain's humor and memorable characters give his work long-lasting popularity. People will be enjoying his stories for years to come.

1 Duplicate the following passage. A master is provided on page 149. Have students follow along as you read it aloud.

> Last Friday night I had a scary experience. I was baby-sitting the two Guterson kids while their parents were at the movies. The kids were asleep in bed, and I was looking forward to a peaceful evening. Then I heard it—a *thud, thud, thud* on the door to the basement. Someone or something was trying to get out.
>
> I walked quietly over to the basement door. What should I do? Call the police? Go to a neighbor's house? Open the door?
>
> "Maybe it's nothing," I told myself. "Maybe it was just the wind, or I was imagining things."
>
> *Thud, thud, thud.* The door shook a little on its hinges.

Ask students when and where this story takes place *(at a neighbor's house last Friday)*. Have them tell whom the story is about *(a babysitter, two kids named Guterson, the kids' parents, and someone or something in the basement)*. Ask them what the story problem is *(The person or animal in the basement is trying to get out!)*.

2 Discuss with students the following elements of a narrative:

- The **setting** is when and where a story takes place. It is important for two reasons. First, it helps the reader visualize the story where it occurs. Also, a setting creates a context for the events that take place. For example, if you are reading a story that takes place at the North Pole, you would know that the characters are very unlikely to face a heat wave. Or, if you are reading a story that takes place in prehistoric times, you would not expect any of the characters to be talking on the telephone.

- **Characters** are the people in a story. The main character is the person who the story is mostly about. One of the reasons good stories are effective is that the characters seem real or interesting, and the reader cares about what happens to them. Remind students that the characters in a story can also be animals or imaginary creatures.

- The **plot** is the series of events that happen in a story. Most stories have a problem, or **conflict,** that the main character must try to resolve. The **resolution** is the solution to the problem. In general, plot is driven by conflict. In other words, the events in a story generally revolve around the conflict, and the events that occur either contribute to the problem or contribute to the solution of the problem.

3 Continue the story by duplicating the following passage and reading it aloud. A master is provided on page 150.

> "Who's there?" I asked, my voice shaking a bit. "What do you want?"
>
> Then the door opened—the front door, not the basement door. Mr. and Mrs. Guterson walked in.
>
> "What a great movie!" Mrs. Guterson said. "You've just got to see—hey, what's wrong?"
>
> "The basement," I mumbled. "There's something . . ."
>
> *Thud, thud, thud.*
>
> "Oh, that's just Sarah," Mrs. Guterson said. She opened the basement door. An orange-and-black cat slipped through, gave me a furious look, and ran upstairs.
>
> "You weren't scared, were you?" said Mr. Guterson.
>
> "No, of course not," I answered.

4 Duplicate and distribute the Story Map on page 148. Work with students to fill in the setting and characters. Then have them complete the plot portion of the map. Possible responses are shown in the Answer Key on page 191.

5 Make additional copies of the Story Map and have them available for students to use at appropriate times during the year.

Setting	Characters

Plot

Problem:

Events:

1

2

3

4

Resolution:

Narrative Elements

Last Friday night I had a scary experience. I was baby-sitting the two Guterson kids while their parents were at the movies. The kids were asleep in bed, and I was looking forward to a peaceful evening. Then I heard it—a *thud, thud, thud* on the door to the basement. Someone or something was trying to get out.

I walked quietly over to the basement door. What should I do? Call the police? Go to a neighbor's house? Open the door?

"Maybe it's nothing," I told myself. "Maybe it was just the wind, or I was imagining things."

Thud, thud, thud. The door shook a little on its hinges.

"Who's there?" I asked, my voice shaking a bit. "What do you want?"

Then the door opened—the front door, not the basement door. Mr. and Mrs. Guterson walked in.

"What a great movie!" Mrs. Guterson said. "You've just got to see—hey, what's wrong?"

"The basement," I mumbled. "There's something . . ."

Thud, thud, thud.

"Oh, that's just Sarah," Mrs. Guterson said. She opened the basement door. An orange-and-black cat slipped through, gave me a furious look, and ran upstairs.

"You weren't scared, were you?" said Mr. Guterson.

"No, of course not," I answered.

Additional Graphic Organizers

On the following pages you will find additional graphic organizers that can be used in a number of different situations to help students comprehend and monitor what they read. Consult the chart below to decide how and when to use each graphic organizer.

Graphic Organizer	Purpose	When and How to Use
K-W-L Chart (page 154)	To help students comprehend a nonfiction selection	*Before Reading:* 1. Identify the topic for students. 2. Have students write what they already **know** about it in the *K* column. 3. Have them write what they **want** to find out in the *W* column. *During Reading:* 4. Have students record what they **learn** in the *L* column.
Q & A Notetaking Chart (page 155)	To help student memorize key facts in a nonfiction selection	*During Reading:* 1. Tell students that as they read they should turn each heading or main idea into a question and write it in column 1. *After Reading:* 2. Have students answer the questions they wrote without opening their books. 3. Have students reread the selection to find answers to any questions they could not answer.
Concept Web (page 156)	To guide students to think of related words or concepts	*Before Reading:* Have students form small groups. List key concepts or vocabulary words on the board. Ask students to discuss meanings, fill out a web for each concept or word by writing it in the center of the web, and then writing related terms in the ovals around the center.
Reflection Chart (page 157)	To help students stop and think about key points or events	*During Reading:* 1. Ask students to note important or interesting passages in the left column. 2. Have them record in the right column their thoughts about each passage noted.
Event Log (page 158)	To help students keep track of story events	*During Reading:* 1. Have students list each event as they read about it. *After Reading:* 2. Students should use the list to give an oral retelling or summary of the selection.

Graphic Organizer	Purpose	When and How to Use
Story Frames (page 159)	To help students summarize story events	*After Reading:* 1. Ask students to draw sketches of key events in the selection. 2. Have them use the sketches to retell the selection orally.
Plot Diagram (page 160)	To help students classify events as being part of the exposition, rising action, climax, or falling action	*After Reading:* 1. Review the terms *exposition, rising action, climax,* and *falling action* with students. 2. Encourage students to use the diagram to list the events that form each of these plot phases.
Character Profile Chart (page 161)	To help students identify character attributes	*During or After Reading:* Have students write the character's name at the center and then list qualities and behaviors that exemplify these qualities in the surrounding boxes.
New Word Diagram (page 162)	To help students understand new vocabulary they encounter	*During or After Reading:* 1. Have students write a new word in the box at the top of the diagram. 2. Encourage them to think of—or look in the dictionary for—synonyms and antonyms of the word and record them in the appropriate boxes. 3. Ask students to think of real people or characters they've read about who they associate with the concept of the word. They can then add the names to the diagram.
Reading Log (page 163)	To encourage students to keep track of what they read	*After Reading:* Have students record on this form each selection they read during the year. Review the form periodically with students.

Topic: _____

K What I Know	W What I Want to Find Out	L What I Learn

Turn the Heading or Main Idea of Each Passage into a Question	Write a Detailed Answer Here
1.	
2.	
3.	
4.	
5.	
6.	
7.	

Quotation or Paraphrase from Text (include page number)	Thoughts About It

Event 1
Event 2
Event 3
Event 4
Event 5
Event 6
Event 7
Event 8
Event 9
Event 10

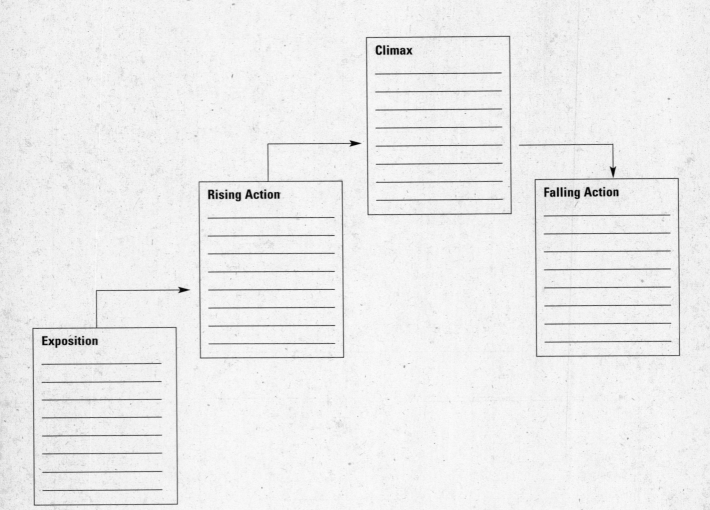

Quality: _____
Example: _____
_____
_____
_____

Quality: _____
Example: _____
_____
_____
_____

Quality: _____
Example: _____
_____
_____
_____

_____
Character's Name

Quality: _____
Example: _____
_____
_____
_____

Quality: _____
Example: _____
_____
_____
_____

Quality: _____
Example: _____
_____
_____
_____

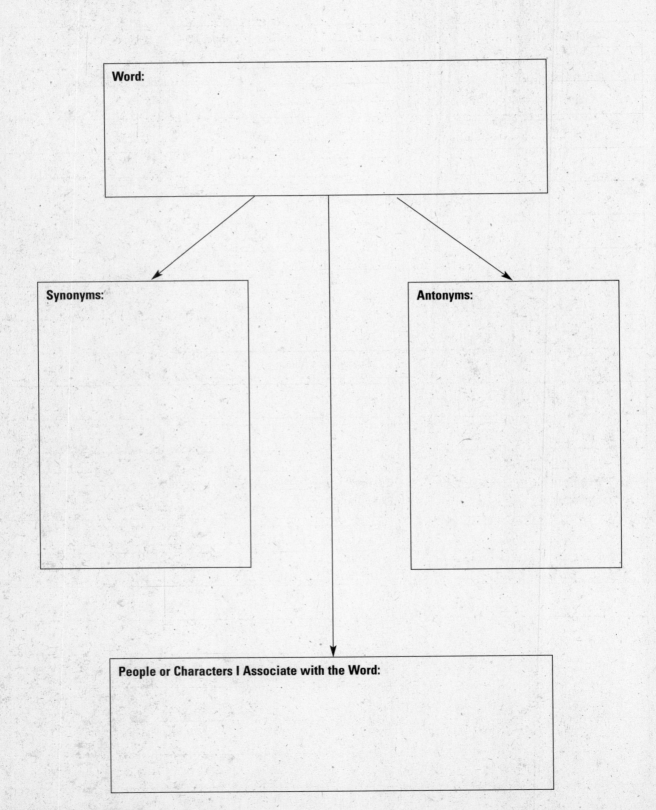

Word:

Synonyms:

Antonyms:

People or Characters I Associate with the Word:

Selection Title	Type of Literature	Date Finished	Reactions

Answer Key

This key answers all questions asked in *The InterActive Reader Plus*, *The InterActive Reader Plus with Additional Support*, and *The InterActive Reader Plus for English Learners*. Pause & Reflect answers have parenthetical notes (Plus, AS, or EL) as necessary to indicate the books to which they apply.

Raymond's Run, page 2
Connect to Your Life, page 2
Answers may include points similar to the following: *I liked the experience because* I played games with my little brother; *The experience was challenging because* my brother would not listen to me.

Key to the Story, page 2
Answers may include points similar to the following:
- learned to pay better attention
- improved in basketball
- learned to be more patient

Reread, page 4
She is the fastest runner.

Mark It Up, page 5
short legs, freckles

Reading Check, page 5
She keeps Raymond on the inside to prevent him from stepping off of the curb or running into the street.

Pause & Reflect, page 6 (Plus)
1. proud, competitive
2. It's hard work to take care of Raymond.

Pause & Reflect, page 6 (AS and EL)
proud, competitive

Pause & Reflect, page 7
Different: Cynthia does not let people know she practices piano. Squeaky does let people know she practices running and spelling. *Similar:* Both practice a lot.

Reader's Success Strategy, page 7
Gretchen: the new girl, the leader of the group, freckle-face; *Mary-Louise:* formerly friends with Squeaky, now hangs out with Gretchen and talks about Squeaky like a dog; *Rosie:* fat, big-mouth where Raymond is concerned

Pause & Reflect, page 9
1. angry
2. Squeaky is the best runner. Nobody should mess with Raymond.

Reread, page 10
Possible response: All Squeaky cares about is running.

Reading Check, page 10
She puts Raymond in the swings, looks for Mr. Pearson to get her race number, and also looks for Gretchen.

Reading Check, page 11
She thinks that he doesn't have the right to call her Squeaky unless she has the right to call him Beanstalk.

Pause & Reflect, page 12 (Plus)
1. jam-packed
2. Mr. Pearson wants Squeaky to let Gretchen win the race.

Pause & Reflect, page 12 (AS and EL)
Mr. Pearson wants Squeaky to let Gretchen win the race.

Reader's Success Strategy, page 13
Squeaky: "get up and slip off my sweatpants" (lines 284–285); "get into place" (line 287); *Gretchen:* "standing at the starting line, kicking her legs out like a real pro" (lines 285–286); *Raymond:* "on line on the other side of the fence, bending down with his fingers on the ground just like he knew what he was doing" (lines 287–289)

Reread, page 13
Drawings should show Squeaky flying over a sandy beach.

Pause & Reflect, page 14
1. Possible details: feels like she's in a dream, imagines she's flying, remembers the smell of apples, thinks about when she was little, imagines a beach, tells herself she must win, looks to see if other racers are near, notices Raymond's run.
2. Raymond runs alongside Squeaky in his own style.

Reading Check, page 15
She realizes that Raymond could be a successful runner.

Pause & Reflect, page 16
1. *For Raymond:* She plans a new career as his running coach. *For herself:* She can become a star in spelling and in playing the piano as well as running.
2. Possible response: I think Squeaky and Gretchen will become friends and that Squeaky will learn to appreciate Raymond more.

Challenge, page 16
Possible response: Squeaky's new understanding of both herself and Raymond is the result of her pride in Raymond's running ability.

Active Reading SkillBuilder, page 17
(Possible responses are provided.)
What Happens: Effect Squeaky takes Raymond walking on Broadway.
Why It Happens: Cause She needs to practice her breathing exercises for the big race.
What Happens: Effect Raymond walks on the inside close to the buildings.
Why It Happens: Cause He might get hurt if he were to walk along the outside curb.
What Happens: Effect Squeaky gets angry with Gretchen, Mary Louise, and Rosie.
Why It Happens: Cause They begin to make fun of Raymond.
What Happens: Effect Squeaky jumps up and down with joy when she sees Raymond at the end of the race.
Why It Happens: Cause She is proud of Raymond because he, too, is a great runner.

Literary Analysis SkillBuilder, page 18
(Possible responses are provided.)
Rising Action
- Squeaky takes Raymond for a walk on Broadway.
- Squeaky tells Gretchen, Mary Louise, and Rosie that she is going to win the big race.
- When the race begins, Raymond runs it too, on the other side of the fence.

Climax
While waiting for the judges' decision about who won the race, Squeaky realizes that Raymond would make a fine runner.

Falling Action
- Squeaky decides that she can be good at things other than running.
- Squeaky is named the winner of the race.
- Gretchen and Squeaky exchange smiles of respect.

Words to Know SkillBuilder, page 19

A. 1. relay   **B.** 1. clutch
    2. clutch   2. sidekick
    3. prodigy   3. periscope
    4. sidekick   4. prodigy
    5. periscope   5. relay

A Mother in Mannville, page 20
Connect to Your Life, page 20
Possible responses are provided. *Lonely:* scary, no one there to help me; *Alone:* peaceful, enjoy the quiet

Key to the Story, page 20
Responses may include points similar to the following: not enough food, clothes with holes, strict teachers

Pause & Reflect, page 23
1. high in the Carolina mountains
2. winter: deep snowdrifts, swirling snow, dense fog; spring: a carpet of pink and white laurel; autumn: flaming maples

Reread, page 24
Although Jerry is small, he has chopped as much wood as a man.

Mark It Up, page 25
It is bedded on courage, but it is more than brave. It is honest, but it is more than honesty.

Reading Check, page 26
She gave him items such as candy and apples as a reward for his thoughtfulness.

Pause & Reflect, page 26
1. hard-working
2. Possible response: When the ax handle breaks, Jerry insists on paying for it. On his own, he decides to stock kindling for the narrator.

Reading Check, page 27
The narrator returns to the cabin at noon on Monday.

Pause & Reflect, page 28
1. Fog prevents her from driving at night.
2. The next morning, he gives the dog part of his own breakfast.

Reader's Success Strategy, page 29
"Why are you not with her? How can she let you go away again?" (lines 238–239); "I must not condemn her without knowing" (lines 252–253)

Pause & Reflect, page 30
1. When Jerry tells the narrator that he has a mother, the narrator feels angry.
2. how she could bear to give him up

Reread, page 31
The narrator becomes distracted by her work.

Reading Check, page 32
Miss Clark doesn't know where he is; he did not eat his lunch; he went off by himself into the laurel; he did not fire the boiler as he was supposed to.

Pause & Reflect, page 32
1. At the end of the story, the narrator finds out that Jerry does not have a mother.
2. Possible response: I thought all along that he was making her up so I was not surprised.

Challenge, page 32
Possible response: Jerry does not want the narrator to feel sorry for him. Jerry wants a mother so badly that he invents one.

Active Reading SkillBuilder, page 33
Students' drawings should show that the woodpile leans against the back of the cabin. The woods stand near the cabin (and probably elsewhere, as well). The stoop should be located at ground level in front of the cabin door; the stone walk leads to that door; the hill stands between the farm and the cabin. The hill may be located near the orphanage farm. The fields of laurel and the mountains may be in the background, and Mannville may be off in the distance.

Literary Analysis SkillBuilder, page 34
Possible responses are provided.
Detail from the Story: The fireplace seems to be the sole source of heat in the cabin.
Inference: This seems to put the story in the past, because today the writer would be likely to bring along a portable electric heater.
Detail from the Story: The woman drives a car.
Inference: This rules out the distant past.
Detail from the Story: The writer pays the boy 10 cents an hour.
Inference: The low hourly rate might indicate a time early in this century.
Detail from the Story: A pair of gloves can be purchased for a dollar.
Inference: This seems to confirm that the time period is early in the 20th century.
Follow Up: The mood is peaceful and somber. The mood is affected by the isolation and the beauty of the mountains. The writer needs an isolated place in which to work, and the high mountains satisfy that need. A cottage on the seashore might also be a suitable setting for the story.

Words to Know SkillBuilder, page 35

A.
1. impel
2. inadequate
3. instinctive
4. blunt
5. kindling
6. ecstasy

B.
1. communion
2. predicated
3. abstracted
4. clarity

The Ransom of Red Chief, page 36

Connect to Your Life, page 36

In the first box students may write that they planned an outdoor activity. In the second box they may write that it rained the day their activity was planned.

Key to the Story, page 36

Possible responses: bribe, kidnapped, stolen, criminal

Reading Check, page 38

Love for one's children is strong in semi-rural communities. Summit is not within the radius of newspapers that send out reporters to stir up talk about such things. Summit couldn't go after the men with anything more than constables, lazy bloodhounds, or a condemnation in the Weekly Farmer's Budget.

Pause & Reflect, page 39 (Plus)

1. kidnap a boy
2. Possible responses: Yes, because they sound like experienced criminals. No, because the first sentence of the story is "It looked like a good thing; but wait till I tell you."

Pause & Reflect, page 39 (AS and EL)

kidnap a boy

Pause & Reflect, page 40 (Plus)

1. playful and violent
2. Red Chief kicked him.

Pause & Reflect, page 40 (AS and EL)

playful and violent

Reader's Success Strategy, page 41

He had a pet possum once. He had five puppies. His father has lots of money. He beat Ed Walker twice on Saturday. He does not like girls.

Reread, page 41

Students may say that the boy is a brat, imaginative, badly behaved, aggressive, or playful.

Pause & Reflect, page 42 (Plus)

1. He enjoys it.
2. He is having bad dreams about the boy.

Pause & Reflect, page 42 (AS and EL)

He enjoys it.

Reading Tip, page 43

rowdy—rough and noisy

dote on—love

reconnoiter—observe

Reread, page 43

Bill sees himself and Sam as the wolves who have kidnapped the "tender lambkin" (Red Chief), and he realizes the boy is going to give them more trouble than they imagined.

Pause & Reflect, page 44 (Plus)

1. Red Chief tries to scalp Bill.
2. afraid

Pause & Reflect, page 44 (EL)

Red Chief tries to scalp Bill

Pause & Reflect, page 45 (Plus)

1. People aren't searching for the boy.
2. He is afraid of being left alone with the boy.

Pause & Reflect, page 45 (AS and EL)

He thinks the boy's family doesn't know he's missing.

Reading Check, page 46

Bill does not want to be left alone with Red Chief.

Pause & Reflect, page 47

1. They want a messenger to bring a reply to a box at the bottom of a fence post.
2. He wants to get rid of the boy as soon as possible and he thinks it wouldn't be human for anybody to pay two thousand dollars for the "forty-pound chunk of freckled wildcat."

Reading Check, page 48

Red Chief wants Bill to play the horse.

Pause & Reflect, page 49 (Plus)

1. You are the hoss [horse]. (line 312)
2. to get some information and post the letter

Pause & Reflect, page 49 (AS and EL)

to get some information and post the letter

Reader's Success Strategy, page 50

Possible response: Sam, you might think that I'm a disloyal person, but I could not help myself. I am a grown person with instincts to defend myself, but I could not control the boy. I sent him home. The plan is off. There have been many people who would suffer death before giving up their profits, but they were not tortured as severely as I have been. I tried to stick to our plan, but I had to give up.

Reading Check, page 50

Bill thinks the boy has gone home.

Pause & Reflect, page 51 (Plus)

1. rides on his back; asks him puzzling questions; kicks him
2. Behind him was the kid, stepping. . . ; The kid stopped about eight feet behind him. (lines 348–351)

Pause & Reflect, page 51 (AS and EL)

rides on his back; asks him puzzling questions; kicks him

Reader's Success Strategy, page 52

8:30—hiding in the tree; 9:30—comes down from the tree to get the note; 10:00—back at the cave; 12:00—knocking on Ebenezer's door to return the boy

Reread, page 52 or 53

He thinks that the neighbors might get angry if they realize that the boy is coming home.

Reading Check, page 53

Sam and Bill pay the boy's father two hundred and fifty dollars to take back the boy.

Pause & Reflect, page 54

1. sorry his adventure is over; exhausted

2. Students may say that they thought the ending was humorous because the two men had to pay the father to finally get rid of the boy. They may say that the way Bill ran away from Summit was also funny.

Challenge, page 54

Students may say that the first twist comes when the boy turns out to be so difficult to handle that the kidnappers become his victims (lines 102–126). Students may also point out that Bill was surprised no one was searching for the boy. Another twist comes when the boy's father offers to accept cash from the kidnappers for taking the boy off their hands (lines 425–436).

Active Reading SkillBuilder, page 55

(Sample responses are provided.)

My Prediction: The boy will say no when the kidnappers offer to take him home.

Actual Event: He said he was having too much fun to go home.

Surprised? No.

My Prediction: Mr. Dorset will agree to the kidnappers' demands.

Actual Event: He does not.

Surprised? Yes.

My Prediction: The kidnappers will pay Mr. Dorset to get rid of the boy.

Actual Event: They pay Mr. Dorset.

Surprised? No.

Literary Analysis SkillBuilder, page 56

(Sample responses are provided.)

What We Expect: How we expect the kidnappers to behave: They will be tough; they'll be mean and will bully the boy.

What Happens: The boy is tough; he is mean and bullies the kidnappers.

Effect on the Reader: Surprise. The kidnappers seem comical.

What We Expect: How we expect Red Chief to react to the kidnapping: He'll be scared, cry, and want to go home.

What Happens: He has fun; he wants to stay.

Effect on the Reader: Interest and amusement; curiosity about what will happen next.

What We Expect: How we expect Red Chief's father to react to the kidnapping: He'll do anything to get his son back.

What Happens: He demands payment to take his son off the kidnappers' hands.

Effect on the Reader: Amusement

Follow Up: Fancy words that the narrator uses include philoprogenitiveness, sturdy yeomanry, contiguous vicinity, and articles of depredation. On page 43, Sam refers to Red Chief as a "lambkin," which is really the opposite of how he views the boy.

Words to Know SkillBuilder, page 57

A. **1.** diatribe
2. impudent
3. palatable
4. commend
5. surreptitiously

B. **1.** collaborate
2. pervade
3. ransom
4. proposition
5. comply

C. **1.** surreptitiously
2. ransom
3. impudent
4. comply
5. palatable

The King of Mazy May, page 58

Connect to Your Life, page 58

Students may say that once they climbed a tree to rescue a kitten and that the kitten's owners were very grateful.

Key to the Story, page 58

Students should shade in the Yukon territory shown on the map.

Pause & Reflect, page 60

1. kind and brave

2. "talk big" with the men (line 20); make bread (line 22); shoot a moose (line 23)

Reread, page 61

People were finding more and more gold in the Mazy May.

Pause & Reflect, page 62 (Plus)

1. Loren Hall's claim might be jumped.

2. steal someone's claim

Pause & Reflect, page 62 (AS and EL)

Loren Hall's claim might be jumped.

Reading Check, page 63

The Irishman means that the creek is very rich with gold.

Mark It Up, page 63

". . . rest the dogs a bit, and then hit the trail as hard as we can."

Pause & Reflect, page 64

1. They realize that Loren Hall has struck gold, and his claim has not been recorded.

2. He may try to stop them.

Reread, page 66

"He was almost breathless with suspense" (line 184); "The creek bank was high and he could not see the men. . . ." (lines 186–188); "his heart beating wildly, and watched the snow rim of the bank above him" (lines 190–191).

Pause & Reflect, page 66 (Plus)

1. 4, 2, 3, 1

2. Students should write either a prediction, summary, or question.

Pause & Reflect, page 66 (AS and EL)

4, 2, 3, 1

Pause & Reflect, page 67

1. bitter cold; shots fired at him; a crooked trail

2. two river islands; mighty Yukon; twilight; great white sea of frozen stillness; breathing of the dogs; churn of the sled.

Reading Check, page 68

Whenever he feels very cold he jumps off the sled and runs behind until he regains warmth.

Reread, page 69

To change dogs he would have to stop the sled; he does not have a moment to spare.

Pause & Reflect, page 70

1. The wrong dog is leading.

2. getting shot

Reading Check, page 71

The bad lead dog was shot and a better lead dog has taken his place.

Pause & Reflect, page 72 (Plus)

1. finds Loren Hall.

2. Students may say that they thought that the men would overtake Walt.

Pause & Reflect, page 72 (AS and EL)

1. His brave actions protected the claims on the Mazy May and made the men of the Yukon proud.

2. Students may say that they thought that the men would overtake Walt.

Challenge, page 72

Students may find it suspenseful when Walt escapes with the sled (lines 179–191). Others may point to the suspenseful moment when one of the stampeders leaps for the sled (lines 192–193). Others may point to the chase near Rosebud Creek when the stampeders began to shoot at Walt (lines 300–314).

Mark It Up, page 72

Students' drawings should include a plan of Walt's route, including the Mazy May Creek and the Yukon River.

Active Reading SkillBuilder, page 73

(Sample responses are provided.)

Question: Will Walt make it to his destination without freezing? Will his pursuers catch up with him?

Visualize: Imagine Walt sitting in a sled pulled by sled dogs. Imagine him jumping off and running alongside of it for a while to stay warm, then jumping back on the sled. Imagine him looking back to see the claim-jumpers behind him, also on a sled pulled by dogs.

Connect: Walt's experience sounds something like going skiing or snowshoeing in really cold weather.

Predict: Walt seems to know a lot about how to survive in the Arctic, but so do his pursuers. I predict that the pursuers will catch up to him, but that Walt will win out in the end.

Clarify: Walt is cold, so he runs alongside the sled to keep warm. Two men are chasing him in another sled.

Evaluate: The story is very suspenseful and full of adventure. At this point, I just want to keep reading to see what will happen next.

Literary Analysis SkillBuilder, page 74

(Sample responses are provided.)

Passages About Walt:

- Walt was well able to stay by himself in the cabin, cook his three meals a day, and look after things.

- He had agreed to keep an eye on the adjoining claim of Loren Hall.

- He was only a boy, but in the face of the threatened injustice to Loren Hall he felt that he must do something.

Passages About Claim-Jumpers:

- He [Walt] had not watched them long before he was sure that they were professional stampeders, bent on jumping all the claims in sight.

- Walt crept along the snow at the rim of the creek and saw them change many stakes, destroy old ones, and set up new ones.

- Loren Hall had struck it rich and his claim was not yet recorded. It was plain that they were going to jump it.

Words to Know SkillBuilder, page 75

A.
1. prospector
2. commissioner
3. peer
4. liable
5. stampede
6. capsize
7. flounder
8. summit
9. antic
10. yaw

B. Accept responses that accurately use at least five Words to Know.

Mother to Son/Speech to the Young, page 76

Connect to Your Life, page 76

Students may provide answers such as: **Subject:** exercise; **Advice:** Try to walk whenever possible. **Subject:** television; **Advice:** Turn off the television and read books or get outside as much as you can.

Key to the Poems, page 76

Students may say that the sentences are directed to a listener and that some words are spelled the way they sound, and that the sentences use informal language.

Reader's Success Strategy, page 78

Possible responses: *Ain't been no* means "has not been a" in lines 2 and 20 and "has not been any" in line 13. *A-climbin'* means "climbing." *Set down* means "sit down."

Reading Check, page 78

No, the mother has faced many obstacles and difficulties in life.

Pause & Reflect, page 78 (Plus)

1. hard to climb

2. She is urging him not to give up on life, even though life may seem like a struggle.

Pause & Reflect, page 78 (AS and EL)

She is urging him not to give up on life, even though life may seem like a struggle.

Reader's Success Strategy, page 79

Each word pair uses imagery to describe negative people.

Read Aloud, page 79

to live in the present

Pause & Reflect, page 79 (Plus)

1. negative

2. Possible response: The speaker tells them to cheer up—life is not always dark and depressing.

3. to live in the present

Pause & Reflect, page 79 (AS and EL)

Possible response: The speaker tells them to cheer up—life is not always dark and depressing.

Active Reading SkillBuilder, page 80

(Sample responses are provided.)

Mother to Son

Clue: The speaker says that her life "ain't been no crystal stair."

Inference: She has had a hard life.

Clue: Her stairs have had tacks, splinters, and places with no carpet.

Inference: She has overcome obstacles, pain, and periods of desolation.

Clue: She kept climbing, even in the dark.

Inference: She has determination and courage.

Clue: Her advice is not to turn back or sit down or fall.

Inference: She is concerned for her son and wants to instill within him the desire to persevere.

Speech to the Young . . .

Clue: The title is "Speech to the Young . . ."

Inference: The speaker is someone older, with experience of life.

Clue: The speaker tells the young to reject the influence of negative people.

Inference: She believes that a positive attitude is necessary to succeed in life.

Clue: She tells the young to live in the present.

Inference: She has learned the value of appreciating the moment.

Literary Analysis SkillBuilder, page 81

(Sample responses are provided.)

Speaker in "Mother to Son": determined, encouraging, realistic, does not give up

Speaker in "Speech to the Young . . .": positive, appreciates the present

Common Qualities: caring, strong, wise, optimistic, sincere

Follow Up: Students may suggest that they would give their children similar advice.

Flowers for Algernon, page 82

Connect to Your Life, page 82

Students may respond to "Your hair looks weird that way" by expressing hurt feelings or anger. Students may respond humorously to "We can tell you're new around here."

Key to the Story, page 82

Students' answers should reveal how much they value intelligence.

Reader's Success Strategy, page 85

Students' time lines should include details similar to the following: March—takes tests that he doesn't understand; Algernon beats him in the maze race; has the operation; doesn't notice any change right away; listens to a TV for sleep-learning; returns to work; coworkers tease him but he doesn't realize it; April—continues to listen to the TV for sleep-learning; coworkers still tease him; beats Algernon; reads difficult books; learns spelling and punctuation; realizes that coworkers tease him; studies more subjects; understands the tests that he didn't understand before; coworkers treat him differently; forced to quit his job; May—level of intelligence becomes extremely advanced; intelligence is so advanced that he has difficulty communicating with people; realizes that he used to laugh at himself when people teased him; wants to use his gift to help others; June—predicts that his intelligence will deteriorate rapidly; begins forgetting things; can no longer understand books and articles that he read; does not want to see anyone; stays in bed for days at a time; decides to move to New York because he doesn't want to be around people that feel sorry for him

Pause & Reflect, page 85 (Plus)

1. wants to be smarter; is afraid of failing; is eager to please
2. can't see any pictures

Pause & Reflect, page 85 (AS and EL)

can't see any pictures

Read Aloud, page 86

Charlie is motivated and determined; he thinks the potential benefits of the experiment outweigh the risks.

Pause & Reflect, page 87 (Plus)

1. Algernon tries to get through the maze.
2. ashamed; worried

Pause & Reflect, page 87 (AS and EL)

1. Algernon
2. ashamed; worried

Reread, page 88

He is very motivated.

Reading Tip, page 88

intellectual, mentality, hostile, uncooperative, apathetic, achievement, comparatively, tremendous

Pause & Reflect, page 89 (Plus)

1. 3, 4, 2, 1
2. Student questions may include: Will Charlie get smarter? Will Miss Kinnian remain a friend? Will the doctors continue to disagree? Will Charlie be happier if the operation succeeds?

Pause & Reflect, page 89 (AS and EL)

3, 4, 2, 1

Pause & Reflect, page 90

1. frightened; superstitious
2. Possible responses: hate that mouse; got to play; take those tests over again; inkblots are stupid; pictures are stupid too; won't make up lies

Reading Check, page 91

Since Algernon had the same operation, it may indicate that Charlie has a good chance of achieving permanent results as well.

Reading Check, page 91

Joe Carp says, "what did they do Charlie put some brains in." Frank Reilly says, "what did you do Charlie forget your key and open your door the hard way." The men make these comments because they are teasing Charlie about the scars on his head.

Reread, page 92

They mean "did something stupid" or "made a mistake." By saying this they are making fun of Charlie's low mental ability.

Pause & Reflect, page 93

1. They laugh at him and make fun of him.
2. a TV for sleep-learning

Reader's Success Strategy or **Reading Tip,** page 94

Effect: Charlie passes out. *Effect:* A policeman finds him and brings him home.

Pause & Reflect, page 95 (Plus)
1. He shows them how he uses a mop to clean the toilet.
2. Charlie's friends encourage him to drink at the saloon. Charlie passes out. A policeman finds him and brings him home.

Pause & Reflect, page 95 (AS and EL)
He shows them how he uses a mop to clean the toilet.

Reading Check, page 95
Charlie feels sorry for Algernon because the mouse is being used in the same experiment and must pass a test to eat. He decides to treat the mouse as a friend rather than as a rival.

Pause & Reflect, page 96 (Plus)
1. Charlie is ashamed that Algernon, a mouse, has beaten him previously, and beating him will show that Charlie is progressing.
2. Charlie begins to feel sorry for the mouse, which is also being used in an experiment. He decides to treat the mouse as a friend rather than as a rival. Students may circle lines 385–388.

Pause & Reflect, page 96 (AS and EL)
Charlie is ashamed that Algernon, a mouse, has beaten him previously, and beating him will show that Charlie is progressing.

Reread, page 97 (Plus)
She feels sorry for Charlie and doesn't want him to see her crying.

Reread, page 97 (AS and EL)
She feels sorry for Charlie because he doesn't realize that his coworkers make fun of him.

Pause & Reflect, page 98 (Plus)
1. He had never before finished such a hard book.
2. spelling, punctuation

Pause & Reflect, page 98 (AS and EL)
He had never before finished such a hard book.

Reading Check, page 99
Charlie kept falling because people were purposely sticking out their feet to trip him.

Pause & Reflect, page 100 (Plus)
1. Possible response: He realizes that his friends only wanted to make fun of him.
2. Possible response: He feels ashamed.

Pause & Reflect, page 100 (AS and EL)
Possible response: He realizes that his friends only wanted to make fun of him.

Pause & Reflect, page 103 (Plus)
1. One sign that Charlie is getting smarter is that his punctuation and spelling have improved.
2. He understands the test this time and sees pictures.

Pause & Reflect, page 103 (AS and EL)
He understands the test this time and sees pictures.

Read Aloud, page 104
He is learning fast and can now analyze his doctors and their behavior.

Reread, page 105
Details may include: how beautiful Miss Kinnian really is; brown eyes; feathery brown hair that comes to the top of her neck; only thirty-four

Pause & Reflect, page 106 (Plus)
1. this was only the beginning; I knew what she meant about levels; leaving her behind made me sad
2. They are frightened of him: His friends at work; They are arguing about him: Dr. Strauss and Dr. Nemur; He is finding her more attractive: Miss Kinnian

Pause & Reflect, page 106 (AS and EL)
They are frightened of him: His friends at work; They are arguing about him: Dr. Strauss and Dr. Nemur; He is finding her more attractive: Miss Kinnian

Reread, page, 107
this was only the beginning; I knew what she meant about levels; leaving her behind made me sad

Pause & Reflect, page 107
1. The people at work want him to leave.
2. Some students may say that he was better off because he was happier and felt closer to the people around him. Other students may say that he was worse off because he did not know that his friends were making fun of him.

Reread, page 108
Responses may include: his elaborate long sentence structure; proper use of "Algernon and I," or words like "quite" and "sensation."

Pause & Reflect, page 110
1. He is not connecting with Miss Kinnian any more; he is alienated from everybody; he turns to books and music.
2. smarter than his doctors; rejected by his fellow workers; aware of his great intelligence

Reread, page 111
Possible response: ashamed and frightened

English Learner Support, page 111
Possible response: They were laughing at him because he was mentally retarded.

Reading Check, page 112
Charlie, like the boy, used to be unaware that people were making fun of him.

Reread, page 112
Possible response: When people laughed at him, he laughed along with them because he wanted to be accepted.

Reading Check, page 113
Charlie has a better understanding of himself and his feelings of inadequacy before the operation.

Pause & Reflect, page 113
1. scared; childlike
2. He knows that they are treating the boy the same way people used to treat him.

Reading Check, page 114
Charlie realizes that the results of the experiment are not permanent and his mental ability will soon begin to deteriorate.

English Learner Support, page 114
Possible response: I'm working too hard; a lifetime of research and thought into a few weeks

Reading Check, page 116
Algernon's mental ability is deteriorating, with symptoms such as memory loss and poor coordination.

Pause & Reflect, page 117 (Plus)
1. sleeps very little
2. T, F, T

Pause & Reflect, page 117 (AS and EL)
T, F, T

Pause & Reflect, page 119
1. becomes absent-minded; thinks of suicide; hides from people
2. Possible responses: Yes, because Charlie is not a mouse, he has more understanding of what is happening to him; No, because he can compare Algernon's situation to his own and watched the mouse deteriorate before death.

Reading Check, page 121
The doctor doesn't believe that Charlie used to be a genius.

Pause & Reflect, page 122 (Plus)
1. His family was wealthy.
2. He thinks that she will laugh at him.
3. Some students may say that questions they had about the experiment were answered. Other students may say they want to know what will happen to Charlie.

Pause & Reflect, page 122 (AS and EL)
1. His family was wealthy.
2. He thinks that she will laugh at him.

Reading Check, page 123
Charlie doesn't want to be around people that feel sorry for him.

Pause & Reflect, page 124
1. Charlie leaves Miss Kinnian. Charlie moves to New York. Charlie feels sad a lot.
2. Some students may say that Charlie is very unhappy at the end of the story. Other students may say that he is happier at the end of the story because he learned many things.

Challenge, page 124
Students may say that Charlie would have had a lonely life because people would be afraid of him.

Active Reading Skillbuilder, page 125
(Sample responses are provided.)
Clue: Charlie says he wants to be smart.
Inference: Charlie knows he is different and wants to fit in with other people.
Clue: Charlie goes to night school to get smarter. Miss Kinnian says he is her best student.
Inference: Charlie possesses determination and is motivated to learn despite his limitations.
Clue: Charlie considers Joe and Frank his friends even though they make fun of him.
Inference: Before the operation, Charlie is innocent and trusting.
Clue: Charlie's journal entry of April 20 tells how sick he feels at realizing what Joe and Frank have been doing to him.

Inference: His new level of intelligence has made him aware of people's flaws and has eroded his innocence.
Clue: Charlie has trouble communicating with Miss Kinnian even when he keeps the conversation on an everyday level.
Inference: He will be as lonely and isolated with his new intelligence as he was before the operation.
Clue: Charlie researches day and night after the symptoms of Algernon's deterioration become apparent.
Inference: Charlie is frightened of becoming what he was before the operation.

Literary Analysis SkillBuilder, page 126
(Sample responses are provided.)
Physical Description: Charlie is 37 years old.
Charlie's Thoughts, Action, and Speech:
- "Their going to use me! Im so exited I can hardly rite."
- Charlie says that Frank and Joe are his best friends.
- "Now I know what it means when they say 'to pull a Charlie Gordon.' I'm ashamed."
- Charlie gets angry at people's treatment of the mentally challenged boy in the restaurant.
- Charlie buries Algernon in his backyard and puts flowers on his grave.
- "Oh, God, please don't take it all away."
- "Im going someplace where nobody knows Charlie Gordon was a genus and now he cant even reed a book or rite good."

Other Characters' Thoughts, Actions, and Speech About Charlie:
- Miss Kinnian says that Charlie is her best night school student.
- Dr. Strauss and Dr. Nemur say that Charlie has good motivation for a person with an IQ of 68.
- Frank and Joe enjoy making a fool of Charlie by playing tricks on him.
- The workers at the factory sign a petition to get rid of Charlie when he becomes intelligent.
- Miss Kinnian looks as if she is scared to see Charlie after the operation.
- Dr. Nemur is intimidated by Charlie's intelligence.

Other Characters' Direct Comments About Charlie:
- "Charlie you don't know it yet but your getting smarter all the time."
- Miss Kinnian says to Charlie, "I have confidence in you. . . ."
- "You used to be a good, dependable, ordinary man—not too bright maybe, but honest. Who knows what you done to yourself to get so smart all of a sudden."

Follow Up: Possible response: Insight into Charlie's thoughts helps increase the sense of tragedy. The reader is more aware of Charlie's intellectual awakening and the contrast between what he was and what he becomes. Charlie's thoughts also bring out themes of the story, such as the fact that people who are different are often rejected or ridiculed by others.

Words to Know SkillBuilder, page 127

A.
1. shrew
2. opportunist
3. absurd
4. specialization
5. introspective
6. tangible
7. syndrome
8. statistically
9. proportional
10. impair
11. regression
12. hypothesis
13. sensation
14. vacuous
15. naïveté

B. The boxed letters spell out *his intelligence.*

The Bet, page 128

Connect to Your Life, page 128

(Possible responses are provided.)

Issue: pollution; **What I Believe:** I think that people should drive less and walk more.

Key to the Story, page 128

voluntary: chosen; enforced: obliged

Reader's Success Strategy or **Reading Tip,** page 130

Sample answers are provided.

Past Events: banker and lawyer make a bet; lawyer spends prison time in banker's house reading many books; *Current Action:* banker regrets making the bet; banker decides to kill lawyer to avoid paying bet; banker reads lawyer's letter

Pause & Reflect, page 131

1. "Execution kills instantly; life imprisonment kills by degrees."
2. Some students may support the banker, while others may support the lawyer.

Reading Check, page 131

They bet two millions that the lawyer won't stay in prison for fifteen years.

Reading Check, page 132

The banker has a lot of money and two millions are nothing to him; the lawyer will lose the best years of his life; the prison time will be more difficult for the lawyer because he will be there voluntarily.

Reread, page 132

The banker thinks that the bet was foolish. Most students will probably agree that the bet was foolish.

Reading Check, page 132

He will communicate by sending notes through a little window.

Pause & Reflect, page 133 (Plus)

1. The lawyer will lose the bet if he leaves the prison before 15 years have passed.
2. Possible responses: Yes, because the lawyer wants to prove his point. No, because no one would choose to stay in prison for 15 years.

Pause & Reflect, page 133 (AS and EL)

The lawyer will lose the bet if he leaves the prison before 15 years have passed.

Reader's Success Strategy, page 133

1870: plays the piano; reads comedies, love stories, crime and fantasy novels; 1871: doesn't play piano; reads only classics; 1874: plays the piano; often does nothing but eat, drink, and lie around; doesn't read; sometimes writes; 1875–1879: studies languages, philosophy, and history; 1880: reads only the New Testament; 1881: reads history of religions and theology; 1883–1885: reads varied subjects such as chemistry, medicine, novels, Shakespeare, philosophy, theology

Reading Check, page 134

The lawyer asked that two shots be fired if his letter, which was written in six different languages, did not contain any mistakes.

Pause & Reflect, page 135 (Plus)

1. reads many books
2. He seems to be ordering books at random.

Pause & Reflect, page 135 (AS and EL)

reads many books

Read Aloud, page 135

The banker is afraid that he will become poor when the lawyer wins the bet. The banker fears he will be forced to depend on the lawyer for money.

Pause & Reflect, page 136

1. He plans to kill the lawyer and let the watchman take the blame.
2. Possible details: "The garden was dark and cold. It was raining. . . . Someone's bed, with no bedclothes on it, stood there, and an iron stove was dark in the corner."

Pause & Reflect, page 138 (Plus)

1. Possible response: The lawyer has suffered terribly during his imprisonment.
2. Possible response: I would feel sorry for him.

Pause & Reflect, page 138 (AS and EL)

Possible response: I would feel sorry for him.

Reread, page 139

Possible response: He scorns the way human beings live their lives and thinks that they are crazy. He does not want to understand them.

Pause & Reflect, page 140

1. He wants to show how little value he puts on money.
2. 4, 2, 3, 1

Challenge, page 140

Sample answer: Although both men change, perhaps the lawyer changes more.

Active Reading SkillBuilder, page 141

(Sample responses are provided.)

1. November 14, 1870: During a dinner party, a banker and a young lawyer enter into a bet. The banker must pay the lawyer two millions if the lawyer is able to remain imprisoned for 15 years.
2. First year of imprisonment: Lawyer plays piano and reads light novels.
3. Second year of imprisonment: Lawyer stops playing piano and reads classics.
4. Second half of sixth year: Prisoner studies languages, philosophy, and history.
5. After tenth year: Lawyer sits without moving and reads the New Testament.
6. Last two years of confinement: Prisoner reads haphazardly.

7. 1885: The night before the agreement comes due, the banker considers murdering the prisoner. He enters the cell and finds the prisoner slumped over a handwritten note.

8. 1885: The day on which the agreement comes due, the prisoner forfeits the bet by leaving his cell before the allotted time is up.

Literary Analysis SkillBuilder, page 142
Time of the Flashback: The night before the bet is to be fulfilled
Event Flashback Refers To: Terms of the bet
Time of the Flashback: The night before the bet is to be fulfilled
Event Flashback Refers To: Lawyer's years of imprisonment
Follow Up: Students may note that the flashback technique allows the events of 15 years to be reviewed quickly, because the banker is recollecting only the highlights. The most important events are those that happen during the last few hours of the bet, and they become the focus.

Words to Know SkillBuilder, page 143
A. 1. capricious
    2. posterity
    3. stipulated
    4. haphazardly
    5. humane
B. 1. immoral
    2. incessantly
    3. rapture
    4. obsolete
    5. renunciation
C. Accept responses that accurately use at least one Word to Know per sentence.

The Treasure of Lemon Brown, page 144
Connect to Your Life, page 144
Possible responses: collect canned food; collect money; talk about the causes and solutions
Key to the Story, page 144
Possible responses: **1.** We hunted for the treasure. **2.** riches; The box was filled with riches. **3.** valuable; The treasure chest was filled with many valuable objects.
Reread, page 146
Greg's grades haven't been good enough.
Pause & Reflect, page 147 (Plus)
1. His father won't let him join the basketball team unless he spends more time studying math.
2. "He stood to go upstairs, thought of the lecture that probably awaited him if he did anything except shut himself in his room with his math book . . ."
Pause & Reflect, page 147 (AS and EL)
"He stood to go upstairs, thought of the lecture that probably awaited him if he did anything except shut himself in his room with his math book . . ."
Reread, page 148
He is torn between what he wants to do and what his father wants him to do.
Pause & Reflect, page 149 (Plus and AS)
1. a broken couch
2. Students may say that they would feel frightened if they were Greg.

Pause & Reflect, page 149 (EL)
a broken couch
Mark It Up, page 150
an old man; black, heavily wrinkled face; halo of crinkly white hair and whiskers; layers of dirty coats; smallish frame; pants bagged to the knee; old shoes; rope for a belt
Reader's Success Strategy, page 150
Possible response: money, jewelry, something that has monetary value
Reading Check, page 151
He was a blues singer.
Read Aloud, page 151
They have similar hair and eyes.
Pause & Reflect, page 152 (Plus)
1. Students may say that he appears to be harmless although he is dirty and ragged.
2. He was a blues singer.
Pause & Reflect, page 152 (AS and EL)
Students may say that he appears to be harmless although he is dirty and ragged.
Reading Check, page 153
The men are looking for Lemon Brown's treasure.
Pause & Reflect, page 154 (Plus)
1. The men think that Lemon Brown has a valuable treasure.
2. Students may say that the men will beat Greg up if they find him.
Pause & Reflect, page 154 (AS and EL)
Students may say that the men will beat Greg up if they find him.
Reading Check, page 155
Greg helped scare the men away by howling.
Reading Check, page 155
Lemon Brown thinks the men will be too scared to come back.
Pause & Reflect, page 156 (Plus)
1. He swallowed hard, wet his lips once more, and howled as evenly as he could. (lines 278–279)
2. not come back
3. Possible response: Greg likes and trusts him.
Pause & Reflect, page 156 (AS and EL)
Possible response: Greg likes and trusts him.
Reading Check, page 157
Lemon Brown gave his harmonica to his son along with some newspaper clippings of reviews of his performances.
Reread, page 157
The items became Lemon Brown's treasure because they showed his accomplishments and symbolized a time when his family was happy and together. The treasure became more important to Lemon Brown after his son died and he realized that his son had treated the items like a treasure as well.
Pause & Reflect, page 158
1. He is proud of him.
2. Some students may feel that Greg has grown and matured through his association with Lemon Brown.

Challenge, page 158
Students may say that Greg realizes that his father has his best interests at heart, as summed up in the last three lines of the story.

Active Reading SkillBuilder, page 159
(Sample responses are provided.)
Event from the Story: Greg gets a letter from school, relating his poor schoolwork.
Event from My Life: This reminds me of a time when I didn't get good grades, and my parents weren't happy with me.
Event from Story: Greg wanders the streets to escape his dad's lecture.
Event from My Life: When I want to get away, I go into the woods behind my house and walk around.
Event from the Story: Greg hears about Lemon's treasure.
Event from My Life: My grandfather used to tell me great stories about his past, and he had a lot of newspaper clippings to show me.

Literary Analysis SkillBuilder, page 160
(Sample responses are provided.)
Character: Lemon Brown
Beginning of Story: homeless person who cares about his treasure more than anything else
End of Story: still homeless, still values his treasure
Static/Dynamic: Static
Character: Greg
Beginning of Story: self-centered teenage boy who wants to play basketball
End of Story: a more thoughtful young person who cares about Lemon and about his own father
Static/Dynamic: Dynamic
Follow Up: Possible response: Greg changes during the course of this story. After he gets to know Lemon and listens to his story, Greg begins to feel some compassion. I think Greg didn't really have a good relationship with his father, but hearing Lemon talk about his son makes Greg realize how lucky he is that his dad is around. I think Greg will have a better relationship with his father now because he will be more likely to listen to what he has to say. I think he will try harder in his schoolwork and may get to play basketball.

Words to Know SkillBuilder, page 161
A. 1. commence 6. beckon
2. tentatively 7. ajar
3. tremor 8. vault
4. ominous 9. probe
5. gnarled 10. impromptu

Stopping by Woods on a Snowy Evening, page 162
Connect to Your Life, page 162
Possible responses: blizzard, wet, shoveling, snowplow, quiet, sledding
Key to the Poem, page 162
He will not see me stopping here.
Reader's Success Strategy, page 164
He expresses concern about whose woods he is stopping by, his horse, and those with whom he has promises to keep.
Reading Check, page 164
The horse shakes his harness bells "to ask if there is some mistake," perhaps wondering why they have stopped and impatient to keep moving.
Mark It Up, page 165
Students' landscape sketches should accurately reflect the scene described in the poem.
Pause & Reflect, page 165
1. attracted
2. The speaker would like to stay longer but must continue the journey.
3. Possible response: "Frozen lake" and "darkest evening" make me think of a quiet and still place.

Active Reading SkillBuilder, page 166
(Possible responses are provided.)
Question: What is the setting?
Answer: darkest evening of the year, between the woods and frozen lake
Question: What is the reaction of the horse at stopping?
Answer: The horse shakes his harness bells.
Question: What is the conflict experienced by the speaker?
Answer: The speaker wants to stay in the woods, but he knows he must continue his journey.
Question: What might his journey represent?
Answer: life
Question: Where is the owner of the woods?
Answer: in the village
Question: When is the speaker's conflict resolved?
Answer: In the last stanza, the speaker decides to continue his journey and not to stay in the woods.
Question: Why does the speaker stop initially?
Answer: He is attracted to the woods, which are lovely, dark, and deep.
Question: Why does the speaker move on?
Answer: He has promises to keep and miles to go before he can sleep.

Literary Analysis SkillBuilder, page 167
bbcb, ccdc, dddd
Follow Up: Students might say he repeats the last line to emphasize the speaker's weariness and the length of his journey. The different rhyme scheme draws attention to the end of the poem.

Legacies, page 168

the drum, page 168

Choices, page 168

Connect to Your Life, page 168
Possible responses: *Things I Do for Myself:* read comic books, play video games; *Things I Do for Others:* wash dishes, mow the lawn

Key to the Poems, page 168
Students' symbols of independence may include an eagle, a lion, a cowboy, or the statue of liberty.

Reader's Success Strategy, page 170
"but the girl didn't want to learn how because she knew even if she couldn't say it that that would mean when the old one died she would be less dependent on her spirit" (lines 5–10); "neither of them ever said what they meant and I guess nobody ever does" (lines 17–19)

Reading Check, page 170
The little girl wants to remain dependent on her grandmother.

Pause & Reflect, page 170 (Plus)
1. The little girl wants to remain dependent on her grandmother.
2. She can't say what she really feels.

Pause & Reflect, page 170 (AS and EL)
She can't say what she really feels.

Reading Check, page 171
The speaker's father says, "the world is a drum tight and hard." The speaker replies, "I'm gonna beat out my own rhythm."

Reader's Success Strategy, page 171
Possible response: by behaving and thinking independently

Pause & Reflect, page 171
1. confident
2. independence

Reading Check, page 172
The speaker feels that it is her task to avoid doing what she does not want to do.

Reader's Success Strategy, page 172
Students should highlight lines 1, 9, 17, and 24.

Reread, page 172
The speaker tells herself to be satisfied.

Pause & Reflect, page 173
1. Students' should place a star next to one of the choices described in the poem.
2. frustrated, sad
3. Perhaps she wanted to express her opinion that human beings must learn to be satisfied with the limited choices they have in life.

Challenge, page 173
(Students should identify the theme of their favorite poem and underline passages that support their opinions.)

Active Reading SkillBuilder, page 174
(Possible responses are provided.)
"Legacies": to express an opinion
"the drum": to express an opinion
"Choices": to inform; to express an opinion

Students may choose other possible author purposes as long as they can explain their reasoning.

Literary Analysis SkillBuilder, page 175
(Possible responses are provided.)

"Legacies"
Little Girl: Yes, ma'am?
Grandmother: I want you to learn to make rolls.
Little Girl: I don't want to make rolls! I want to be dependent on your spirit when you are gone because I will miss you so much.
Grandmother: Lord, these children. I don't understand them and they don't understand me.

"Choices"
Speaker: I know I can't control everything in life—I can control only my own feelings.
Friend: What do you mean?
Speaker: I can work with what I do have and face situations with strength and a positive attitude.
Friend: Will emotions get in the way?
Speaker: No, emotions will save me. They will help me deal with situations I cannot control.

The Diary of Anne Frank, page 176
Connect to Your Life, page 176
Possible response: violence in schools

Preview, page 178
Born Into Danger: She was Jewish and faced persecution by the Nazis.
The Nazis in Power: Hitler blamed the Jews for the depression.
Trapped in Holland: In 1940, Germany invaded Holland.
A Life in Hiding: They hid in the "Secret Annex," a small attic area.
Discovery and Death: Except for Mr. Frank, all residents of the Secret Annex died.

Read Aloud, page 180
Miep Gies and Mr. Kraler do not live in the Secret Annex. They are workers in Mr. Frank's business.

Reader's Success Strategy, page 180
Students' diagrams should show the three rooms and small attic space of the Secret Annex. The largest room should be in the center, and a door to the bathroom should be labeled on the right. Students may label the stairwell and entrance to the Secret Annex off of the closet-sized room on the left. Diagrams might also show the rooftops and church tower in the background.

Pause & Reflect, page 181 (Plus)
1. the top floor of a warehouse and office building in Amsterdam, Holland
2. a bookcase

Pause & Reflect, page 181 (AS and EL)
the top floor of a warehouse and office building in Amsterdam, Holland

Answer Key (continued)

Reading Check, page 182
Amsterdam has too many painful memories for Mr. Frank.

Reread, page 183
Monday, the sixth of July, 1942; three years earlier

Pause & Reflect, page 184 (Plus)
1. Miep Gies
2. Possible responses: distraught, comforted

Pause & Reflect, page 184 (AS and EL)
Possible responses: distraught, comforted

Pause & Reflect, page 185 (Plus)
1. Jews were not allowed to own businesses, ride bikes, go to Dutch schools, ride in automobiles, ride in streetcars.
2. The Franks went into hiding.

Pause & Reflect, page 185 (AS and EL)
Jews were not allowed to own businesses, ride bikes, go to Dutch schools, ride in automobiles, ride in streetcars.

Reader's Success Strategy, page 185
The Franks and the Van Daans move into the Secret Annex. (July, 1942)

Reading Check, page 186 (AS)
Mrs. Van Daan is worried that the Franks have been stopped by the police because they have not arrived on time.

Reading Check, page 186 (EL)
The Franks are late because they took side streets to avoid the police.

Reading Check, page 188
They will be bringing the residents food and news each day.

Reading Check, page 189
They must have looked suspicious with Petronella walking down the street wearing a fur coat in July and Peter carrying a cat.

Reread, page 189
Possible response: never going outside and not being able to move around or make noise during the daytime

Pause & Reflect, page 190
1. Possible responses: Mr. Van Daan—late forties, tall, well dressed; Mrs. Frank—young, gentle, reserved; Mr. Frank—confident; Anne Frank—13 years old, lively; Margot Frank—beautiful, quiet, shy
2. tense

Reading Check, page 191
Mr. Van Daan helped Mr. Frank adjust when Mr. Frank first immigrated to the Netherlands.

Read Aloud, page 192
Possible response: She is friendly and outgoing.

Reader's Success Strategy, page 193
Similar: They both like cats. They both went to the same school.
Different: Anne is outgoing and has a lot of friends. Peter is quiet and likes to be alone.

Reading Check, page 193
He can not be forced to wear it now that he is in hiding.

Reading Check, page 194
They left dishes in the sink and beds unmade.

Reread, page 194
She cannot throw it away because it is a symbol of Judaism.

Pause & Reflect, page 195
1. Anne was more popular, and Peter was more of a loner.
2. Possible responses: Yes, because they need each other in this difficult time. No, because they are very different and will not get along.

Reread, page 196 (Plus)
She is overjoyed.

Reread, page 196 (AS and EL)
Even though we are locked away from the outside world, no one can put a lock on our thoughts and minds.

Reading Check, page 197
They freeze in fear that someone downstairs has heard him.

Reader's Success Strategy, page 198
Students should label the room on the right as Anne and Margot's room. Peter's room should be labeled as the room on the left. Mr. and Mrs. Frank sleep in the middle room and Mr. and Mrs. Van Daan sleep in the attic room.

Reading Check, page 198
According to Mr. Frank, they would suffer the same fate as the Franks.

Pause & Reflect, page 199 (Plus)
1. Possible response: Even though we are locked away from the outside world, no one can put a lock on our thoughts and minds.
2. She dislikes it and feels afraid.

Pause & Reflect, page 199 (AS and EL)
She dislikes it and feels afraid.

Reader's Success Strategy, page 201
Students may highlight parts of the dialogue between Anne and her mother in lines 63–75. Students' paragraphs may include these points: Mrs. Frank wishes Anne would be more respectful and act mature. Anne just wants to have fun and thinks her mother is too serious.

Reading Check, page 201
She is afraid that she will forget how to dance.

Reading Check, page 202
Peter blushes because his mother is teasing him.

Reread, page 203
Possible response: I think that I would be nervous all the time. I might lose my appetite or feel shaky. I would probably lose my temper and yell at my parents.

Read Aloud, page 203
Possible response: Yes, the boys and girls in my class tease each other and fool around just like this.

Pause & Reflect, page 204
1. lively, outgoing
2. His father thinks that Peter does not spend enough time on his studies.

Reading Check, page 204
Illness would be a problem because they would not be able to call or visit a doctor.

Reading Check, page 205
He thinks that Anne is homesick.

Pause & Reflect, page 206
1. Possible response: Anne thinks her mother overreacts.
2. Possible response: Mr. Frank is a better father because he seems to really care about his children, their schoolwork, etc.

Reading Check, page 207
It is precious to her because her father gave it to her before he died.

English Learner Support, page 207
Students should draw a picture of bees buzzing around a jam pot.

Reading Check, page 208
Peter hasn't done his schoolwork.

Reread, page 210
Possible response: I think Miep is glad to help because she is saving their lives and willing to risk her own to do so.

Reader's Success Strategy, page 211
Possible responses: Mr. Frank: calm, helpful, cooperative, tries to make the best of the situation; Mrs. Frank: pleasant, helpful, tries to make the best of the situation, wishes Anne would be courteous and obedient; Mr. Van Daan: disgruntled, rude, antagonistic; Mrs. Van Daan: rude, disruptive

Reading Check, page 211
Mr. Van Daan has been complaining that Anne talks to much and has suggested that she keep quiet.

Pause & Reflect, page 212
1. Possible responses: Yes, because their quarrels are the result of living in hiding in close quarters. No, because they are difficult people who would behave this way even if they were not living in hiding.
2. Possible response: Yes, because she is so outgoing.

Reading Check, page 213
Margot lets people take advantage of her.

Read Aloud, page 214
She feels as though everyone is against her. The others have only praise for Margot and only criticism for Anne.

Reading Check, page 214
Mrs. Frank didn't think it was a good idea to invite the Van Daans.

Pause & Reflect, page 215
1. Possible response: No, because it seems like she is always criticizing Anne.
2. Possible response: Anne is more rebellious and outspoken than Margot.

Reading Check, page 216
The dentist must hide from the Nazis.

Reread, page 216
Possible response: He does not hesitate even for a moment. He is kind and willing to help.

Reread, page 217
Mr. Van Daan says that his opinion is not important since the rooms belong to Mr. Frank; Mr. Van Daan means that he does not want Mr. Dussel to join them.

Reading Check, page 217
Mr. Frank does not want the girls in Peter's room because Peter's cat has caught some rats in there.

Reader's Success Strategy, page 218
Students should revise their diagrams to show that Margot has moved to her parents' room (the common room), and Mr. Dussel has moved into Anne's room.

Reading Check, page 219
They don't like the Nazis.

Pause & Reflect, page 220 (Plus)
1. Another person, Mr. Dussel, moves in with them.
2. Possible responses: Yes, because he will be killed if they do not allow him to join them. No, because his presence is a threat to all of them since they might not have enough food.

Pause & Reflect, page 220 (AS and EL)
Possible responses: Yes, because he will be killed if they do not allow him to join them. No, because his presence is a threat to all of them since they might not have enough food.

Reading Check, page 220
Mr. Frank wants the adults to have a glass of cognac to welcome Mr. Dussel.

Reread, page 221
Possible response: He feels ashamed because his father is complaining that Mr. Dussel's arrival will cut into their rations.

Reading Check, page 221
They are apprehended and taken to the death camp.

Reread, page 222
Jopie has been taken away by the Nazis.

Reading Check, page 222
Mr. Frank notices Anne's reaction and he doesn't want everyone to become frantic and upset about the news.

Reading Check, page 223
Mr. Dussel didn't think he would be targeted by the Nazis because he considers himself Dutch and his family has lived in Holland for generations.

Reader's Success Strategy, page 223
Possible answers: "I'm a man who's always lived alone." (line 767) "I have an allergy for fur-bearing animals." (line 778)

Reading Check, page 224
Part of the street and the canal can be seen from their window.

Reread, page 224
Possible responses: Yes, because Anne is kind and considerate to him. No, because there is too much tension and fear in their living conditions.

Reader's Success Strategy, page 225
Mr. Dussel moves into the Secret Annex (September 1942)

Reading Check, page 225
Anne and Mr. Dussel aren't getting along with each other.

Pause & Reflect, page 226
Conditions on the outside have become much worse.

Challenge, page 226
Possible response: The quarrels will increase. Someone, like Mrs. Van Daan or Mr. Dussel, will break down.

Active Reading SkillBuilder, page 227
(Possible responses are provided.)

Scene One
Characters: Mr. Frank, Miep Gies
Setting: November 1945, top floor of warehouse
Main Events: Miep gives Mr. Frank his daughter's diary. He begins to read it.

Scene Two
Characters: Mr. Frank, Miep, Mr. and Mrs. Van Daan, Mrs. Frank, Mr. Kraler, Peter, Anne, Margot
Setting: July 1942, top floor of warehouse
Main Events: The families set rules for how they will live in the rooms. Mr. Frank gives Anne a diary, and she starts to write in it.

Scene Three
Characters: Mr. Frank, Miep, Mr. and Mrs. Van Daan, Mrs. Frank, Mr. Kraler, Peter, Anne, Margot, Mr. Dussel
Setting: September 1942, top floor of warehouse
Main Events: The Franks and the Van Daans quarrel. Anne spills milk on Mrs. Van Daan's fur coat. Mr. Dussel moves in. Dussel criticizes Anne.

Literary Analysis SkillBuilder, page 228
(Possible responses are provided.)
Flashback Clues
Auditory: Anne's voice comes in as Mr. Frank begins to read; then his voice fades out and hers continues alone.
Visual: The lights dim slowly to darkness; the curtain falls. When the next scene starts, the setting is altered: more people are in the room, Mr. Frank and Miep look younger, and Miep is not pregnant.
Dialogue: They make plans for how they are going to live in the hidden rooms.

Words to Know SkillBuilder, page 229

A.		B.	
1.	c	1.	vile
2.	c	2.	insufferable
3.	a	3.	conspicuous
4.	b	4.	loathe
5.	a	5.	indignantly

The Lady, or the Tiger?, page 230
Connect to Your Life, page 230
Students should describe the choices they faced and how they made their decision.
Pause & Reflect, page 232
1. quiet and kind
Pause & Reflect, page 232
He reacts mildly and pleasantly to problems because it pleases him to solve them.
Reread, page 233
chance, or fate
Mark It Up, page 234
two doors, exactly alike and side by side
Reading Check, page 234
He marries the lady regardless of whether he already has a wife.

Pause & Reflect, page 235 (Plus)
1. Possible response: First an accused man is placed in an arena and forced to choose between two doors. Behind one door there is a tiger who will eat the man. Behind the other door is a lady who will marry the man.
2. Possible response: In the story, who will be placed in the arena?
Pause & Reflect, page 235 (AS and EL)
Possible response: In the story, who will be placed in the arena?
Reread, page 235
If the door of the lady, then he must be innocent. If the door of the tiger, then he must be guilty.
Pause & Reflect, page 236 (Plus)
1. The system of justice was popular in the kingdom because people never knew whether they would witness a bloody slaughter or a hilarious wedding.
2. Possible response: It is totally unfair because the person's fate is not based on whether or not it has been proven that he is guilty or innocent.
Pause & Reflect, page 236 (AS and EL)
The system of justice was popular in the kingdom because people never knew whether they would witness a bloody slaughter or a hilarious wedding.
Reread, page 236
Possible response: The king will place the young man in the arena.
Reread, page 237
Either way, the young man will not be able to marry the king's daughter. If the young man chooses the lady, he will be married to her. If he chooses the tiger, he will die.
Reading Check, page 237
The trial will decide whether or not the young man had done wrong in allowing himself to love the princess. It will also decide whether the young man will live or die.
Pause & Reflect, page 238 (Plus)
1. young, proud, romantic, beautiful
2. The king decides to put the young man on trial in the arena.
Pause & Reflect, page 238 (AS and EL)
proud, semibarbaric
Mark It Up, page 238
". . . she had possessed herself of the secret of the doors. She knew in which of the two rooms that lay behind those doors stood the cage of the tiger, with its open front, and in which waited the lady." (lines 203–207)
Reread, page 239
The princess is jealous of the woman behind the door.
Reading Check, page 239
No, because he had expected her to know it. He understands her and knew that she would not rest until she learned it.
Pause & Reflect, page 240 (Plus)
1. The princess is jealous. The lady is lovely, and the princess has seen the lady and the young man talking.
2. jealous and quick to anger
Pause & Reflect, page 240 (AS and EL)
jealous and quick to anger

Reread, page 240

He trusts the princess.

Reader's Success Strategy or **Reading Tip,** page 241

Possible response: It would be best to send him to the lady because she truly loves him and doesn't want him to die even if they can't be together. It would be best to send him to the tiger because she couldn't bear to see him with another woman.

Pause & Reflect, page 242

1. Possible responses: I think the lady came out because the princess could not bear to let her young man die. I think the tiger came out because the princess could not bear to see her young man married to someone else.

2. Students should write either a question or an answer.

Challenge, page 242

Possible responses: I like the way the author ended the story because I keep thinking about it. Sometimes, I think the lady will come out and sometimes I think the tiger will come out. It all depends on how I feel about the princess. The ending makes me want to analyze her motives.

Mark It Up, page 242

Students should draw a picture of a lady or a tiger.

Active Reading SkillBuilder, page 243

(Possible responses are provided.)

Stated Facts: She loved the young man with ardor. She had much power and influence in the kingdom. She knew what was behind each door.

Inferred Facts: She will not want her lover to be torn apart by the tiger. She will not want her lover to be married to the maiden. She was jealous of the maiden.

My Knowledge: Strong-willed people sometimes do outrageous things just to shock other people. Love and jealousy are both very strong emotions that can make people act irrationally. A beautiful princess could easily find another lover.

Conclusion: Students may choose either ending, but should support it with the facts they listed in their charts.

Literary Analysis SkillBuilder, page 244

(Possible responses are provided.)

Clues Leading to the Lady's Door: She felt horror when she thought of the cruel fangs of the tiger. She could almost hear the shrieks and see the blood that the awful tiger would cause.

Clues Leading to the Tiger's Door: Her soul burned in agony when she pictured him rushing to meet the maiden. She could imagine her one despairing shriek lost in the merriment of the wedding.

Words to Know SkillBuilder, page 245

1. imperious
2. destiny
3. valor
4. subordinate
5. assert
6. decree
7. doleful
8. procure
9. exuberant
10. retribution

The Tell-Tale Heart, page 246

Connect to Your Life, page 246

Responses may include the following: A good horror story should have a monster, have a surprise ending, take place in a spooky place, have a character who is insane, feature grizzly details.

Key to the Story, page 246

Answers may include the following: A nervous person is jumpy, jittery, has hands that shake, looks worried, is over sensitive.

Pause & Reflect, page 248 (Plus)

1. He decides to kill the old man, because he cannot stand the old man's eye, a pale, blue eye—the eye of a vulture.

2. nervous, healthy, sane

Pause & Reflect, page 248 (AS and EL)

He decides to kill the old man, because he cannot stand the old man's eye, a pale, blue eye—the eye of a vulture.

Reread, page 249

For seven nights, the narrator carefully creeps into the old man's room and shines a lantern on the old man's closed eye.

Reading Check, page 249

Each morning, the narrator visits with the old man and chats pleasantly as if nothing has happened.

Reader's Success Strategy or **Reading Tip,** page 250

Rising action: For seven nights, the narrator creeps into the old man's room but doesn't kill him because the old man doesn't open his eye. *Climax:* On the eighth night, the narrator sees the old man's eye and murders him. *Falling Action:* The narrator dismembers and conceals the body. Police officers arrive to search the premises. The narrator confesses to his crime because he thinks he hears the beating of the old man's heart.

Reread, page 250

The old man wakes up.

Pause & Reflect, page 251 (Plus and AS)

1. nothing but the wind in the chimney; it is only a mouse crossing the floor; it is merely a cricket which has made a single chirp

2. filled with terror

Pause & Reflect, page 251 (EL)

nothing but the wind in the chimney; it is only a mouse crossing the floor; it is merely a cricket which has made a single chirp

Reread, page 252

Possible response: The beating of the heart will increase the madness of the narrator. He will kill the old man.

Read Aloud, page 252

Possible response: Poe's use of short sentences and repetition speeds up the story, making the reader feel tense and anxious.

Pause & Reflect, page 253 (Plus)

1. a low, dull, quick sound, such as a watch makes when enveloped in cotton (lines 125–126); a hellish tattoo, i.e. the beating of a drum (line 133)

2. It increases the narrator's fury at the old man.

Pause & Reflect, page 253 (AS and EL)

a low, dull, quick sound, such as a watch makes when enveloped in cotton (lines 125–126); a hellish tattoo, i.e. the beating of a drum (line 133)

Reread, page 253

Possible response: No, the narrator isn't sane because he murdered and dismembered the old man just because he couldn't stand the old man's eye.

Reading Check, page 254

A neighbor heard a shriek and suspected foul play.

Pause & Reflect, page 254

1. He cuts up the body and places the parts underneath the floor.
2. tells them that the old man is away in the country; urges them to search the house; invites them to sit in the room where the body is hidden

Read Aloud, page 255

frantic

Pause & Reflect, page 256

1. The narrator confesses because he thinks that the police can hear the beating of the old man's heart.
2. Possible response: The narrator's guilt and his fear of being discovered torment him with the imaginary sound.

Challenge, page 256

Students might say that the narrator would have initially gotten away with the crime but that, in time, his madness would have given him away.

Mark It Up, page 256

Students' drawings should accurately reflect one of the narrator's comparisons.

Active Reading SkillBuilder, page 257

(Possible responses are provided.)

Narrator

Details from Text: "I was never kinder to the old man than during the whole week before I killed him";
"I smiled . . . I bade the gentlemen welcome"; "I felt myself getting pale"; "I arose and argued about trifles, in a high key and with violent gesticulations"; "I paced the floor"; "I swung the chair"

Visualization: Students may draw or describe a man with wild, nervous eyes who paces around like a caged animal, or whose smile seems unnaturally cheerful.

Old Man

Details from Text: "He had the eye of a vulture—a pale blue eye, with a film over it"; "the old man sprang up in the bed, crying out—'Who's there?'"; "groan of mortal terror"

Visualization: Students may draw or describe an old man with a large, deformed, or somehow hideous eye, perhaps looking frightened.

Setting

Details from Text: "about midnight"; "His room was black as pitch . . . the shutters were close fastened"; "a single dim ray . . . shot from out the crevice and fell full upon the vulture eye"

Visualization: Students may draw or describe a darkened room with a single ray from a lantern shining across it.

Literary Analysis SkillBuilder, page 258

(Possible responses are provided.)

Example: "I undid the lantern cautiously—oh, so cautiously—cautiously . . . just so much that a single thin ray fell upon the vulture eye."
Mood Created: Suspense, anticipation
Example: "I heard a slight groan . . . of mortal terror."
Mood Created: Horror, fright, apprehension
Example: "With a loud yell, I threw open the lantern and leaped into the room."
Mood Created: Surprise and horror

Words to Know SkillBuilder, page 259

A. 1. audacity   B. 1. stealthily
    2. conceived   2. crevice
    3. hypocritical   3. stifled
    4. acute   4. vehemently
    5. vex   5. derision

The boxed letters spell out *his eye*.

The Monkey's Paw, page 260

Connect to Your Life, page 260

Possible response: Event/situation: I would like to move to a new city. How this would affect my life: I wouldn't know anyone and would have to start a new school.

Key to the Story, page 260

Students should list the names of movies and explain what made each movie scary.

English Learner Support, page 262

Possible responses: "the night was cold and wet, but in the small parlor" (lines 1–3); "I'm listening" (line 16)

Reread, page 262

beastly, slushy, out-of-the-way; pathway's a bog; road's a torrent

Pause & Reflect, page 263 (Plus)

1. the son
2. isolated and lonely

Pause & Reflect, page 263 (AS and EL)

isolated and lonely

Reading Check, page 264

It looks like an ordinary paw, dried to a mummy.

Read Aloud, page 265

The previous owner had wished for his own death.

Reading Check, page 265

He kept it as a whim. He considered selling it but thinks it has caused too much mischief already; people may not buy it anyway.

Pause & Reflect, page 266 (Plus)

1. has a spell on it; looks ordinary; grants three wishes
2. anxious and afraid

Pause & Reflect, page 266 (AS and EL)

has a spell on it; looks ordinary; grants three wishes
anxious and afraid

Reading Check, page 266

He seems afraid of the paw and thinks it should be discarded.

Reader's Success Strategy, page 267

Student may include these points: The Whites seem fascinated by the paw. They joke about the paw as if they don't take its powers seriously. They ignore the sergeant major's advice about the paw

Reading Check, page 267

Herbert thinks that the sergeant major's stories were not truthful.

Pause & Reflect, page 267

1. The Whites joke about the monkey's paw; the sergeant-major is afraid of it and wants it destroyed.
2. Possible responses: Yes, because it seems to have magic powers. No, because the paw has never brought anyone happiness.

Reread, page 268

The family is skeptical of the paw's power.

Reading Check, page 268

Mr. White wishes for two hundred pounds to pay off the house.

Pause & Reflect, page 269 (Plus)

1. "I wish for two hundred pounds," said the old man distinctly. (lines 189–190)
2. Possible response: The mood changes from playfulness to unease, fear, and depression.
3. Possible response: I would feel very uneasy and afraid of what might happen next.

Pause & Reflect, page 269 (AS)

1. Possible response: The mood changes from playfulness to unease, fear, and depression.
2. Possible response: I would feel very uneasy and afraid of what might happen next.

Pause & Reflect, page 269 (EL)

Possible response: The mood changes from playfulness to unease, fear, and depression.

Pause & Reflect, page 270

1. Mr. White is afraid of the paw; Herbert and Mrs. White are still joking about it.
2. moved in his hand

Mark It Up, page 271

ill at ease; gazed at her furtively; strangely silent

Reading Check, page 272

He was caught in the machinery at work.

Pause & Reflect, page 273 (Plus)

1. He tells Mr. and Mrs. White that their son has died in an accident at work.
2. The company has sent them the money as compensation for their son's death. It is the amount that Mr. White wished for.

Pause & Reflect, page 273 (AS and EL)

The company has sent them the money as compensation for their son's death. It is the amount that Mr. White wished for.

Reader's Success Strategy or **Reading Tip,** page 273

Expectations: They thought their wish might not be granted. If their wish was granted, they expected to receive the money without consequence. *Results:* They received two hundred pounds because Herbert was killed at work.

Reader's Success Strategy, page 274

Students may include these points: The Whites decide to wish for money. The monkey's paw moves when Mr. White makes the wish. Herbert sees faces in the fire that make him feel uneasy.

The Whites joke about their wish of the night before. A man from Herbert's workplace tells Mr. and Mrs. White that their son has died in an accident and that they will receive two hundred pounds (the amount they wished for) as a result. Mr. and Mrs. White mourn the death of their son. Students' summaries may note that the characters and mood shifted from playful and lighthearted to fearful, uneasy, and depressing.

Reader's Success Strategy, page 275

Students may predict that the Whites' second wish might result in further misfortune.

English Learner Support, page 275

"lit the candle"

Pause & Reflect, page 275

1. wish for Herbert to be alive again
2. He is afraid that his mutilated son might appear before him in the room.

Reading Check, page 276

He feels relieved.

Reread, page 277

The Whites have been waiting for a sign that Herbert has been brought back to life. Mrs. White forgot that he had been buried two miles away and that it would take him a long time to walk home from the cemetery.

Reading Check, page 277

He uses his last wish to retract his second wish.

Pause & Reflect, page 278

1. Possible response: No, because I didn't want to know what was behind it.
2. He wishes for Herbert to return to the grave.

Challenge, page 278

They asked for money and were punished. They tried to bring their son back from the dead and came close to seeing a horrific sight.

Active Reading SkillBuilder, page 279

(Possible responses are provided.)

Passage: "If the tale about the monkey's paw . . ."

Passage Clarified: Herbert doesn't think the visitor's stories are very truthful.

Passage: "Unconscious of his wife's shriek, . . ."

Passage Clarified: The old man collapsed, unconscious of everything around him.

Literary Analysis SkillBuilder, page 280

(Possible responses are provided.)

Conflict

- Mr. White wishes for money.
- The major conflict is that the Whites receive money but at the cost of their son's life. They are miserable and now wish to undo their initial action.
- The Whites have internal conflict as they struggle with their grief. Their external conflict is seen in their isolation from each other. A more obvious external conflict is the desire of Mrs. White for a second wish and Mr. White's refusal to make the wish.

Rising Action

- There is a considerable interval of time between Mr. White's second wish and its fulfillment during which nothing happens. The suspense heightens as Mrs. White waits with excited anticipation, and Mr. White awaits the results with dread.
- A very faint knocking is ignored by Mr. White.
- The knocking becomes louder, and Mr. and Mrs. White argue over whether to open the door.

Climax

- Mr. White makes his third wish.
- The last wish is used up, so the Whites have no way to change the past.

Falling Action

When the knocking stops and the street is seen to be deserted, the conflict between Mr. and Mrs. White is over because Herbert is gone for good and the wishes are all used. The internal conflict of their grief is not resolved, however.

Words to Know SkillBuilder, page 281

A.
1. surveying
2. peril
3. fate
4. credulity
5. grimace

B.
1. B
2. B
3. C
4. A
5. C

C. Accept responses that accurately use at least three Words to Know.

Paul Revere's Ride, page 282
Connect to Your Life, page 282
Responses may include the following: displaying the flag, running for public office, going to a Fourth of July parade

Pause & Reflect, page 285
1. two lanterns; two if by sea (line 10)
2. cheerful

Reread, page 287
tense, suspenseful, eerie

Pause & Reflect, page 289
1. the tramp of feet, a graveyard, startled pigeons
2. Students might say by sea, since the men are "marching down to their boats on shore."

Reading Check, page 291
Revere pauses to see if his friend will light the second lamp.

English Learner Support, page 291
Students may cite references to the horse on page 288, "saddle" (line 70, page 290), and "hoofs" (line 73, page 290).

Pause & Reflect, page 291
1. Revere sounded the alarm that started the Revolutionary War.
2. 2, 3, 1

Pause & Reflect, page 293
1. meetinghouse windows, songs of birds, bleating of sheep
2. "As if they already stood aghast/at the bloody work they would look upon." (lines 99–100)

Pause & Reflect, page 295
1. The colonists attack the British, who flee.
2. Students may say that the most exciting part is when Revere is galloping through the night.

Challenge, page 295
Some students will say that the inaccuracies do not affect the drama of the poem, especially the symbolic meaning of Revere's dramatic ride. Other students will feel that the poet should have included the facts.

Active Reading SkillBuilder, page 296
(Possible responses are provided.)
Lines from Poem: Beneath, in the churchyard, . . . "All is well!" (lines 42–48); **Paraphrase:** Beneath him lay a cemetery. It was so quiet that he could hear the wind, which was like a night guard, whispering, "All is well!"
Lines from Poem: And the meeting-house windows, . . . the bloody work they would look upon (lines 97–100); **Paraphrase:** The windows of the meeting house seemed to stare at him with horror, as if they knew about the bloodshed that would happen later.
Lines from Poem: And one was safe and asleep . . . Pierced by a British musket-ball (lines 107–110); **Paraphrase:** The man who would be the first to die in battle was safe in his bed that morning.
Lines from Poem: How the farmers gave them ball for ball, / From behind each fence and farmyard wall (lines 113–114); **Paraphrase:** how the farmers, hiding behind fences and walls, returned each shot that the British fired
Lines from Poem: For, borne on the night-wind . . . people will waken and listen to hear (lines 125–128); **Paraphrase:** If we are ever again in great danger, the proud history of Revere's message will once again rouse people to action.

Literary Analysis SkillBuilder, page 297
(Possible responses are provided.)
Rising Action *Event:* His friend climbs the tower of the Old North Church. *Event:* Revere sees two lanterns and starts riding. *Event:* He crosses through Medford, Concord, and Lexington.
Climax *Event:* The British soldiers battle with the farmers and finally flee.
Falling Action *Event:* Revere's voice echoes through our history.

from **Harriet Tubman,** page 298
Connect to Your Life, page 298
Responses may include the following: the right to hang out with my friends, the right to play soccer after school, the right to vote

Pause & Reflect, page 301 (Plus)
1. Harriet Tubman
2. Slaves were escaping.

Pause & Reflect, page 301 (AS and EL)
Harriet Tubman

Reading Check, page 301
by singing a forbidden spiritual about Moses

Reread, page 302

Harriet Tubman had to take escaped slaves all the way to Canada because the Fugitive Slave Law allowed slave owners to recover escaped slaves even if the slaves reached free states.

Reader's Success Strategy or **Reading Tip,** page 302

Similar: known as Moses; announced her arrival by singing; *Different:* eleven in her group this time; largest group she had ever conducted; had to go all the way to Canada this time because the Fugitive Slave Law was being enforced; had only gone as far as Philadelphia in other trips

Pause & Reflect, page 303

1. She had never been to Canada before. She had never led a group as large as this one.
2. "If they were caught, the eleven runaways would be whipped and sold south, but she—she would probably be hanged." (lines 97–99)

Pause & Reflect, page 304 (Plus)

1. Possible response: They were turned away because the place had been searched the week before.
2. Students' questions should accurately reflect information in the story.

Pause & Reflect, page 304 (AS and EL)

Possible response: They were turned away because the place had been searched the week before.

Reader's Success Strategy, page 304

Problem: The fugitives fear pursuit. *Solution:* Tubman paints wondrous word pictures. *Problem:* The fugitives are tired and irritable. *Solution:* Tubman urges them on by telling stories.

Reread, page 305

Possible responses: lack of food, lack of sleep, never feeling safe, being cold all the time

Reading Check, page 305

She described Thomas Garret and told the fugitives that he would give them all a new pair of shoes when they arrived at his house. She told the fugitives the story to give them hope and urge them forward.

Pause & Reflect, page 306 (Plus)

1. She painted wondrous word pictures.
2. strong and kind, friend to runaways, hates Quakers

Pause & Reflect, page 306 (AS and EL)

She painted wondrous word pictures.

Reading Check, page 306

She was afraid that the group would be turned away again.

Pause & Reflect, p 307

1. He and his wife fed them in the lamp-lit kitchen, their faces glowing as they offered food and more food, urging them to eat, saying there was plenty for everybody, have more milk, have more bread, have more meat.
2. Possible response: They will be turned away from the next stop and/or Tubman will have trouble with someone in the group.

Reread, page 308

They were too tired, hungry, and frightened to care.

Reader's Success Strategy, page 308

Problem: One of the runaways wants to go back. *Solution:* Tubman threatens him with a gun and tells him that he must continue or die.

Read Aloud, page 309

Possible response: She is desperate to have them continue. She is afraid the man will give them away.

Reading Check, page 309

He decided to continue.

Reading Check, page 310

He was tortured and killed.

Reread, page 310

They now trust her completely. The runaways do not flee when Tubman falls asleep during one of her spells.

Pause & Reflect, page 311 (Plus)

1. If a runaway returned, the master or overseer would force the runaway to turn traitor.
2. threatens to use violence; says, "We got to go free or die"; tells stories about the Middle Passage

Pause & Reflect, page 311 (AS and EL)

If a runaway returned, the master or overseer would force the runaway to turn traitor.

Reading Check, page 311

He published his record of the fugitives he helped along the Underground Railroad.

Reader's Success Strategy, page 312

Students should trace the following points: Dorchester County, Maryland; Wilmington, Delaware; Philadelphia, Pennsylvania; Burlington, New Jersey; New York, New York; Syracuse, New York; Rochester, New York; St. Catharines, Ontario

Pause & Reflect, page 312

1. 1, 4, 2, 3
2. It had taken almost a month to complete this journey; most of the time had been spent getting out of Maryland.

Reader's Success Strategy, page 313

Pros: freedoms it offered, ex-slaves owned homes and could live in whatever part of town they chose and send their children to the schools; Cons: severe cold, hard work, bleak, barren countryside

Reading Check, page 313

Not only did freedom grant the right to change jobs and keep wages, but it allowed the right to vote, sit on juries, and be elected to office.

Pause & Reflect, page 314 (Plus)

1. She rented a small frame house in the town and set to work to make a home. The fugitives boarded with her. They worked in the forests, felling trees, and so did she. Sometimes she took other jobs, cooking or cleaning house for people in the town. She cheered on these newly arrived fugitives, working herself, sometimes begging for them.
2. Students may say they are impressed by her courage and determination.
3. Students' questions and answers should accurately reflect information in the story.

Pause & Reflect, page 314 (AS and EL)

1. She rented a small frame house in the town and set to work to make a home. The fugitives boarded with her. They worked in the forests, felling trees, and so did she. Sometimes she took other jobs, cooking or cleaning house for people in the town. She cheered on these newly arrived fugitives, working herself, sometimes begging for them.

2. Students may say they are impressed by her courage and determination.

Challenge, page 314

Students could say that freedom cost them physical and emotional pain, their home and belongings, family members and friends whom they left behind, and the risk of being captured and killed.

Active Reading SkillBuilder, page 315

(Possible responses are provided.)

Question: Why did Tubman plan to take the slaves to Canada?
Answer: The Fugitive Slave Law made it unsafe for escaped slaves even in the northern United States.

Question: How did Tubman encourage the others to keep going after they were turned away at the farmhouse? **Answer:** She described Canada to them, making it sound wonderful. She knew how to encourage them but also make them afraid enough to keep walking.

Question: How did Tubman handle escaping slaves who turned against her? **Answer:** She carried a gun that she used to threaten anyone who wanted to turn back.

Literary Analysis SkillBuilder, page 316

(Possible responses are provided.)

Ordinary Human Qualities: "she was as tired and discouraged as they were"; "She kept thinking, Eleven of them. Eleven thousand dollars' worth of slaves"; "She hesitated before she approached the door, thinking, Suppose that he, too, should refuse shelter"; she was "short, muscular"

Extraordinary Human Qualities: "Then she thought, Lord, I'm going to hold steady on to You, and You've got to see me through"; "She lifted the gun, aimed it at the despairing slave. She said, 'Go on with us or die'"; "The runaways . . . did not steal the gun. . . . They had come to trust her implicitly, totally."

Words to Know SkillBuilder, page 317

A. 1. E   3. G   5. A   7. C
        2. B   4. F   6. D

B. 1. dispel   5. instill
        2. disheveled   6. indomitable
        3. fastidious   7. eloquence
        4. mutinous   8. cajoling

Roughing It, page 318
Connect to Your Life, page 318
Possible response: loved pet-sitting because I like being around animals; hated babysitting my brothers and sisters because they never listen to me.

Key to the Essay, page 318
Possible response: stuntperson, race car driver

Pause & Reflect, page 321 (Plus)

1. The narrator doesn't want to work.

2. unsuccessful

Pause & Reflect, page 321 (AS and EL)
The narrator doesn't want to work.

Reader's Success Strategy or **Reading Tip,** page 321
Job: blacksmith *What Happened?:* fired for spending all his time trying to fix the bellows so it would blow itself *Job:* bookstore clerk *What Happened?:* bothered by customers that disturbed his reading; given an unlimited leave of absence *Job:* drug store clerk *What happened?:* poisoned people with prescriptions *Job:* compositor *What Happened?:* too slow *Job:* private secretary, silver-miner, silver-mill operative *What Happened?* amounted to less than nothing

Reread, page 323
He gave out the wrong prescriptions and made his customers sick.

Pause & Reflect, page 323 (Plus)

1. grocery clerk; blacksmith; compositor

2. He spent all his time reading and was annoyed with the customers who bothered him.

Pause & Reflect, page 323 (AS and EL)
grocery clerk; blacksmith; compositor

Reading Check, page 325
He became frustrated when dirt fell all over him as he was trying to shovel it out of the shaft.

Reread, page 325
He thought his own letters were not very good and the editors should have known better than to print them.

Pause & Reflect, page 327

1. city editor.

2. Possible response: He takes the job because otherwise he would have to depend on someone else to support him, and that would be humiliating.

Reading Check, page 329
His job is to investigate the news and write news articles for the paper.

Pause & Reflect, page 329 (Plus and AS)

1. Possible response: Always let your readers think that you are writing the truth.

2. Students may say that it is good advice, since it is important to put in the extra effort to get all the facts, and when you do, people will take your work seriously.

Pause & Reflect, page 329 (EL)
Possible response: Always let your readers think that you are writing the truth.

Reader's Success Strategy, page 331
"But I made affluent use of it. I multiplied it by sixteen, brought it into town from sixteen different directions, made up sixteen separate items of it, and got up such another sweat about hay as Virginia City had ever seen in the world before." (lines 166–171)

Reading Check, page 331
He filled two columns by exaggerating the hay truck's activity.

Read Aloud, page 331

He seems so happy about it.

Reread, page 333

The narrator is unable to lie because he is surrounded by reporters from other papers. They will know that he's lying.

Reading Check, page 333

He felt as though he had finally found the right career. He thought that he was particularly suited for the job.

Pause & Reflect, page 334

1. A hay-truck came into town. A desperado murdered a man. A wagon train arrived from "Indian country."
2. Possible responses: Yes, because he had to fill up his column and there was no news. No, because his articles invented the truth.
3. Students' opinions should accurately reflect information in the story.

Challenge, page 334

Students' should include appropriate details from the story.

Active Reading SkillBuilder, page 335

(Possible responses are provided.)

Inference: restless; **Clue:** doesn't stay long at any job

Inference: proud and resourceful; **Clue:** doesn't like to be dependent on others, finds ways to avoid it

Inference: highly imaginative; **Clue:** made up an entire Indian fight

Literary Analysis SkillBuilder, page 336

(Possible responses are provided.)

Exaggeration: "I had engaged briefly in the study of blacksmithing, but wasted so much time trying to fix the bellows so that it would blow itself, that the master turned me adrift in disgrace"

Inference: Narrator is ingenious but lazy.

Exaggeration: "I made the toss, and landed the mess just on the edge of the shaft and it all came back on my head and down the back of my neck. I never said a word, but climbed out and walked home. I inwardly resolved that I would starve before I would make a target of myself and shoot rubbish at it with a long-handled shovel"

Inference: He doesn't like manual labor, and he doesn't like to appear foolish.

Exaggeration: "I multiplied it by sixteen, brought it into town from sixteen different directions, made sixteen separate items of it, and got up such another sweat about hay as Virginia City had never seen in the world before"

Inference: He's imaginative and not afraid of taking liberties with the truth.

Words to Know SkillBuilder, page 337

A. Across
1. lavish
4. contrive
6. affluent
8. board
9. emigrant

Down
1. legitimate
2. vocation
3. proprietor
5. barren
7. endow

B. Accept responses that accurately use five Words to Know.

One Million Volumes, page 338
Connect to Your Life, page 338

Responses may include some of the following: comic books, series books, special interest magazines.

Reader's Success Strategy or **Reading Tip,** page 340

(Sample answers are provided.)

Grandfather's Stories: made us see that we were part of the universe; created a thirst for knowledge; guides in the world of nature and knowledge; taught the magic of words *Books:* have the magic power of words; allow participation in the wisdom of mankind; quenches the thirst of the imagination; held as much magic as the words of the old ones

Pause & Reflect, page 341

1. to imagine, to thirst for knowledge
2. wisdom and knowledge

Reading Check, page 341 (AS)

He felt confused yet determined.

Reading Check, page 342

Worlds lie waiting to be discovered in each book.

Pause & Reflect, page 342

1. they are a deadly power if misused (line 54)
2. snow, piled high, lost many sheep and cattle, trees groaned and broke, raging blizzard, awful destruction

Reading Check, page 343

He could take out books with his library card. The card was his "ticket into the same worlds [his] grandfather had known, worlds of magic that fed the imagination."

Reader's Success Strategy, page 343

Students may note the following points: both provide wisdom and knowledge; both inspire a thirst for wisdom and knowledge; both fuel the imagination

Pause & Reflect, page 344 (Plus)

1. Possible response: Reading allowed Anaya to enter worlds that fed the imagination.
2. Students may respect or admire Anaya.

Pause & Reflect, page 344 (AS and EL)

1. Possible response: Reading allowed Anaya to enter worlds that fed the imagination.
2. Possible response: It is important to preserve the literature of all cultures today, just as it has been important to preserve the oral stories and traditions of our own culture for generations.

Challenge, page 344

Possible response: Anaya's use of powerful and interesting images supports his purpose of showing that reading can be a source of wonder and knowledge. Students may underline the description of a million books (lines 78–79). Students may also underline the description of the library (lines 101–107).

Active Reading SkillBuilder, page 345

(Possible responses are provided.)

To Entertain: "That was the winter the snow came, he would say, it piled high and we lost many sheep and cattle, and the trees groaned and broke with its weight. I looked across the llano and saw the raging blizzard. . . ."

To Inform: "And now there are a million volumes for us to read here at the University of New Mexico Library."

To Persuade: "Books on every imaginable subject, in every field, a history of the thought of the world which we must keep free of censorship, because we treasure our freedoms."

To Express an Opinion: "Words are a way, he said, they hold joy, and they are a deadly power if misused."

What was Anaya's main purpose?

Students may conclude that Anaya's main purpose was to entertain, since he includes many amusing anecdotes from his childhood, or to express an opinion, since he obviously feels very strongly that books are precious. Accept all well-supported responses.

Literary Analysis SkillBuilder, page 346

(Possible responses are provided.)

Words and Phrases: "the swirl of the Milky Way which swept over us"; **Ideas and Feelings They Convey:** creates vivid image of the night sky

Words and Phrases: "we were bound to the infinity of that cosmic dance of life"; **Ideas and Feelings They Convey:** conveys wonder at the hugeness of the universe

Words and Phrases: "My tattered library card was my ticket into . . . worlds of magic that fed the imagination"; **Ideas and Feelings They Convey:** creates an ironic contrast between the ordinariness of a library card and the wonder of the worlds it opens up to readers

Follow Up: Accept responses that show a careful choice of words to convey ideas, feelings, and images.

Words to Know SkillBuilder, page 347

A.		B.	
1.	B	1.	induce
2.	D	2.	Censorship
3.	A	3.	ignite
4.	E	4.	paradox
5.	C	5.	litany

Academic and Informational Reading Answer Key

Reading a Magazine Article, page 350

Mark It Up

1. cowboys; cowboys at work and cowboys at play
2. Students should draw a star beside the italicized paragraph beneath the title.
3. Students should circle the photo featuring a helicopter. Students should put a checkmark beside the rodeo photo.
4. events at a typical rodeo
5. six
6. Students should underline the following sentence: "The cowboy grabs the steer's horns and wrestles the animal to the ground."

Reading a Textbook, page 352

Mark It Up

1. the West
2. Students should circle the words under the heading "Terms & Names."
3. Students should circle the following sentence under "Main Idea": "Miners, ranchers, and cowhands settled in the West seeking economic opportunities."
4. Students should put a checkmark beside the passage under the heading "A Voice from the Past." Nat Love wrote the excerpt.
5. Nat Love was an African-American cowhand who became a rodeo star.
6. Students should circle Great Plains. Students should underline the following parenthetical sentence: "(See map on page 558.)"

Reading Graphs, page 354

Mark It Up

1. Students should box the bar graph.
2. Students should circle the pie representing 31% of kids who do not get an allowance.
3. $1.47

Reading a Transit Map, p. 355

Mark It Up

1. The purpose of this map is to show the elevated/subway train stations for the Red, Blue, Purple, and Yellow Lines.
2. The symbols mean that a particular station will have wheelchair accessibility when an agent is on duty.
3. Students should circle stations 35th, 30th, and 27th.
4. Students should underline the station at 30th Street.
5. The Red Line runs north and south. Students should put an "X" by the Purple Line to show that it runs in the same direction as the Red Line.

Reading a Diagram, p. 356

Mark It Up

1. The diagram is about balanced and unbalanced forces. Students should draw a box around the diagram's title, at letter A.
2. The black arrows represent the different forces at work. *First picture:* down arrow—gravity; up arrow—ground. *Second picture:* down arrow—gravity; up arrow—crane. *Third picture:* down arrow—gravity; up arrow—ground.
3. Students should draw a star next to the middle picture.
4. The shorter arrow pointing down represents the force of gravity on the car; the longer arrow pointing up represents the force of the crane pulling up on the car.
5. The car rises up from the ground because the force of the crane on the car is greater than the force of gravity on the car.
6. Students should circle the longer arrow, pointing up.
7. Students should draw an X next to the first and last pictures.

Main Idea and Supporting Details, page 358
Mark It Up
1. Students should circle and write the following sentence under "Main Idea": "Nothing can escape the gravity of a black hole."
2. Students should write the three remaining sentences in the boxes labeled "Detail."

Problem and Solution, page 359
Mark It Up
1. Students should underline the first sentence in the last paragraph: "A community nature garden would be a great thing for the city."
2. Students could circle any sentence in the second paragraph except for the first sentence.
3. Possible answers: Yes, I think it's a good idea, because it's an interesting project for kids and adults, and a great use of open space. or No, I think it would be better to build a playground or a basketball court on that space.

Sequence, page 360
Mark It Up
1. Students should circle *On a recent Saturday, spent the day, At 6:45 A.M. the day of filming, At 7:45 A.M., till 9:30 A.M., It was 20 minutes before, we had five minutes,* and *By 1:30 P.M.*
2. Students should underline *My day started off with, After that, After, again, Finally, then, Before, after that first take, two more times, then, Then,* and *After.* There may be some overlap between time words and phrases and order words and phrases.
3. (Sample answers are provided.)
   6:45 A.M.: *Report to set.* Go through registration and wardrobe check. Then get assigned to a section and wait in that section.
   7:45 A.M.: Eat breakfast; then wait some more.
   9:30 A.M.: Finally, take part in the big scene! Listen to directions; after that, go to a stairwell and stand smooshed with 75 other people.
   9:50 A.M.–1:30 P.M.: Walk down stairwell, being careful not to look at camera. Do two more takes; then take a five-minute break.
   1:30 P.M.: At last, shooting is over. Gather in gym, report to wardrobe, and return costume. After that, stand in line to get paid, and then leave.

Cause and Effect, page 362
Mark It Up
1. Students should underline "it was going slowly." The phrase is an effect.
2. Students should circle *because, caused, as a result, therefore.*
3. Possible responses:
   Cause: The boilers exploded.
   Effect: Hundreds of passengers were killed instantly.

Cause: The newspapers were covering Abraham Lincoln's death.
Effect: The *Sultana* tragedy was barely reported.

Comparison and Contrast, page 364
Mark It Up
1. Students should circle *both.*
2. Students should underline *Another big difference is, but,* and *but.*
3. (Sample answers are provided.)
   Bosnia: mountains, hills, beautiful meadows and forests, strict schools, give teachers respect, number grades, country is at war
   Both: schools have rules, teachers ask students questions, schools have dress codes *or* can wear jeans to school, Elvisa loves both places
   United States: tall buildings, students express themselves freely *or* students talk without being called on, letter grades, country is at peace

Argument, page 366
Mark It Up
1. Students should circle the following words and phrases: *Many people believe; Others disagree; They claim.*
2. Students should underline the opinions "Many people believe that life before television was happier than life today" and "They claim that television has many advantages as an educational tool."
3. Students should box the statement "People were not violent because they did not watch violent programs."
4. **For Television**
   Television keeps people informed about current issues and events.
   Television programs can help children learn valuable social skills.
   It can teach children how people live, work, and deal with misfortune.
   Some public programs also promote activities such as visits to museums, libraries, bookstores, and zoos.
   Against Television
   People read books and magazines for information.
   Families spent more time together.
   Children used their imaginations to write and tell stories.
   Children participated in outdoor activities instead of spending hours in front of the television.

Social Studies, page 368
Mark It Up
1. economic effects of the war and resistance by slaves
2. Students should circle *income tax* and *greenbacks.* They should underline *a tax on greenbacks* and *a new paper currency.*
3. Students should put a star next to the part of the graphic that reads *$18.00—Confederate Soldier's Monthly Pay.*

4. to bring under control or to conquer; Students should put a box around the vocabulary tip in the margin and the quotation near the bottom of the page.

5. Cause: Food could not get to market. *or* Trains carried war materials, not food.
Cause: The Confederate army seized food.

Science, page 370
Mark It Up

1. Star distances; I found this information in the title at letter A.
2. Students should circle the term *light-year* in the text to the left of letter B. They should underline the sentence where that term is found: "A **light-year** is the distance that light travels in one year, about 9.5 trillion kilometers."
3. 680 years old
4. Students should draw a star near letter D.
5. Students should circle the third, fourth, fifth, and sixth sentences in the last paragraph.
6. The close star appears to move between January and July, but it actually stays in the same place.

Mathematics, page 372
Mark It Up

1. A multi-step equation is solved using two or more steps, or by transforming the equation more than one time. Students should circle the Goal at letter B and/or the last sentence of the Vocabulary Tip at letter D.
2. Students should draw a box around the Key Words in the left column: *like terms* and *distributive property.*
3. The question will be answered in the paragraph to the right of the photo, beneath the subhead at the top of the page. Students should put a star next to the part of the page described above.
4. nine
5. You undo the addition and then undo the multiplication. Students should underline the sentence under the subhead *Solution.*

Reading an Application, page 374
Mark It Up

1. section 1: ENTRANT INFORMATION; section 2: TEAM MEMBER INFORMATION; section 3: SCHOOL INFORMATION; section 4: PROJECT INFORMATION
2. grade 7, grade 8, or high school
3. Students should underline the following requests: "A COPY OF THE ABSTRACT MUST BE ATTACHED TO THIS ENTRY FORM" and "A COPY OF THE ENDORSEMENT(S) AND ABSTRACT MUST BE ATTACHED TO THIS ENTRY FORM." entry form, endorsement(s), and abstract
4. 04
5. D
6. Students should fill out the application according to all instructions, being sure to correctly identify the category number of their made-up project.

Reading a Public Notice, page 376
Mark It Up

1. all members of the community *or* all users of the South Blaine Public Library's computers
2. follow the library's rules for Internet use
3. Students should underline *Net etiquette, or manners on the Internet.*
4. Students should circle the name of the library and its address and telephone number at the top of the page and the two sentences at the bottom of the page.
5. Students should put a star next to the library's address at the top of the page.
6. B

Reading a Web Page, page 378
Mark It Up

1. Students should circle *http://www.lookquick.com/search/+gold+rush+California* and *http://www.museumca.org/goldrush/fever.html.*
2. *gold, rush,* and *California*
3. Students should put a star by *Natives & Immigrants.*
4. Students should put a box around *guest book.*
5. C

Reading Technical Directions, page 380
Mark It Up

1. Students should underline the direction "Touch Clock pad."
2. The letters "EE" will appear on the display.
3. How to create your own cooking programs. Students should box the **Note,** "See page 10 to create your own cooking programs."
4. Students should circle the **Note,** "Choose P-30 for thawing or defrosting foods."
5. B

Product Information: Warranties, page 382
Mark It Up

1. 90 days
2. Students should underline the phrase beginning "cosmetic damage" and ending with "including the antenna."
3. a bill of sale or receipted invoice
4. Students should circle "1-(800)-111-1111."
5. D

Reading a Train Schedule, page 383
Mark It Up

1. to Turner City
2. Monday through Friday
3. Students should circle any three of the following: Kenwood, North Springs, Hollow Lake, Santa Ana.
4. C

Comprehension Mini-Lesson Answer Key

Main Idea and Details

Main Idea	Details
Paragraph 1: Implied Main Idea: People are fascinated with the idea of time travel.	• Philosophers and scientists, including Albert Einstein, have studied the concept of time. • Writers have written stories about time travel in the past and future. • Movies like *Star Trek* and *The Terminator* show the possibilities of time travel.
Paragraph 2: Although time travel may not be possible in the near future, history has taught us that advanced technology is capable of the impossible.	• In the beginning of the 20th century, many people doubted that humans would ever fly. • Today we can get from one ocean to another in a matter of hours. • Likewise, the thought of flying to the moon seemed an impossibility, but today we have the spacecraft to get us there and back. • Perhaps someday we'll have a machine capable of transporting people into the past or future.

Sequence

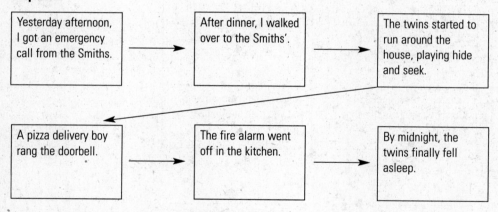

Yesterday afternoon, I got an emergency call from the Smiths. → After dinner, I walked over to the Smiths'. → The twins started to run around the house, playing hide and seek.

A pizza delivery boy rang the doorbell. → The fire alarm went off in the kitchen. → By midnight, the twins finally fell asleep.

Cause and Effect

Cause	→	Effect(s)
The narrator's mother decided the family should learn about nature.	→	The family went on a camping trip. They had an awful time.
The family brought the wrong kinds of camping supplies.	→	The family will do more research when planning the next vacation.

Comparison and Contrast

Television
small screen

weak sound

quiet, personal experience

gives little opportunity to feel the reactions of a large audience

Both
show an image on screen

have sound

Movie Theaters
magnified screen that can make the image more intense and real

stronger sound system than television

moviegoer shares his or her emotions with the rest of the audience

Making Inferences

Selection Information + **What I Know** = **My Inference**

Selection Information		What I Know		My Inference
Donna drums her fingers while the phone rings.	+	Drumming fingers suggest impatience.	=	Donna is getting impatient with the person she's calling.
She slams the phone down, sits stiffly in her chair, and taps her foot.	+	These movements indicate growing impatience or anger.	=	Donna's impatience with her friend has turned to anger.
Donna hears footsteps coming up the steps and runs out the door.	+	Footsteps running up the steps suggest that someone has arrived.	=	Donna's friend has arrived, and she runs out to meet the person.

Predicting

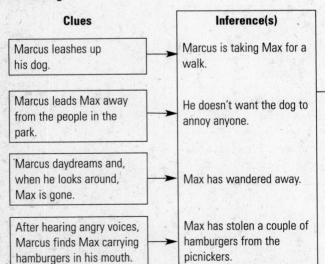

Clues

Marcus leashes up his dog.

Marcus leads Max away from the people in the park.

Marcus daydreams and, when he looks around, Max is gone.

After hearing angry voices, Marcus finds Max carrying hamburgers in his mouth.

Inference(s)

Marcus is taking Max for a walk.

He doesn't want the dog to annoy anyone.

Max has wandered away.

Max has stolen a couple of hamburgers from the picnickers.

Prediction(s)

The picnickers will be very angry with Marcus.

Marcus will not let Max off the leash in the park again.

Fact and Opinion

Fact	Opinion
• His work is still read by many people today. • Many of his short stories and novels have been made into movies. • Recently, Disney Studios released *Tom and Huck*, a retelling based on two of Twain's popular novels.	• It seems that Mark Twain's popularity will never end. • As long as his popularity continues, Mark Twain's literary work will be read and enjoyed by many people one hundred years from now.

Narrative Elements

Setting at the Gutersons' house last Friday night	**Characters** the narrator, the two Guterson kids, their parents, and possibly someone or something in the basement

Plot

Problem: The narrator is baby-sitting when he or she hears noises at the basement door. Who or what is trying to get in the house?

Events:

1. The narrator walks to the door and hears the noises again.

2. The narrator asks who is there.

3. The parents get home. The narrator tries to explain what is wrong.

Resolution: The parents explain that the cat wants to be let in.